EMERGENT LITERACY
AND LANGUAGE DEVELOPMENT

CHALLENGES IN LANGUAGE AND LITERACY
Elaine R. Silliman and C. Addison Stone, Series Editors

Frame Work in Language and Literacy:
How Theory Informs Practice
Judith Felson Duchan

Phonological Awareness: From Research to Practice
Gail T. Gillon

Handbook of Language and Literacy:
Development and Disorders
*C. Addison Stone, Elaine R. Silliman,
Barbara J. Ehren, and Kenn Apel, Editors*

Language and Literacy Learning in Schools
Elaine R. Silliman and Louise C. Wilkinson, Editors

Children's Comprehension Problems in Oral
and Written Language: A Cognitive Perspective
Kate Cain and Jane Oakhill, Editors

Brain, Behavior, and Learning in Language
and Reading Disorders
Maria Mody and Elaine R. Silliman, Editors

Instruction and Assessment for Struggling Writers:
Evidence-Based Practices
Gary A. Troia, Editor

Emergent Literacy and Language Development:
Promoting Learning in Early Childhood
Paula M. Rhyner, Editor

Emergent Literacy and Language Development

Promoting Learning in Early Childhood

Edited by Paula M. Rhyner

Series Editors' Note by Elaine R. Silliman and C. Addison Stone

THE GUILFORD PRESS
New York   London

© 2009 The Guilford Press
A Division of Guilford Publications, Inc.
72 Spring Street, New York, NY 10012
www.guilford.com

Printed in the United States of America

This book is printed on acid-free paper.

Last digit is print number: 9   8   7   6   5   4   3   2   1

Library of Congress Cataloging-in-Publication Data

Emergent literacy and language development : promoting learning in early
childhood / edited by Paula M. Rhyner.
    p. cm. — (Challenges in language and literacy)
  Includes bibliographical references and index.
  ISBN 978-1-60623-300-9 (hardcover: alk. paper)
  1. Language arts (Preschool)   2. Children—Language.   I. Rhyner,
Paula M.
  LB1140.5.L3E43 2009
  372.6—dc22

                                                        2009011208

With love and gratitude to
my parents, Joseph and Frances Pecyna,
and
my family—Mark, Luke, Emma, and Casey

About the Editor

Paula M. Rhyner, PhD, CCC-SLP, is Professor in the Department of Communication Sciences and Disorders at the University of Wisconsin–Milwaukee (UWM). She is a Board Recognized Specialist in Child Language and has served in various roles on the Specialty Board on Child Language, including that of Chair. Dr. Rhyner is a member of the editorial board for *Communication Disorders Quarterly*, and served as an Associate Editor for *Language, Speech, and Hearing Services in Schools*. She directs the Child Language Lab at UWM, which conducts interdisciplinary research in areas related to development and disabilities in children from birth through 5 years of age. Her published research on language assessment and intervention and her interest in emergent literacy and early language acquisition led her to collaborate with the series editors and the other contributing authors to create this book.

Contributors

Dolores E. Battle, PhD, CCC-SLP, Department of Speech–Language Pathology, Buffalo State College, State University of New York, Buffalo, New York

Sonia Q. Cabell, PhD, Curry School of Education, University of Virginia, Charlottesville, Virginia

Eileen K. Haebig, BS, Department of Communicative Disorders, University of Wisconsin–Madison, Madison, Wisconsin

Elizabeth Hester, PhD, CCC-SLP, Department of Communication Disorders, State University of New York at New Paltz, New Paltz, New York

Barbara W. Hodson, PhD, CCC-SLP, Department of Communication Sciences and Disorders, Wichita State University, Wichita, Kansas

Laura M. Justice, PhD, CCC-SLP, School of Teaching and Learning, College of Teaching and Human Ecology, The Ohio State University, Columbus, Ohio

Joan N. Kaderavek, PhD, CCC-SLP, Department of Early Childhood, Physical, and Special Education, Judith Herb College of Education, University of Toledo, Toledo, Ohio

Paula M. Rhyner, PhD, CCC-SLP, Department of Communication Sciences and Disorders, University of Wisconsin–Milwaukee, Milwaukee, Wisconsin

Froma P. Roth, PhD, CCC-SLP, Department of Hearing and Speech Sciences, University of Maryland, College Park, Maryland

Elizabeth Vander Veen, BA, Department of Speech, Language, and Hearing Sciences, Purdue University, West Lafayette, Indiana

Judith Vander Woude, PhD, CCC-SLP, Department of Communication Arts and Sciences, Calvin College, Grand Rapids, Michigan

Anne van Kleeck, PhD, CCC-SLP, Callier Center for Communication Disorders, School of Behavioral and Brain Sciences, University of Texas at Dallas, Dallas, Texas

Kaycee M. West, MS, CCC-SLP, Elmbrook School District, Brookfield, Wisconsin

Series Editors' Note

Given our nation's renewed attention to early childhood education, this volume represents a timely addition to The Guilford Press series Challenges in Language and Literacy. The aim of the series is to integrate interdisciplinary perspectives on language and literacy with empirically based programs and practices for promoting effective learning outcomes in diverse students. Past policy debates about preschool programs have tended to highlight the potential for improvement of early educational success, while discussions about the longer-term economic and social impact of less than adequate early childhood education programs remained in the background. However, there is increasing recognition of the potential for both economic and educational outcomes, and this dual focus serves to highlight the value of renewed focus on effective preschool programs. A major virtue of this volume is its presentation of evidence regarding key components of effective programs, as well as specific recommendations to practitioners regarding promising practices for implementing such programs.

Preschool Education: Long-Term Benefits

Long-term data trends show that, across ethnic groups, preschool enrollment has surged in the past two decades. In 2005, almost 66% of 4-year-olds and 40% of 3-year-olds were receiving a preschool education through an uncoordinated mix of public and private programs (Barnett, 2008). Furthermore, targeted federal programs such as Head Start, and state-funded programs combined with government subsidies for child care, have been successful in providing greater access to 3-year-olds from low-income families (Barnett & Yarosz, 2007). However, enhanced access has not necessarily resulted in increased quality of preschool education. Marked variations persist in the quality of the educational experiences of young children, particularly in publicly funded programs. In the public domain, boundaries are often ambiguous between programs that primarily provide long hours of child care because of parental employment needs and those that chiefly emphasize learning and development (Barnett & Yarosz, 2007).

From an economic perspective, Heckman (2008) offers evidence that enhancing "yields on investment" (p. 312) means social policies must be directed to the harnessing of children's human capital throughout their schooling, from preschool through high school. A national commitment of this kind requires the economic will to invest financially in (1) well-designed and implemented preschool programs, in spite of the large costs required initially, and (2) follow-up programs during the elementary and secondary years that meet standards of excellence. Heckman's argument is that the later intervention is offered, the less likely it is that there will be economic returns. In other words, "Investments at different stages of the life cycle are complementary and require follow-up to be effective" (Heckman, 2008, p. 316).

Instead of relying on economic analysis, meta-analyses of early childhood interventions (e.g., Barnett, 2008) are another option. Outcomes indicate that "rigorous studies find not only immediate gains, but lasting benefits for learning and educational achievement" (Barnett, 2008, p. 16), including decreases in delinquency and crime (Heckman, 2008). A major issue for resolution is whether fiscal investment should be directed to universal prekindergarten or targeted programs (e.g., Head Start). Another issue is whether combining child care with preschool programs might better enhance economic advantages for families by expanding parental employment opportunities. Nevertheless, the economic consequences of an inadequate literacy education in preschool are motivating potential revitalizations of federal policy initiatives for early childhood education.

Effective Preschool Programs:
Integrating Language Learning and Emerging Literacy

In the end, policy initiatives must be translated into everyday practices that originate from scientific evidence. This is the challenge that Paula M. Rhyner and the contributing authors take on in a comprehensive manner in this book. Chapters focus on two interdependent dimensions: (1) the dynamic aspects of oral language in relation to emerging literacy, and (2) the role of oral language in young children's developing self-regulation of their own learning.

In the preschool literature, there is consensus across disciplines that the roots of becoming a literate learner can be traced to the blossoming of young children's oral language systems (e.g., Dickinson & Tabors, 2001; Foorman, Anthony, Seals, & Mouzaki, 2002; National Institute of Child Health and Human Development [NICHD] Early Child Care Research Network, 2005). However, despite this general agreement, less accord exists on the actual roles that specific oral language components play in promoting advances in developing literacy. For example, in regard to beginning reading, the NICHD Early Child Care Research Network (2005) concluded that existing assessments of reading readiness with preschool children were premised on reading models that viewed oral language skills as primarily consisting of vocabulary. In contrast to this discrete view, a more comprehensive model would approach oral language along two interrelated dimensions: as a synergistic system whose effects on emerging literacy cannot be predicted from its parts and as a major platform through which young children are launched into learning how to learn (NICHD Early Child Care Research Network, 2005).

Rhyner and the contributors assume this all-inclusive voice in stitching together potential bidirectional relationships between aspects of oral language experience and emerging literacy foundations. Conceptual frameworks are then translated into clear instructional goals and practices that are equally applicable to three varied groups of preschool children: (1) those with typically developing oral language systems, (2) those who may have profiles consistent with delayed language development, and (3) those whose engagement of oral language for literacy purposes may differ as the product of their cultural and linguistic heritages. All professional staff, from classroom teachers to speech–language pathologists, who are concerned with building preschool programs meeting the dual standards of educational excellence and the promotion of lifelong resilience in young children, will find that the current volume provides a valuable road map for reaching these goals.

ELAINE R. SILLIMAN
C. ADDISON STONE

References

Barnett, W. S. (2008, September). *Preschool education and its lasting effects: Research and policy implications.* Boulder and Tempe: Education and the Public Interest Center & Education Policy Research Unit. Retrieved December 22, 2008, from *epicpolicy.org/publication/preschool-education.*

Barnett, W. S., & Yarosz, D. J. (2007, November). *Preschool policy brief of the National Institute for Early Education Research.* Retrieved December 22, 2008, from *www.nieer.org.*

Dickinson, D. K., & Tabors, P. O. (2001). *Beginning literacy with language.* Baltimore: Brookes.

Foorman, B. R., Anthony, J., Seals, L., & Mouzaki, A. (2002). Language development and emergent literacy in preschool. *Seminars in Pediatric Neurology, 9,* 173–184.

Heckman, J. J. (2008). Schools, skills, and synapses. *Economic Inquiry, 46,* 289–324.

National Institute of Child Health and Human Development Early Child Care Research Network. (2005). Pathways to reading: The role of oral language in the transition to reading. *Developmental Psychology, 41,* 428–442.

Acknowledgments

There are many people who provided the support, encouragement, and assistance that were important to me in bringing this book to completion. I am grateful to Elaine R. Silliman and C. Addison Stone, the Series Editors for Challenges in Language and Literacy, for the opportunity to partner with the contributing authors to develop a book that adds critical insights to the understanding of the relationship between emergent literacy and early language acquisition. The mentoring, guidance, and feedback that Elaine and Addison provided were invaluable to me throughout the preparation of this book. I also want to thank Rochelle Serwator and Anna Nelson at The Guilford Press for their support and assistance in the publication process.

My sincere gratitude is extended to the contributing authors, whose expertise, talents, and efforts were essential to creating a resource for early childhood professionals that informs their efforts to foster the development of children's knowledge and skills in emergent literacy and early language. The authors' enthusiasm for the collaborative development of this book was energizing to me as the editor. I especially want to thank my coauthors, Eileen K. Haebig and Kaycee M. West, for their diligent efforts toward the completion of our chapter. They each brought a vital perspective to the preparation, organization, and writing of the chapter. For their assistance in researching the literature, verifying references, and proofreading, I would like to acknowledge and express my heartfelt thanks to Samantha Drews, Eileen K. Haebig, and Renee Marti Humpal. I appreciate the considerable time and effort that they spent on these critical tasks.

I want to convey my appreciation to the people whom I value as close friends and colleagues. They continually provided me with support in various ways and always at just the right times. Above all, I am most grateful to my husband, Mark, and my children, Luke and Emma, for everything that they did for me (big and small) to give me the time that I needed to focus on this book. Their love, patience, support, understanding, encouragement, and humor have always been constant sources of strength and happiness for me.

Contents

Introduction

PAULA M. RHYNER

A child's success in school is strongly influenced by the knowledge and skills that he or she has acquired before entering school (Duncan et al., 2007). Thus, a child's experiences as an infant, toddler, and preschooler are critical to the acquisition of a set of "tools" (or knowledge and skills) that the child can draw on to facilitate academic success. Literacy is one area examined extensively for connections between knowledge and skills before and after entering school (Fritjers, Barron, & Brunello, 2000; Hammill, 2004; Scarborough & Dobrich, 1994; Storch & Whitehurst, 2002).

Interest in children's acquisition of the knowledge and skills that pertain to literacy has increased over the last two decades within disciplines such as general education, special education, early childhood education, psychology, and speech–language pathology. Following Marie Clay's suggestion in 1966 that children demonstrate literacy-related behaviors even when they are not able to read and write, investigators in these disciplines turned their attention to defining "emergent literacy" (Teale & Sulzby, 1986). Their goals were to delineate the knowledge and skills that characterized the emergent literacy stage and describe the process of emergent literacy development. As research findings revealed that children's literacy development began even before they were exposed to formal reading instruction in school (Clay, 1991; Snow, Burns, & Griffin, 1998; Teale & Sulzby, 1986), interest increased in young children's

1

emergent literacy development and in the relationship between emergent and later literacy development. Consequently, there has been a surge of information from various disciplines on these two goals. Further, there has been growing recognition of the relationship between the acquisition of early oral language and emergent literacy knowledge and skills (Snow et al., 1998). In fact, the available longitudinal research has shown that children who were identified as having oral language impairments during the preschool years were at greater risk for oral and written language impairments as they progressed through school, even if their language impairments appeared to have been remediated by the time they began kindergarten (Aram, Ekelman, & Nation, 1984; Aram & Nation, 1980; Bishop & Adams, 1990; Catts, Fey, Zhang, & Tomblin, 1999).

From a professional perspective, it has been the responsibility of speech–language pathologists to engage in the prevention of communication disorders (American Speech–Language–Hearing Association, 1988). Recently, professional responsibility has been expanded with respect to reading and writing development (American Speech–Language–Hearing Association, 2001). As a result, it is important for speech–language pathologists and other early childhood specialists (e.g., teachers, psychologists, and day care providers) to have an understanding of the emergent literacy stage and of the relationship between emergent literacy and early language acquisition. Such understanding will increase the effectiveness of these specialists in their collaborative efforts with parents to foster the emergent literacy and early oral language development of young children. Thus, the major purpose of this book is to provide a framework for understanding the emergent literacy stage and the linkages between emergent literacy and early language acquisition.

The focus of this book is on building a bridge to connect our knowledge on emergent literacy learning and early oral language learning with instruction so that greater effectiveness can be achieved by specialists within early childhood educational settings. The construction of this bridge draws on the expertise of this book's contributing authors, which include clinical researchers who are engaged in the study of emergent literacy and early oral language acquisition. Thus, the content of each chapter reflects the expertise and specialty areas that the authors emphasize in their research.

Chapter 1 offers an overview of emergent literacy for early childhood specialists. The chapter begins with a definition of "emergent literacy" and a discussion of the notion that the emergent literacy stage is the beginning of a continuum of literacy development. The chapter progresses with descriptions and comparative analyses of three main perspectives on, and their corresponding frameworks for, understanding the emergent literacy stage, followed by the implications of the perspectives for fostering children's emergent literacy development. Chapter 2 addresses the importance of book sharing for the development of meaning for both children's emergent literacy and early oral language acquisition. In Chapter 3, the development of children's phonological awareness and its relationship to development in other areas of language and emergent literacy are examined. The focus of Chapter 4 is on children's early writing and spelling development and their bidirectional influence on early oral language acquisition. The interrelationship of children's early language learning and their early story and expository discourse is considered in Chapter 5. In Chapter 6, the connection between emergent literacy and cultural and linguistic diversity is discussed with regard to assessment and intervention with young children.

Throughout this book, the "supports" for our bridge are provided in each chapter by the relevant and current evidence on young children's emergent literacy and early oral language development. These supports are critical to maintaining and guiding the construction of the "substructure" of our bridge, which is the assessment of young children's emergent literacy and early oral language acquisition. The assessment substructure then serves as a basis for the intervention "roadbed" for the bridge that in turn links emergent literacy and early oral language acquisition. The "superstructure" of the bridge is then created through each chapter with examples and case studies specific to early childhood settings. Building sturdy bridges between emergent literacy and early oral language acquisition is critical to children's development. This bridge building requires that early childhood specialists collaborate with parents to support children's journey along the continuum of literacy and language learning with the mutual goal of ensuring their success in school.

References

American Speech–Language–Hearing Association. (1988). Position statement on the prevention of communication disorders. *ASHA, 30*(3), 90.

American Speech–Language–Hearing Association. (2001). Position statement of the roles and responsibilities of speech–language pathologists with respect to reading and writing in children and adolescents (position statement, executive summary of guidelines, technical report). *ASHA Supplement, 21,* 17–27.

Aram, D., Ekelman, B. L., & Nation, J. (1984). Preschoolers with language disorders: 10 years later. *Journal of Speech and Hearing Research, 27,* 232–244.

Aram, D., & Nation, J. (1980). Preschool language disorders and subsequent language and academic difficulties. *Journal of Communication Disorders, 13,* 159–170.

Bishop, D. V. M., & Adams, C. (1990). A prospective study of the relationship between specific language impairment, phonological disorders, and reading retardation. *Journal of Child Psychology and Psychiatry, 31,* 1027–1050.

Catts, H. W., Fey, M. E., Zhang, X., & Tomblin, B. (1999). Language basis of reading and reading disabilities: Evidence from a longitudinal investigation. *Scientific Studies of Reading, 3*(4), 331–362.

Clay, M. M. (1966). *Emergent reading behaviour.* Unpublished doctoral dissertation. University of Aukland, New Zealand.

Clay, M. M. (1991). *Becoming literate: The construction of inner control.* Portsmouth, NH: Heinemann.

Duncan, G. J., Dowsett, C. J., Claessens, A., Magnuson, K., Huston, A. C., Klebanov, P., et al. (2007). School readiness and later achievement. *Developmental Psychology, 43*(6), 1428–1446.

Fritjers, J. C., Barron, R. W., & Brunello, M. (2000). Direct and mediated influences of home literacy and literacy interest on prereaders' oral vocabulary and early written language skill. *Journal of Educational Psychology, 92,* 466–477.

Hammill, D. D. (2004). What we know about correlates of reading. *Exceptional Children, 70,* 453–468.

Scarborough, H. S., & Dobrich, W. (1994). On the efficacy of reading to preschoolers. *Developmental Review, 14,* 245–302.

Snow, C. E., Burns, M. S., & Griffin, P. (1998). *Preventing reading difficulties in young children.* Washington, DC: National Academy Press.

Storch, S. A., & Whitehurst, G. J. (2002). Oral language and code-related precursors to reading: Evidence from a longitudinal structural model. *Developmental Psychology, 38,* 934–947.

Teale, W. H., & Sulzby, E. (1986). Emergent literacy as a perspective for examining how young children become writers and readers. In W. H. Teale & E. Sulzby (Eds.), *Emergent literacy: Writing and reading* (pp. vii–xxv). Norwood, NJ: Ablex.

CHAPTER ONE

Understanding Frameworks for the Emergent Literacy Stage

PAULA M. RHYNER
EILEEN K. HAEBIG
KAYCEE M. WEST

The study of emergent literacy reflects a somewhat recent change in perspective on the reading and writing development of young children (Strickland & Morrow, 1988). The change is based on the recognition that children acquire knowledge and skills before learning to read and write, which are related in some way to their later reading and writing development. In addition, as the body of knowledge on emergent literacy grows, so does interest in the relationship between early language acquisition and emergent literacy. In fact, there is a notable increase in the research on the relationship among early language, emergent literacy, and later literacy development. This interest arises at least in part from an acknowledgment that "reading is a linguistic activity" (Snow, Tabors, & Dickinson, 2001, p. 3) that requires knowledge about the structure of words. Children's first knowledge about the words of their language is acquired through the development of oral language skills. In turn, the word knowledge that children acquire via oral language development is important to learning about printed words. It even has been suggested that "without oral language, it might be impossible to develop the ability to read and write" (Glazer, 1989, p. 19).

A variety of component areas of children's early oral language development are proposed as essential to emergent literacy development. These include semantics (Adams, 2002), syntax (Dickinson, McCabe, Anastasopoulos, Peisner-Feinberg, & Poe, 2003; Storch & Whitehurst, 2002), phonology (Wagner, Torgesen, & Rashotte, 1994; Whitehurst & Lonigan, 1998, 2002), and pragmatics (Owens, 2007; Roth, Speece, Cooper, & De La Paz, 1996; Storch & Whitehurst, 2002). Although the exact ways in which the associated knowledge and skills within each component area are related to children's emergent literacy development have not been determined, frameworks have been offered in an attempt to describe the relationship. We begin with an overview of emergent literacy.

To address the relationship between early language acquisition and emergent literacy effectively, it is necessary to develop an understanding of the available frameworks for the emergent literacy stage. Thus, after a brief discussion of the general construct of emergent literacy, we examine three emergent literacy perspectives for typically developing children. As with other areas of child development, a universally accepted model that provides comprehensive answers to questions about emergent literacy in children does not exist. In fact, a search of the literature reveals only a few identified "models" of emergent literacy; some researchers have presented viewpoints on emergent literacy without providing the structure of a "model." These models and viewpoints serve as a basis for understanding emergent literacy. For the purposes of this chapter, the models and viewpoints are referred to as "frameworks" for the emergent literacy stage. These frameworks have been organized into three main perspectives. Determining similarities and differences among the perspectives is important to building an understanding of the emergent literacy stage. In the final section, we discuss the implications of the three perspectives for fostering emergent literacy development in young children.

An Overview of Emergent Literacy

Defining Emergent Literacy

Descriptions of the available frameworks for the emergent literacy stage typically begin with a definition of the term "emergent literacy." According to Teale and Sulzby (1986), Marie Clay coined the term "emergent literacy" in 1966 to refer to the behaviors of very young children which reflected an understanding of reading and writing when children were not yet reading and writing in a conventional sense. Teale and Sulzby (1986) further developed Clay's concept of emergent literacy, emphasizing the importance of considering both reading and writing together as comprising *literacy*. Teale and Sulzby (1986) also recognized that *emergent* conveyed the perspective that children were "in the process of becoming literate" (p. xix).

In general, what children learn about reading and writing before they are considered readers and writers is referred to as emergent literacy *knowledge* and the ways that children demonstrate that knowledge (i.e., the observable behavior) is referred to as emergent literacy *skills*. There is consensus that emergent literacy involves the knowledge, skills, and attitudes that begin to develop before, but are related to, conventional reading and writing (McNaughton, 1995; Reese, Cox, Harte, & McAnally, 2003; Teale & Sulzby, 1986). There is a lack of agreement, however, on the exact set of knowledge and skills that characterize emergent literacy and on the patterns of acquisition that can be expected for typically developing children (Sénéchal, LeFevre, Smith-Chant, & Colton, 2001). As the body of research on emergent literacy grows, it is likely that a better understanding of the knowledge and skills and patterns of acquisition will evolve.

Emergent Literacy Knowledge as a Continuum of Development

The difficulty in delineating a widely agreed upon set of knowledge and skills seems to offer support for the notion that emergent literacy represents the beginning of a continuum of literacy development in children. Teale and Sulzby (1986) reviewed the early reading research and concluded that the findings, which could be summarized as follows, supported the concept of a continuum:

1. Literacy development begins early in life and long before formal literacy instruction in elementary school.
2. There is an interrelationship between oral language skills (listening and speaking) and written language skills (reading and writing) such that the skills develop concurrently

and interrelatedly rather than in some sequence (e.g., oral language development preceding written language development, etc.). In addition, children's cognitive development during early childhood is important to their literacy development.

3. The *functions* of literacy (e.g., ordering a meal from a menu at a restaurant, obtaining information on an event, inviting friends to a birthday party) are as important as the *forms* of literacy (e.g., letters, words, sentences) to the child's literacy development in early childhood.

4. Children's active exploration of print within their environment and their social interactions with adults (particularly their parents) within reading and writing contexts (e.g., reading books together, making a sign to show support for a favorite football team, following a cookie recipe) provide important opportunities for adults to model literacy behaviors for children to learn.

5. There is variability for typically developing children in the age and sequence of acquisition of emergent literacy knowledge and skills across the continuum of literacy development.

Timing of the Emergent Literacy Stage

The concept that emergent literacy is the beginning of the continuum of literacy development makes it difficult to delineate a "stage" of development as emergent literacy. This difficulty is further complicated by the observation that there are no definitive "endpoints" between emergent, early, and conventional literacy development in children (Justice, 2006). Although it might be suggested then, that emergent literacy development should not be referred to as a "stage," Justice (2006) states that the use of stage terminology "allows categorization of skills and an estimation of where children are along on a continuum of development" (p. 8). Thus, the phrase "emergent literacy stage" is used to refer to the period of time during which children acquire a variety of emergent literacy knowledge and skills.

Despite the challenges in defining the emergent literacy stage, there is considerable agreement on the approximate timing of the stage for typically developing children. This agreement appeared to be based on the concept of "reading readiness," which emerged in the 1920s. The readiness concept suggested that there was a period of time during the preschool years in which children developed skills necessary for reading and writing (Teale & Sulzby, 1986). The exact age at which the emergent literacy stage begins for typically developing children has not been determined but there is general agreement that the stage begins long before children are able to read and write (Fields & Spangler, 2000; Teale & Sulzby, 1986). Some authors suggest that, because of the close relationship between emergent literacy and early language acquisition, the emergent literacy stage begins at birth (Clay, 1991; Justice, 2006; Neuman & Roskos, 1993; Strickland & Morrow, 1988). For typically developing children in the United States, the emergent literacy stage is expected to last until around age 5 years, when children enter kindergarten (Justice, 2006). With the beginning of kindergarten, children become exposed to formal instruction in reading and writing via the preschool curriculum.

Perspectives on the Emergent Literacy Stage

Despite the variability among the available models of and viewpoints on the emergent literacy stage, each offers a framework in which to consider children's emergent literacy. In addition, the frameworks can be categorized on the basis of their primary perspective. For example, some frameworks have a developmental perspective, attempting to describe a progression in the acquisition of emergent literacy knowledge and skills (e.g., Goodman, 1986; McCormick & Mason, 1986; Strommen & Mates, 2000; van Kleeck, 1998); others delineate the components of emergent literacy (i.e., knowledge and skills) that children acquire (e.g., Storch & Whitehurst, 2002; van Kleeck, 1998). Still other frameworks focus on child and environmental influences on emergent literacy acquisition (e.g., McNaughton, 1995; Wasik & Hendrickson, 2004). Thus, the frameworks for the emergent literacy stage can be categorized according to three main perspectives: a developmental perspective, a components perspective, and a child and environmental influences perspective.

There have been changes over time in the emphases of the available frameworks for the emergent literacy stage. The earliest frameworks, which provided a developmental perspective, were more general in their description of changes in children's conceptual understanding about the reading process and/or emergent literacy skills. The emphases in the frameworks then shifted to a more specific focus with an effort to identify the component knowledge and skills associated with emergent literacy. It is possible that the shift in perspective reflected increasing knowledge about the emergent literacy stage, which had resulted from increased research.

The most recent frameworks acknowledge the influence of child and environmental factors on development during the emergent literacy stage. This change in perspective reflects a growing belief in the child development field that growth in any area results from a complex interaction of child and environmental variables. This belief is further evidenced in child-centered, holistic approaches in early childhood education and intervention.

In the following sections, we discuss the various frameworks within each of the three main perspectives: the developmental perspective, the components perspective, and the child and environmental influences perspective. One qualification is in order: Although each framework is categorized according to its primary approach to the emergent literacy stage, some frameworks are included within multiple perspectives to allow for a more complete description.

Developmental Perspective

Among the earliest approaches to describing the emergent literacy stage were those with a developmental perspective. These developmental frameworks provide a general approach to describing changes in children's conceptual knowledge about literacy and/or emergent literacy skills. Included within this perspective are frameworks by Goodman (1986), McCormick and Mason (1986), Strommen and Mates (2000), and van Kleeck (1998). A common assumption among these frameworks is that the understanding of the relationship between print and meaning occurs first, followed by an understanding of print form.

The Goodman (1986) Framework

Goodman's framework (1986) delineates five areas in which children's knowledge and skills progress in their developing the "roots of literacy." These include (1) print awareness in situational contexts,

(2) print awareness in discourse, (3) functions and forms of writing, (4) oral language to talk about written language, and (5) metacognitive and metalinguistic awareness about written language.

According to Goodman (1986), evidence of a child's print awareness in situational contexts is observed when the child begins to learn and recognize print in the environment, such as logos for restaurants and food companies. The development of print awareness in discourse is supported as a child is exposed to print within the context of books, magazines, video games, computer games, websites, and newspapers. Through experiences with different print media, the child learns that each serves a particular purpose. For example, an individual can read a newspaper or online websites to find out about the weather for the day or for several days, events that occurred locally, or events that have occurred around the world. After being introduced to these media, the child learns how to manipulate them. Learning how to "read" a book by turning the pages from the front to the back of the book and reading from left to right (in English) are examples of ways to manipulate print media.

In the development of the functions and forms of writing, a child begins to write by scribbling or drawing lines to represent letters or typing strings of letters while using a computer. Use of oral language to talk about written language is observed when the child begins to understand and talk about the functions of print. For example, the child may describe a book as something that tells a story using words or pictures. Lastly, metacognitive and metalinguistic awareness about written language is observed when the child begins to understand the meanings of literacy terms, such as "letter" and "page," and uses words to describe what he or she reads. The progression through these "roots of literacy," according to Goodman (1986, p. 6), enables children to acquire emergent literacy knowledge and skills.

The McCormick and Mason (1986) Framework

Another framework for the emergent literacy stage within the developmental perspective was offered by McCormick and Mason (1986), who suggested that children progress through a "hierarchy" of knowledge and skills when learning to read. This hierarchy is comprised of three emergent literacy levels: functions of print, form of print, and coordination of the form and function of print.

For the first level, the functions of print, children's understanding of literacy is context-dependent (i.e., closely connected with the environment in which the print occurs). They begin to read environmental print such as street signs, yet may not be able to read those same words in different situations (McCormick & Mason, 1986). Within this level, children learn that meaningful words can be represented in printed form (i.e., they understand that print has a function).

When children learn about grapheme–phoneme correspondences and begin to experiment with this understanding through increased reading exposure and invented spelling, they have reached the second level of emergent literacy, the form of print (McCormick & Mason, 1986). Here they can apply phonetic analysis to printed words because their attention to print shifts from function to form; hence, children begin to learn about the structure of printed words via their letter–sound understanding, rather than relying solely on contextual cues provided by pictures or environmental situations (e.g., street signs or restaurant logos).

During the final coordination stage of the emergent literacy hierarchy, children apply their understanding of print function and print form concurrently. Since children develop clearer and more efficient ways to decode printed words, such as by noting orthographic redundancy and phonologic patterns, they are able to give more attention to word meanings (McCormick & Mason, 1986). In this last stage, children learn to use their skills for both print function and form in order to read, just as conventional readers do. Although McCormick and Mason (1986) did not explicitly address changes in children's conceptual knowledge about the reading process, their hierarchy suggests that the development of the underlying knowledge of the reading process builds from the function of print to the form of print to the coordination of the form and function of print. The child's success at the higher levels of the hierarchy is dependent on successful development of the underlying knowledge at the preceding level or levels.

The Strommen and Mates (2000) Framework

The Strommen and Mates (2000) developmental framework focuses directly on a developmental progression of children's understanding about becoming a reader. The framework evolved from a longitudinal study of 18 children from the age of 3 years through the completion of kindergarten. Children were met with individually on a periodic basis to document their ideas about the nature of reading. The study goals were to determine whether children (1) were similar in their concepts about what readers do, and (2) demonstrated a similar sequence in their development of these concepts. The results from children's ideas about the nature of reading revealed a uniform sequence in the development of these ideas, although there were differences and overlap in the ages at which the concepts emerged. A set of six concepts about reading were observed during the emergent literacy stage:

1. Reading is one aspect of an interpersonal routine—book reading is viewed as a social routine in which the book itself has a minor role.
2. Readers focus on the book—book reading is viewed as a social routine in which the book is the focus of the routine.
3. Readers construct a sequenced account—they rely on the illustrations rather than the print to construct a meaningful story.
4. Readers reconstruct a specific account—they recognize that the content of a story is unique to each book; in reconstructing a story, the words can change, but the meaning must stay the same.
5. Readers refer to print to reconstruct texts—printed text is needed to reconstruct a story; however, the relationship between decoding print and reading is not always understood.
6. Readers reconstruct texts by using multiple strategies to interpret the language encoded by print—there is the understanding that they must accurately interpret written language using a variety of language and decoding strategies (e.g., graphophonemic, semantic, and syntactic information), in addition to the illustrations, in order to be able to read.

This developmental framework for the emergent literacy stage (Strommen & Mates, 2000) suggests that children's understanding of the reading process progresses from a notion about the social-interactive nature of book sharing to an understanding of the complex interaction among linguistic knowledge, decoding skills, and printed text. The progression reveals an initial focus on observable reading behaviors (e.g., turning pages, looking at illustrations, moving from the front to the back of the book, etc.) and a later focus on actual reading skills (e.g., sounding out words, decoding text, and extracting meaning from printed text). According to Strommen and Mates (2000), "though children expressed their ideas in many different ways and reached various conclusions at widely different ages, we saw consistent evolution of these ideas as each child slowly came to see an accurate interpretation of the language encoded by print as the key to reading" (p. 210). The developmental progression through these different conceptual processes illustrates the ways that children learn the functions, content, and purpose of print materials.

The van Kleeck (1998) Framework

The framework for the emergent literacy stage that van Kleeck (1998) developed explains the knowledge and skills that children acquire and is therefore primarily included within the components perspective (see next section). However, in addition to describing the components of emergent literacy, van Kleeck addressed the developmental progression of emergent literacy knowledge and skills, and therefore this aspect of her model is included in this discussion of the developmental perspective. Specifically, van Kleeck (1998) suggested that there are two general stages of emergent literacy during which children acquire the knowledge and skills described in her components framework.

During the first stage, which occurs from infancy to approximately 3 to 4 years of age, children discover that print is meaningful through their exposure to print and terms related to book reading such as "book" and "page." Children in the first stage also begin to retell stories in their own words while looking at pictures in books and may begin to learn to rhyme and name letters. Further, the emphasis on the print–meaning relationship is evident in the behavior of both the adult and the child during shared book reading. For example, adults tend to convey the meanings associated with pictures in the books via strategies such as labeling objects and people and describing objects or events during book sharing with infants and toddlers.

During the second stage, older preschool children begin to learn about print form and early form–meaning correspondences while continuing to learn about print meaning across a range of literacy environments. Adults make more specific and direct references to the form of printed text using print-related terms such as "capital" (letter) and "word" during book sharing. During the second stage, children also learn how to write letters and match letters with their associated sounds, create more detailed stories, and strengthen their ability to predict events in stories that are orally read to them. (See Vander Woude, van Kleeck, & Vander Veen, Chapter 2, this volume, for an in-depth discussion of book sharing and the development of meaning.)

Summary

The frameworks described in this section use different approaches to explain the development of emergent literacy. Consistent with a developmental perspective, each framework addresses (albeit in a somewhat general way) the progression in children's acquisition of knowledge and skills (e.g., print meaning, print form, and the coordination of print meaning with print form) that occurs during the emergent literacy stage. McCormick and Mason (1986) and van Kleeck (1998) describe stages of development within the emergent literacy stage, noting the integrated relationship of the stages and the increased extent to which children's literacy development mirrors conventional reading through each stage. In contrast, the Goodman (1986) and Strommen and Mates (2000) frameworks emphasize a progressive change throughout the emergent literacy stage in print-related skills and conceptual knowledge about reading, respectively. Separate stages are not denoted within the emergent literacy stage. A summary of the key elements of the frameworks within the developmental perspective is provided in Table 1.1.

Components Perspective

Recognition of a preliteracy stage (i.e., the emergent literacy stage) caused researchers to further investigate this period and identify the knowledge and skills developed during it. One result of this research emphasis was the development of frameworks that attempted to delineate the "components" of the emergent literacy stage. In contrast to the developmental frameworks, which describe a general sequence in the acquisition of emergent literacy knowl-

TABLE 1.1. Components of the Four Developmental Frameworks

Goodman (1986)	McCormick and Mason (1986)	Strommen and Mates (2000)	van Kleeck (1998)
Roots of literacy	Hierarchy	Concepts about reading	Stages
1. Print awareness in situational contexts 2. Print awareness in connected discourse 3. Functions and forms of writing 4. Oral language to talk about written language 5. Metacognitive and metalinguistic awareness about written language	1. Functions of print 2. Print form 3. Coordination of print form and function	1. Reading is one aspect of an interpersonal routine in which the book has a minor role 2. Reading is a social routine in which readers focus on the book 3. Readers construct a sequenced account (story) by relying on the illustrations rather than the print 4. In reconstructing a story, readers can change the words, but the meaning must stay the same 5. Readers refer to printed text to reconstruct a story but might not understand the relationship between decoding print and reading 6. Readers use multiple strategies to interpret the language encoded by print	1. Emphasis on print–meaning relationship 2. Emphasis on print form and early form–meaning correspondences

edge and skills, the primary focus of the components frameworks is on the specific knowledge and skills that characterize the emergent literacy stage. In other words, the components frameworks attempt to address the questions (1) "What do children learn about reading and writing (knowledge) before they are readers and writers in the conventional sense?" and (2) "How do they demonstrate that knowledge (skills)?"

A components perspective on the emergent literacy stage presents a challenge related to the comprehensiveness of the description; that is, any description of the knowledge and skills associated with the emergent literacy stage must be neither too broad nor too narrow in its focus. According to Whitehurst and Lonigan (1998), "recent years have seen an almost unbounded definition of literacy that is often extended to any situation in which an individual negotiates or interacts with the environment through the use of a symbolic system" (p. 849). Just as a broad view of the emergent literacy stage might include knowledge and skills that are only tangentially related to literacy development, a narrow view might result in some critical knowledge and skills being overlooked.

The components frameworks for the emergent literacy stage include those proposed by Storch and Whitehurst (2002) and van Kleeck (1998, 2003). A summary of each framework is presented here followed by a comparison of their similarities and differences.

The Storch and Whitehurst (2002) Framework

Storch and Whitehurst (2002) developed a components framework for the emergent literacy stage based on the perspective that children gain literacy knowledge and skills throughout the stage that influence later literacy development. This framework evolved from an earlier components framework that Whitehurst and Lonigan (1998) developed, which described inside-out skills (children's knowledge of the rules for translating print into sounds and sounds into print) and outside-in skills (children's understanding of the context in which the writing that they are trying to read or write occurs).

The Storch and Whitehurst (2002) framework categorizes children's emergent literacy knowledge and skills as *code-related skills* and *oral language skills*. Code-related skills are comprised of conventions of print (e.g., directionality of reading), beginning forms of writing (e.g., writing one's name), grapheme knowledge (e.g., identifying letters of the alphabet), grapheme–phoneme correspondence (e.g., knowledge that the letter *m* makes the /m/ sound, and phonological awareness (e.g., knowledge that the word "book" begins with the /b/ sound). Oral language skills include semantic knowledge (word knowledge, expressive and receptive vocabulary), syntactic knowledge (knowledge of word order and grammatical rules), narrative discourse (e.g., telling a story), and conceptual knowledge (e.g., knowledge of the world). The oral language and code-related skills that are acquired during the emergent literacy stage constitute the foundation for conventional literacy.

The Storch and Whitehurst (2002) framework shows an early relationship between code-related skills and oral language skills, with these skill areas having a strong reciprocal effect on each other and on early reading development during the preschool and kindergarten years. After kindergarten, code-related and oral language skills become independent of each other with regard to reading development; that is, the code-related skills continue to influence a child's reading development in the first and second grades, but no longer influence the child's oral language skills (Storch & Whitehurst, 2002). Additionally, Storch and Whitehurst (2002) claim that oral language skills have little or no direct influence on reading development in the first and second grades and indirectly affect reading comprehension in the third and fourth grades. Instead, they state that code-related skills learned in kindergarten, such as phonological processing and print concepts, heavily affect a child's ability to read (for some contradictory evidence, see van Kleeck & Norlander, 2008). It is important to emphasize, however, that the early interaction of code-related and oral language skills provides a foundation for reading achievement at least in the early grades of school. For example, Storch and Whitehurst (2002) found that 38% of kindergarten code-related skills were drawn from the code-related skills in the preschool period (e.g., phonological processing and orthographic representation), which also significantly predicted reading achievement in the first and second grades. These code-related skills enabled children to convert printed words to their spoken counterparts, thus driving reading comprehension. Although the influence of code-related skills on emergent literacy is apparent, Storch and Whitehurst (2002, p. 944) stress that oral language skills and code-related skills should not be taught in isolation:

> Though improving code-related skills, such as phonological awareness and print knowledge, may necessarily be a focus of intervention in those children who have not yet acquired sufficient skill in reading words, we must not wait until children have solved the decoding puzzle to begin instruction in oral language skills, such as vocabulary and syntax.

Storch and Whitehurst (2002) emphasize the coordination and interaction of oral language and code-related skills throughout the preschool and kindergarten years. They also explain that these skills continue to develop and influence conventional literacy acquisition. Like Storch and Whitehurst (2002), van Kleeck (1998, 2003) offered a framework that describes the knowledge and skills that children develop throughout the emergent literacy stage.

The van Kleeck (1998, 2003) Framework

The framework that van Kleeck described in 1998 represents another early components framework for the emergent literacy stage. This framework, which evolved from a model of later reading processes first developed by Seidenberg and McClelland (1989) and then elaborated on by Adams (1990), illustrates the interrelationship among four components: (1) the context processor, (2) the meaning processor, (3) the orthographic processor, and (4) the phonological processor. The framework, which van Kleeck discussed further in 2003, specifies the skills that are associated with each processor. van Kleeck (1998) also includes a developmental focus within her components framework, which is discussed in the section "Developmental Perspective."

The *context processor* enables children to comprehend and interpret text that is being read to them before they can read and that they will read themselves later on in their literacy development (van Kleeck, 1998, 2003). Context processor skills include world knowledge (e.g., concept development), syntactic knowledge (e.g., knowledge of grammar and word order), narrative development (e.g., knowledge of story grammar), book conventions (e.g., knowledge of how to use books), abstract language (e.g., inferential language), and functions of print (e.g., to share information).

The *meaning processor* is important to children's ability to apply lexical knowledge to the meanings of individual words (van Kleeck, 1998, 2003). The meaning processor skills are comprised of word awareness (a form of metalinguistic awareness), which involves the understanding that words are units of language and are not part of their referents, and vocabulary development (a semantic language skill).

The *orthographic processor* involves the ability to recognize individual letter units that enable the child to identify individual letters and sequences of letters. Orthographic processor skills are those that pertain to print conventions and letter knowledge (van Kleeck, 1998, 2003).

Lastly, the *phonological processor* enables the child to use phonological awareness skills to convert printed letters to sounds and sound sequences (i.e., words). The phonological processor skills include syllable segmentation, rhyming, and phoneme segmentation (van Kleeck, 1998, 2003). Syllable segmentation is the ability to divide a word into separate syllables. For example, *mother* is divided into two syllables: *moth-er*. Rhyming involves the ability to isolate and change one consonant or consonant cluster at the beginning of a word to create a new word with a similar sound (e.g., isolating and changing the first consonant in *bat* to create *rat*). Phoneme segmentation occurs when a word is divided into phonemes or sound units. For example, *bus* is divided into three units: *b-u-s*.

Summary

The components frameworks that are presented in this section show similarities and differences in the knowledge and skills (i.e., the components) that are viewed as characteristic of the emergent literacy stage. For example, both Storch and Whitehurst (2002) and van Kleeck (1998, 2003) include letter knowledge, phonological awareness, language skills (e.g., semantics, syntax, narrative discourse), and conventions of print. The differences in the components of the Storch and Whitehurst (2002) and van Kleeck (1998, 2003) frameworks arise primarily from differences in the level of specificity in the general categories and the components included within those categories, as illustrated in Table 1.2. The information in the table shows greater specificity in both the general categories and the components for the van Kleeck (1998, 2003) framework.

Although the Storch and Whitehurst (2002) and van Kleeck (1998, 2003) frameworks primarily offer a components perspective on emergent literacy, both frameworks acknowledge that children's exposure to language and literacy shape their emergent literacy development. For example, exposure to environmental print is important to the early development of sight word knowledge. Other factors, such as children's internal motivation to read, also can influence their emergent literacy development. Recognition that factors within the child and the environment are significant to emergent literacy development resulted in the development of frameworks for the emergent literacy stage that are based in this recognition.

TABLE 1.2. Elements Included in Each of the Components Frameworks

Storch and Whitehurst (2002)	van Kleeck (1998, 2003)
Code-related skills	Context processor
• Conventions of print • Beginning forms of writing • Grapheme knowledge • Knowledge of grapheme–phoneme correspondence • Phonological awareness	• Word knowledge • Syntactic knowledge • Narrative development • Book conventions • Abstract language • Functions of print
Oral language skills	Meaning processor
• Semantic knowledge • Syntactic knowledge • Narrative discourse • Conceptual knowledge	• Word awareness • Vocabulary development
	Orthographic processor
	• Print conventions • Letter knowledge
	Phonological processor

	• Phonological awareness
	  • Syllable segmentation
	  • Rhyming/onset and rime
	  • Phoneme segmentation

Child and Environmental Influences Perspective

The most recent frameworks for the emergent literacy stage reflect the growing acknowledgment of child development studies across various disciplines that a child's progression through different stages results from the influence of child and environmental factors either acting separately or in some complex interaction. Frameworks within this category differ in the extent to which they address the child and environmental influences and in the specific child and environmental influences that they consider. Child influences can include factors within the child that might positively or negatively affect emergent literacy development (Wasik & Hendrickson, 2004), such as (1) the child's participation in literacy-related activities, (2) language proficiency, (3) cognitive abilities, (4) interest in literacy, (5) attention, and (6) overall health. The environment includes (1) the physical settings in which the child typically functions (e.g., home, day care, preschool), (2) the people with whom the child interacts somewhat regularly (e.g., parents, siblings, day care providers, preschool teachers), (3) the literacy materials to which the child is exposed consistently (e.g., books, magazines, signs, crayons, pencils, paper), and (4) the literacy experiences and opportunities that are provided within the child's environments (e.g., joint book reading with an adult, group book reading with a teacher, ordering from a menu, drawing a picture of a favorite activity). Two frameworks that emphasize the role of child and/or environmental influences on the emergent literacy stage are those of McNaughton (1995) and Wasik and Hendrickson (2004).

The McNaughton (1995) Framework

McNaughton's (1995) socialization model of child development provides a framework for considering the influence of a child's environment on the acquisition of emergent literacy knowledge, skills, and processes. According to McNaughton's (1995) framework, a child's emergent literacy development is structured within initial family experiences, built from specific activities, and formed into systems of expertise, which then are applicable in some way to all of the child's primary environments. The framework suggests that the activities in which the family engages with the child and the resulting system of learning and development are based on four distinct and identifiable components of family literacy practices. These are (1) *family practices*, (2) *activities* (child and family), (3) *systems for learning and development*, leading to *expertise*, and (4) *relationships between settings*.

Family practices are how children are socialized, thus creating ways of thinking, acting, and using language that are considered appropriate by the various cultural and social communities with which the family identifies. For example, a general social and cultural expectation of families in developed countries is that their children will become literate (McNaughton, 1995). As a result, families expose their children to a range of functions of written language within different contexts. Very young children's experiences range from observing the different uses of written language (e.g., watching a sibling read a book) to being directly involved in such events (e.g., book sharing with a parent).

A family's literacy practices can be observed within the reading and writing *activities* that occur routinely for that family. These activities have goals and rules that are followed. The child can accomplish the activities alone, with siblings, or with the entire family. For example, a family might celebrate friends' and relatives' birthdays by sending birthday cards that the family members have signed (McNaughton, 1995). The goal of the activity is to acknowledge and celebrate someone's birthday; personal notes might also be written that share additional information. As McNaughton notes, such an activity requires that certain conventions are followed, such as signing the card below the text and writing from left to right and top to bottom, including both the mailing and return addresses as well as a postage stamp in appropriate locations on the envelope. Overall, many of the decisions with regard to the goals and rules of each activity are based on the family's cultural and social routines.

Systems for learning and development occur within the family and interact with the activities that provide learning contexts. McNaughton (1995) describes two systems of learning and development. The first occurs when the family is directly involved in activities with the child, such as book sharing. The second occurs when the child explores writing and reading alone. Through both systems, the child develops *expertise* in the areas that are being introduced through participation in the various activities. For example, through book sharing with a parent, the child is becoming an expert on what a book is, how it is read, and the purpose of reading. The child learns how to turn the pages and begins to understand that the pictures represent the text that is being read. Lastly, literacy practices, activities, and systems can be found in settings other than the family environment, such as day care centers, preschools, church events, playgroups, and other community settings. Thus, there is a *relationship between settings* that influences how the child learns and develops different areas of expertise when participating in similar activities within and across a variety of settings. As just one example, if a child learns how to interact with books during book-sharing experiences with a parent, he or she then can use the same book-sharing knowledge and skills in play with another child and with books in a preschool classroom.

The Wasik and Hendrickson (2004) Framework

In studies on family literacy practices with children from infancy through preschool, Wasik and Hendrickson (2004) developed a framework to "organize an analysis of major variables in family literacy practices" (p. 157) that influences literacy development in very young children. Four major variables addressed in the framework are (1) *parental characteristics*, (2) *child characteristics*, (3) *home literacy environment*, and (4) *parent–child relationships*.

The three types of *parental characteristics* that Wasik and Hendrickson (2004) identified include culture and ethnicity, parental beliefs, and socioeconomic status. Culture and ethnicity affect areas such as the expectations for education, the patterns for language use in bilingual families (e.g., primary language used at home, language of the community, bilingual education), the preferences for types of literacy activities (e.g., storytelling, book sharing), and the structure of tasks (e.g., question-asking, task routines, and parental teaching strategies). Parental beliefs include the family's beliefs about the importance and role of the educational system in the literacy development of their children. The family's socioeconomic status has an effect on factors such as the amount of time spent in literacy-related activities, financial resources available for literacy-related materials and experiences, the underlying purpose of family literacy activities (e.g., literacy to perform functions of daily living, literacy to entertain), and other factors that support children's literacy development. These variables might include parents' educational background and the quality of parent–child interactions. Culture and ethnicity, parental beliefs, and socioeconomic status are especially important to consider because of the variability among families in terms of these parental characteristics.

Child characteristics include the child's level of engagement and social interaction in literacy-related activities, as well as language proficiency, cognitive abilities, developmental achievements, motivation, attention, and health conditions that might affect language and literacy development. According to Wasik and Hendrickson (2004), each of the child characteristics can influence the extent to which a child can use the support that the environment provides for early literacy learning. For example, the substantial body of research demonstrating that preschool children with language delays are at a significant risk for later difficulties in learning to read (Boudreau & Hedberg, 1999; Nathan, Stackhouse, Goulandris, & Snowling, 2004; Snowling, Bishop, & Stothard, 2000) indicates that factors within the child can influence emergent literacy development.

The *home literacy environment* includes such aspects as book sharing between parents and children, parents reading aloud with their children, print materials being available to the children, and parents' positive attitudes toward literacy activities (Wasik & Hendrickson, 2004). The home literacy environment is comprised of both direct and indirect literacy-related events. Direct literacy-related events are those in which the child engages, such as book sharing with a parent or labeling the printed letters of the alphabet. Indirect literacy-related events are those about which the child learns through the observation of individuals as they engage in those activities (e.g., reading the newspaper, writing notes). Wasik and Hendrickson (2004) acknowledge that "the home environment is complex, multilayered, and multidimensional, involving both physical and interpersonal features" (p. 162). They emphasize that the characteristics of the home literacy environment interact with the parental and child characteristics in influencing a child's acquisition of emergent literacy knowledge and skills.

The last aspect concerns social–emotional and interpersonal aspects of *parent–child relationships* that relate to literacy practices. According to Wasik and Hendrickson (2004), parent–child literacy interactions are central to fostering a child's emergent literacy skills. Specifically, nurturing parent–child relationships characterized by warm, supportive, and compassionate parental interactions have been correlated with higher language and literacy achievement. Wasik and Hendrickson (2004) further note that although positive parent–child relationships do not wholly account for a child's success or failure with achieving emergent literacy skills, the absence of such relationships can be a detrimental factor in a child's emergent literacy development.

Despite agreement in the literature that there is an interaction between the home literacy environment, parental and child characteristics, and the parent–child relationship, it is difficult to determine the exact nature of the interaction in influencing children's emergent literacy development (McNaughton, 1995; Wasik & Hendrickson, 2004). Consequently, it is important to consider the influence of each variable on emergent literacy development for a particular child.

Summary

Ultimately, the parent and child characteristics, the home literacy environment, and the parent–child relationships interact to influence a child's acquisition of emergent literacy knowledge, skills, and processes. Such a multidimensional approach provides a framework for understanding how a child acquires different components of emergent literacy; however, additional evidence is needed to relate environmental influences to children's acquisition of specific emergent literacy knowledge and skills.

McNaughton (1995) primarily concentrates on family literacy activities that allow children, who are "novices" to reading and writing, opportunities to learn from others in the family and gain expertise in whatever skills are being modeled. In a different light, Wasik and Hendrickson (2004), focus on the influences of family dynamics and how they can affect the development of emergent literacy. Despite this difference, there are parallels in their frameworks. These two frameworks focus on the social, cultural, and interactive influences that comprise children's literacy environments.

Whitehurst and Lonigan (1998) and van Kleeck (1998) also consider the importance of a child's environment on the emergent literacy stage, even though the environment is not explicitly listed as a component in their respective frameworks. Home literacy environments, through direct and indirect input, foster language learning opportunities in addition to nonlanguage outcomes, such as concepts of print and rhyming skills (Whitehurst & Lonigan, 1998). In a similar vein, McNaughton (1995) and van Kleeck (1998) also addressed the influence of joint activities and environmental opportunities, such as shared book reading, dramatic play, and parental modeling of advanced literacy skills on literacy learning. The unifying theme that underlies these frameworks (McNaughton, 1995; van Kleeck, 1998; Wasik & Hendrickson, 2004; Whitehurst & Lonigan, 1998) is that any attempt to describe children's emergent literacy development must take into consideration the literacy environments in which children participate.

Implications of the Perspectives for Fostering Emergent Literacy Development

Children likely develop literacy skills from birth (e.g., Justice, 2006; Teale & Sulzby, 1986). Immediately following birth, children are exposed to oral language, which, for example, builds vocabulary and phonological repertoires that will be important in learning to read. In addition, later academic achievement can often be predicted from the emergent literacy skills children possess when they enter kindergarten (Whitehurst & Lonigan, 1998).

Since emergent literacy has important consequences for a child's life (particularly in school), parents, day care providers, educators, and speech–language pathologists may actively seek information on ways to aid children's emergent literacy development. The frameworks discussed in this chapter fall within three main perspectives on the emergent literacy stage. The implications of the perspectives for fostering children's emergent literacy development alone and in combination are considered in this section. The focus of the discussion on implications is general in nature; Chapters 2 through 6 in this volume provide detailed information on emergent literacy assessment and intervention approaches and strategies.

Developmental Perspective

Efforts to aid children's emergent literacy that are based on the developmental perspective emphasize targeting knowledge and skills that build upon one another in facilitating the child's progression toward conventional literacy. Therefore, such efforts require an understanding of how children generally acquire emergent literacy knowledge and skills, despite a lack of information on the sequence of acquisition. For example, in discussing the hierarchy of development during the emergent literacy stage, McCormick and Mason (1986) stressed the importance of evaluating each child's emergent literacy development to determine the child's progress within the hierarchy in order to provide appropriate literacy guidance. Hence, a child who is working toward developing an understanding of the functions of print (a first-level skill) should not be expected to understand letter–sound correspondences (a second-level skill). McCormick and Mason (1986) suggested the use of "easy-to-read little books" to support the development of print functions because these books follow a predictable pattern, allowing children to construct meaning from the print. In addition, little books serve as a means of fostering positive parent–child literacy activities. While reading the little books to a child, the parent or other adult can point to words that represent pictures in the book. Adults also can facilitate children's learning the different functions of print by reading and pointing to words that the child sees in the environment (e.g., on traffic signs, menus, billboards, packages, and computer games).

Strommen and Mates (2000) emphasize the developmental changes in children's understanding of reading. They believe that, while providing support for emergent literacy development, professionals must also:

- Formulate a hypothesis regarding the child's idea of reading (i.e., level of understanding).
- Introduce new skills for and ideas about reading (i.e., identify skills and ideas that build on and are more complex than previously acquired skills).
- Set goals for reading performance that consider the child's ideas about reading (i.e., specify targets for the identified skills and ideas).

These recommendations are consistent with the belief that the concepts about reading development that children hold influence their actual reading development. By understanding how children develop literacy knowledge and skills, parents and professionals can determine appropriate strategies to facilitate development during the emergent literacy stage.

Components Perspective

Fostering children's emergent literacy development within a components perspective involves identifying and targeting specific knowledge and skills that children acquire during the emergent literacy stage. Examples of specific emergent literacy knowledge and skills that can be targeted within a components perspective are print meaning and print form.

Print Meaning

Assisting children in acquiring print meaning skills centers on the understanding that printed text conveys meaning. Knowledge and skills that are related to print meaning are important to the development of reading comprehension. McCormick and Mason (1986) proposed that an important first step in the acquisition of emergent literacy knowledge and skills is for children to learn that print has a function and carries meaning. They, along with other researchers, recommended the incorporation of parent–child shared book-reading experiences as a means of promoting development of print meaning. Shared book reading and dialogic reading are considered effective in promoting print meaning and other emergent literacy knowledge and skills, such as print awareness, story schema, and plot structure (McCormick & Mason, 1986; Roth & Baden, 2001;

van Kleeck, 2003; Whitehurst & Lonigan, 1998). Dialogic reading, in which the adult uses "What?" questions, open-ended questions, and expansions during shared reading to help the child become the storyteller (Whitehurst & Lonigan, 1998), is strongly advocated as a strategy to facilitate development of print meaning and other emergent literacy knowledge and skills (e.g., Lonigan, Anthony, Bloomfield, Dyer, & Samwel, 1999; Morgan & Goldstein, 2004; Roth & Baden, 2001; Wasik & Hendrickson, 2004; Whitehurst & Lonigan, 2002).

Print Form

Another example of an emergent literacy skill that can be targeted via approaches that are based on a components perspective is print form. The development of decoding abilities is dependent on children's knowledge and skills pertaining to print form (Storch & Whitehurst, 2002; van Kleeck, 2003). Approaches that include a focus directly on print form knowledge and skills have been referred to as bottom-up, parts-to-whole, and explicit approaches to emergent literacy (e.g., Justice & Kaderavek, 2004; van Kleeck, 1998). Storch and Whitehurst (2002) suggest that phonological awareness training facilitates the acquisition of code-related skills to enhance word recognition. In addition, it can aid development of knowledge and skills associated with the phonological and orthographic processors that are included in the components framework of van Kleeck (2003).

Child and Environmental Influences Perspective

Approaches to fostering emergent literacy development that fall within this perspective emphasize comprehensive family literacy practices that eventually enable children to achieve conventional literacy (Wasik & Hendrickson, 2004). One example of implementation is a coaching approach in which parents engage in dialogic reading, learn to scaffold children's literacy learning, and encourage children's active participation to help them learn from adult partners and gain expertise about reading. Parents are taught to ask appropriate questions and to prompt children to comment on and ask questions about books during shared book reading. Lonigan et al. (1999) examined the effects of shared book-reading interventions with preschool children. Both typical shared-reading and dialogic reading interventions positively affected the emergent literacy skills tested. Specifically, the children whose parents used the dialogic reading intervention performed better on measures of descriptive language use and the children whose parents used the typical shared-reading intervention performed better on measures of listening comprehension and alliteration detection. These results indicate that increased exposure to shared-reading experiences enhances children's acquisition of emergent literacy skills. (See Vander Woude et al., Chapter 2, this volume, for additional information on the effects of shared book reading on emergent literacy development.)

Additional changes within a child's literacy environment can improve emergent literacy skills as well. Wayne, DiCarlo, Burts, and Benedict (2007) studied the effects of environmental modifications (e.g., including literacy props) and teacher mediation (e.g., modeling use of a literacy prop or encouraging the child to use the prop) on preschool children's emergent literacy skills. Results revealed that these modifications displayed an increase in the use of literacy behaviors (e.g., looking at a book, listening to a book, looking at letters or words in the environment, writing, etc.).

Children's emergent literacy knowledge and skills can be further enhanced through shared book-reading activities if adults gradually release their role as the "reader" and allow children to become more active participants in book-sharing experiences (van Kleeck, 2003). Adults continue to provide necessary support through abstract comments and questions during reading activities that allow children to develop emergent literacy skills.

Combined Perspectives

Although approaches that are based on a single perspective can effectively promote children's emergent literacy development, there is consensus in the literature that approaches that reflect the use of combined perspectives offer a comprehensive approach to intervention (Storch & Whitehurst, 2002; van Kleeck, 2003; Whitehurst & Lonigan, 1998).

The embedded–explicit approach to emergent literacy that Justice and Kaderavek (2004) describe provides an example of a combined perspectives approach. The basic goals involve development of (1) basic literacy skills linked with reading achievement (e.g., phonological awareness, print concepts, letter knowledge) via explicit instruction, and (2) a positive literacy learning attitude in children and an understanding of the function and intention of literacy via literacy-embedded activities. The first goal is consistent with a components perspective, whereas the second goal reflects the perspective that centers on child and environmental influences. Implementation focuses on incorporating well-developed daily oral and written opportunities for children that enable natural, meaningful, intentional, and deeply contextualized interactions. (Kaderavek, Cabell, & Justice, Chapter 4, this volume, presents a case study that illustrates application of the embedded–explicit approach.)

General Considerations

The various perspectives on emergent literacy development in children can cause confusion when parents, day care providers, educators, and speech–language pathologists search for ways to teach emergent literacy. Decisions about approaches, instructional strategies, literacy materials, and literacy activities can be further complicated by factors associated with the child, such as speech or language impairments. Three of the most researched factors affecting children's emergent literacy development that can place children at risk for literacy problems include the social effects of low socioeconomic status (Justice, Chow, Capellini, Flanigan, & Colton, 2003; Lonigan et al., 1999; Morgan & Goldstein, 2004), language delay/impairments (Justice et al., 2003), and hearing impairments (Kaderavek & Justice, 2002). Even in the case of children without these characteristics, it is important to remember that a single model for fostering emergent literacy development that serves all children does not exist. It is necessary to consider the needs of each child in selecting a perspective or combination of perspectives that can be used to choose an effective approach to promoting children's emergent literacy development.

Conclusion

This chapter has provided a summary and comparative analysis of frameworks within three main perspectives whose purpose is to account for the emergent literacy stage. Although there is no single framework that represents a comprehensive approach to understanding the emergent literacy stage, consideration of the similarities and differences among the available frameworks enables parents, educators, day care providers, and speech–language pathologists to make better informed decisions about the most effective ways to support children's emergent literacy development. As the body of research on the emergent literacy stage increases, it is possible that the picture of patterns of acquisition, as well as the connections between emergent literacy knowledge and skills associated with the stage, will become more clearly identified. Whether this possibility becomes a reality, it is essential to keep in mind that the emergent literacy stage marks the beginning of a journey on a continuum of literacy that has far-reaching effects on children's lives.

DISCUSSION QUESTIONS

1. Discuss the strengths and limitations of each perspective on the emergent literacy stage.

2. Choose a framework within each perspective on the emergent literacy stage. Explain how each framework could be applied within a preschool classroom to foster the emergent literacy development of children with a specific language impairment.

3. Consider the perspectives on the emergent literacy stage. Discuss how you might approach the development of a new framework for the emergent literacy stage that is consistent with one of the perspectives presented in this chapter.

EXERCISES

1. Prepare a handout for parents of children from birth through 5 years of age that describes activities that parents can use to support their children's emergent literacy development at these various ages.

2. Design a preschool classroom environment that will effectively promote children's emergent literacy development. Describe ways to incorporate literacy props throughout the environment.

3. Identify three objectives pertaining to emergent literacy knowledge and skills for a preschool classroom. Describe an activity that addresses each objective and explain how the activity could be implemented via collaboration between the classroom teacher and the speech–language pathologist.

References

Adams, M. (1990). *Beginning to read: Thinking and learning about print.* Cambridge, MA: MIT Press.

Adams, M. J. (2002). Alphabetic anxiety and explicit, systematic phonics instruction: A cognitive science perspective. In S. B. Neuman & D. K. Dickinson (Eds.), *Handbook of early literacy research* (pp. 66–80). New York: Guilford Press.

Boudreau, D. M., & Hedberg, N. L. (1999). A comparison of early literacy skills in children with specific language impairment and their typically developing peers. *Journal of Speech, Language, and Hearing Research, 8,* 249–260.

Clay, M. M. (1991). *Becoming literate: The construction of inner control.* Portsmouth, NH: Heinemann Educational Books.

Dickinson, D. K., McCabe, A., Anastasopoulos, L., Peisner-Feinberg, E. S., & Poe, M. D. (2003). The comprehensive language approach to early literacy: The interrelationships among vocabulary, phonological sensitivity, and print knowledge among preschool-aged children. *Journal of Educational Psychology, 95*(3), 465–481.

Fields, M. V., & Spangler, K. L. (2000). *Let's begin reading right: A developmental approach to emergent literacy.* Columbus, OH: Merrill.

Glazer, S. M. (1989). Oral language and literacy development. In D. S. Strickland & L. M. Morrow (Eds.), *Emerging literacy: Young children learn to read and write* (pp. 16–26). Newark, DE: International Reading Association.

Goodman, Y. M. (1986). Children coming to know literacy. In W. H. Teale & E. Sulzby (Eds.), *Emergent literacy: Writing and reading* (pp. 1–14). Norwood, NJ: Ablex.

Justice, L. M. (2006). Emergent literacy: Development, domains, and intervention approaches. In L. M. Justice (Ed.), *Clinical approaches to emergent literacy intervention* (pp. 3–27). San Diego: Plural.

Justice, L. M., Chow, S., Capellini, C., Flanigan, K., & Colton, S. (2003). Emergent literacy intervention for vulnerable preschoolers: Relative effects of two approaches. *American Journal of Speech–Language Pathology, 12*(3), 320–332.

Justice, L. M., & Kaderavek, J. N. (2004). Embedded–explicit emergent literacy intervention: I. Background and description of approach. *Language, Speech, and Hearing Services in Schools, 35,* 201–211.

Kaderavek, J., & Justice, L. M. (2002). Shared storybook reading as an intervention context: Practices and potential pitfalls. *American Journal of Speech–Language Pathology, 11*(4), 395–406.

Lonigan, C. J., Anthony, J. L., Bloomfield, B. G., Dyer, S. M., & Samwel, C. S. (1999). Effects of two shared-reading interventions on emergent literacy skills of at-risk preschoolers. *Journal of Early Intervention, 22*(4), 306–322.

McCormick, C. E., & Mason, J. M. (1986). Intervention procedures for increasing preschool children's interest in and knowledge about reading. In W. H. Teale & E. Sulzby (Eds.), *Emergent literacy: Writing and reading* (pp. 90–115). Norwood, NJ: Ablex.

McNaughton, S. (1995). *Patterns of emergent literacy: Processes of development and transition.* New York: Oxford University Press.

Morgan, L., & Goldstein, H. (2004). Teaching mothers of low socioeconomic status to use decontextualized language during storybook reading. *Journal of Early Intervention, 26*(4), 235–252.

Nathan, L., Stackhouse, J., Goulandris, N., & Snowling, M. J. (2004). The development of early literacy skills among children with speech difficulties: A test of the "critical age hypothesis." *Journal of Speech, Language, and Hearing Research, 47,* 377–391.

Neuman, S. B., & Roskos, K. (1993). *Language and literacy in the early years: An integrated approach.* Fort Worth, TX: Harcourt, Brace, Jovanovich.

Owens, R. E., Jr. (2007). *Language development: An introduction.* New York: Allyn & Bacon.

Reese, E., Cox, A., Harte, D., & McAnally, H. (2003). Diversity in adults' styles of reading books to children. In A. Van Kleeck, S. A. Stahl, & E. B. Bauer (Eds.), *On reading books to children: Parents and teachers* (pp. 37–57). Mahwah, NJ: Erlbaum.

Roth, F. P., & Baden, B. (2001). Investing in emergent literacy intervention: A key role for speech–language pathologists. *Seminars in Speech and Language, 22*(3), 163–173.

Roth, F. P., Speece, D. L., Cooper, D. H., & De La Paz, S. (1996). Unresolved mysteries: How do metalinguistics and narrative skills connect with early reading? *Journal of Special Education, 30*(3), 257–277.

Seidenberg, M. S., & McClelland, J. L. (1989). A distributed, developmental model of word recognition and naming. *Psychological Review, 96*(4), 523–568.

Sénéchal, M., LeFevre, J., Smith-Chant, B. L., & Colton, K. V. (2001). On refining theoretical models of emergent literacy: The role of empirical evidence. *Journal of School Psychology, 39*(5), 439–460.

Snow, C. E., Tabors, P. O., & Dickinson, D. K. (2001). Language development in the preschool years. In D. K. Dickinson & P. O. Tabors (Eds.), *Beginning literacy with language: Young children learning at home and school* (pp. 1–26). Baltimore: Brookes.

Snowling, M., Bishop, D. V. M., & Stothard, S. E. (2000). Is preschool language impairment a risk factor for dyslexia in adolescence? *Journal of Child Psychology and Psychiatry and Allied Disciplines, 41*(5), 587–600.

Storch, A. S., & Whitehurst, G. J. (2002). Oral language and code-related precursors to reading: Evidence from a longitudinal structural model. *Developmental Psychology, 38*(6), 934–947.

Strickland, D., & Morrow, L. (1988). New perspectives on young children learning to read and write. *The Reading Teacher, 42,* 70–71.

Strommen, L. T., & Mates, B. F. (2000). What readers do: Young children's ideas about the nature of reading. In M. Robinson, J. McKenna, &

J. Wedman (Eds.), *Issues and trends in literacy education* (2nd ed., pp. 200–212). Boston: Allyn & Bacon.

Teale, W. H., & Sulzby, E. (1986). Emergent literacy as a perspective for examining how young children become writers and readers. In W. H. Teale & E. Sulzby (Eds.), *Emergent literacy: Writing and reading* (pp. vii–xxv). Norwood, NJ: Ablex.

van Kleeck, A. (1998). Preliteracy domains and stages: Laying the foundations for beginning reading. *Journal of Children's Communication Development, 20,* 33–51.

van Kleeck, A. (2003). Research on book sharing: Another critical look. In A. van Kleeck, S. A. Stahl, & E. B. Bauer (Eds.), *On reading books to children* (pp. 271–320). Mahwah, NJ: Erlbaum.

van Kleeck, A., & Norlander, A. E. (2008). Fostering form and meaning in emerging literacy using evidence-based practice. In M. Mody & E. R. Silliman (Eds.), *Brain, behavior, and learning in language and reading disorders* (pp. 275–314). New York: Guilford Press.

Wagner, R. K., Torgesen, J. K., & Rashotte, C. A. (1994). Development of reading-related phonological processing abilities: New evidence of bidirectional causality from a latent variable longitudinal study. *Developmental Psychology, 30*(1), 73–87.

Wasik, B. H., & Hendrickson, J. S. (2004). Family literacy practices. In C. A. Stone, E. R. Silliman, B. J. Ehren, & K. Apel (Eds.), *Handbook of language and literacy: Development and disorders* (pp. 154–174). New York: Guilford Press.

Wayne, A., DiCarlo, C. F., Burts, D. C., & Benedict, J. (2007). Increasing the literacy behaviors of preschool children through environmental modification and teacher mediation. *Journal of Research in Childhood Education, 22*(1), 5–17.

Whitehurst, G. J., & Lonigan, C. J. (1998). Child development and emergent literacy. *Child Development, 69,* 848–872.

Whitehurst, G. J., & Lonigan, C. J. (2002). Emergent literacy: Development from prereaders to readers. In S. B. Neuman & D. K. Dickinson (Eds.), *Handbook of early literacy research* (pp. 11–29). New York: Guilford Press.

CHAPTER TWO

Book Sharing and the Development of Meaning

JUDITH VANDER WOUDE
ANNE VAN KLEECK
ELIZABETH VANDER VEEN

Repeatedly participating in semantically rich and meaningful early literacy activities increases children's knowledge about their world, the language they are learning, and how people communicate within those activities (for a review, see Dickinson & McCabe, 2001). Shared book reading between children and adults is one such early literacy activity that ideally includes discussions about the text and pictures that facilitate children's understanding of essential vocabulary, their development of text inferencing skills, and their ability to engage in school-like patterns of discourse, such as learning how to verbally display their knowledge. Proficient vocabulary, inferencing, and discourse skills are foundational for academic success and are particularly related to later skilled reading comprehension.

The nature of adults' book-sharing discussions is of critical importance to how well children are able to derive meaning from, and participate in, the book-sharing activity. As such, we first briefly review evidence on the development of early book-sharing discussions. We synthesize key research that illuminates how many middle-class adults naturally change their methods for mediating print meaning as young children mature cognitively and linguistically. After summarizing the development of book-sharing conversations, we contrast the findings on developmental changes in strategies for reading to children who are typically developing with those found in book-sharing interactions with young children who have language delays. Finally, we outline book-sharing assessments and interventions shown to be effective for fostering children's literal and inferential language skills.

As part of this discussion, we highlight a dimension of print meaning that is rarely considered in interventions directly, but that nonetheless occurs frequently in book sharing with older preschool children from middle-class families—engagement with the information of books that requires inferencing. Children's ability to engage in inferencing is increasingly acknowledged to be particularly important to later higher levels of text comprehension that are critical for academic success (e.g., Block & Pressley, 2002).

Benefits of Engaging in Early and Frequent Shared Book Reading

Early and frequent shared book reading can be important for learning new vocabulary even before children have learned to speak. In mainstream culture families, shared book reading often begins with infants even before the age of 7 months (e.g., DeBaryshe, 1993; Richman & Colombo, 2007). Infants potentially derive benefit from such early book-sharing routines because around the age of 5 months they are able to recognize relatively abstract two-dimensional stimuli and discriminate between pictures and objects (DeLoache, Strauss, & Maynard, 1979), and by approximately 6 months old, they are able to maintain joint attention on objects and pictures during interactions (Rogoff, Malkin, & Gilbride, 1984). Later, around the age of 9 months, infants begin exploring pictures manually by scratching, grasping, or trying to manipulate them in some way; and around the age of 15 months, children begin both pointing at and manually exploring the pictures in books. Finally, at 19 months, toddlers begin to show their understanding of the relationship between representation and referent by pointing to pictures almost exclusively (DeLoache, Pierroutsakos, Uttal, Rosengren, & Gottlieb, 1998; DeLoache et al., 1979; DeLoache, Uttal, & Pierroutsakos, 2000).

If parents read to their infants from the time they have developed skills of joint attention and the ability to recognize two-dimensional stimuli, their infants are more likely to have better oral language skills (DeBaryshe, 1993; Karrass & Braungart-Rieker, 2005; Raikes et al., 2006) and early literacy skills (Bus, 2003) in their preschool years than parents who begin reading to their children later in their development. In a study of the book-sharing habits of 2,581 low-income mothers, Raikes and her colleagues (2006) found that daily book sharing predicted children's vocabulary and comprehension of language at 14 months of age and their language and cognition at 24 and 36 months of age, respectively. Bus, Sulzby, and Kaderavek (cited in Bus, 2003) found that children who began participating in routine book sharing with their mothers before they were 14 months of age exhibited better early literacy skills when they were 24 to 36 months of age. These children were able to better internalize the story's content, including actual phrases, events, and vocabulary, than children who started sharing books after they were 14 months old. Bus (2003) asserted that children do not simply memorize the content of stories, but instead the children's routine experiences with books help them to internalize the information in books so that they can recognize story structures and vocabulary with greater ease.

In addition to the positive effects of very early book sharing, the frequency of children's participation in book sharing is also related to greater increases in vocabulary and early literacy skills (Crain-Thoreson & Dale, 1992; Vivas, 1996; Wells, 1985). Indeed, simply asking parents or day care providers of preschool children to share books for at least 15 minutes three times a week and teaching them ways to encourage the toddlers to talk more about pictures during book sharing appears to significantly increase children's language abilities (e.g., Bus, 2003; Crain-Thoreson & Dale, 1999; DeBaryshe, 1993; Whitehurst et al., 1988; Whitehurst & Lonigan, 2001). However, to be maximally effective, as we discuss next, young children need to be engaged in book-sharing conversations in developmentally appropriate ways.

Development of Conversational Strategies

Studies suggest that it is not just the presence or absence of book sharing with young children, nor even the amount of book sharing that takes place, but rather the interactional book-sharing conversations that are most beneficial to children's language and literacy development. Mol, Bus, de Jong, and Smeets (2008) conducted a meta-analysis of 16 early literacy studies that compared the relative benefits of interactive conversations during book sharing to book sharing without conversations for increasing children's vocabulary. They found that interactive conversations during book sharing were most effective for increasing children's vocabulary growth if the children were typically developing and between the ages of 2 and 3 years; conversely, they found reduced effects for children who were 4 to 5 years old. Mol and colleagues (2008) suggested that older children are developmentally more able to independently enjoy and understand the stories without much external parental support and are better able to initiate conversations if they do not understand vocabulary in the text than younger children. Mol and colleagues (2008) also found significantly reduced effects of book sharing on the vocabulary development of children at risk for language and literacy impairments. Children were defined as at risk based on families' low-income or reportedly low maternal educational status. In view of the results of Mol and colleagues' (2008) meta-analysis, the content of the book-sharing conversations, the optimal developmental ages for conversational content, and children's at-risk status differentially influenced children's learning from book-sharing activities. In the following section, we review selective research to demonstrate how parents naturally evolve the conversational strategies they use to coconstruct meaning with their maturing children.

Responsive Interactive Strategies

Observations of the different ways parents naturally use conversational strategies with their infants, toddlers, and preschool children provide a framework for constructing developmentally appropriate assessments and interventions for children at risk for language and early literacy delays. From observational data, we know that parents often use consistent teacher-like labeling routines during book-sharing conversations to help their children develop vocabulary and to help parents determine what their children have learned (Ninio & Bruner, 1978; Sénéchal, Cornell, & Broda, 1995; van Kleeck, Vander Woude, & McDonald, 2006). The labeling routine often consists of an "attentional evocative," defined as an utterance designed to get a child's attention, a "query" or question, then a "label," given in response to the parent's question and a "feedback" utterance, which is a parent's evaluation of the child's labeling response. If the child is not yet able to provide the labels, the parent consistently takes the child's turn and models the correct responses; the parent therefore uses natural and intuitive adjustments, as needed, to help the child participate successfully in the book-sharing conversations over time.

To illustrate, van Kleeck, Vander Woude, and McDonald (2006) observed the same 10 mother–child dyads over an 18-month period, from the time the children were 6 months old until they were 24 months old. Throughout the 18 months, the mothers focused on labeling pictures of nouns on average at least six times more often than pictures of verbs. The mothers also appeared to use different types of questions over time to help their children participate successfully in the book-sharing context. When the children were between 6 and 18 months of age, the mothers used many questions about specific lexical items in which the answers were embedded in the question, such as "Where?" questions (e.g., "Where is the bear?") and yes–no questions (e.g., "Is this a bear?"). When the mothers used "Where?" questions and yes–no questions, the children only had to respond minimally by simply pointing or indicating "yes" or "no" to participate in the book-sharing conversations. After the children were 18 months old and had larger expressive vocabularies, the parents began using more questions about specific lexical items without embedding answers (e.g., "What is that?"). Most importantly, the parents in the van Kleeck, Vander Woude, & McDonald (2006) study focused on helping their children establish meaning from the shared book-reading activity through a variety of means that were especially appropriate for their children's different linguistic and cognitive developmental stages.

Focus on Developing Comprehension of Meaning

A similar pattern of natural and intuitive conversational adjustments emerged in another longitudinal study on the development of 10 mothers' corrections of children's errors in responding during shared book reading (Vander Woude, van Kleeck, & Bormann, 2005). In this study, which observed mothers sharing books with their young children from the ages of 6 to 48 months, mothers began correcting children's incorrect responses to requests for labels of items in books at about 11 to 12 months of age, which corresponded with their children's development of their first words. When the children were between 12 and 20 months old, their mothers focused primarily on correcting semantic (and just a few phonetic) errors. When their children were 22 months old, the mothers began making more syntactic corrections; however, later at 36 and 48 months, the mothers made very few syntactic corrections. Syntactic corrections at 22 months were primarily expansions of the children's telegraphic utterances. These expansions focused on the developmental "errors" children make before they mastered more adult-like grammar, as shown in the following excerpt from a conversation between a young boy and his mother while reading a book together when the child was 22 months old:

1. Mother:	Do you feed Cody?	(question)
2. Child:	Mouth	(answer)
3. Mother:	Yes,	(feedback and
	and do you feed	question)
	her bones?	
4. Child:	In mouth	(answer)
5. Mother:	Mhm (agrees)	(feedback)
6. Child:	Mouth	(repeat answer)
7. Mother:	In her mouth	(corrective expansion)

In the above excerpt, the child's mother made a connection to his real-life experiences by asking him if he feeds his dog, Cody, in line 1. Even though the child did not answer his mother's question as expected with a "yes" or a "no" answer in line 2, his mother affirmed his answer and then continued the dialogue by talking about what he specifically feeds his dog in line 3. In his response, the child added a preposition to his answer (*in*) in line 4. Subsequently in line 7, his mother expanded his utterance in line 6 (*mouth*) by adding the pronoun *her*. Although there was evidence of the mothers correcting their children's syntax more frequently around the age of 22 months, they continued to focus overwhelmingly on correcting semantic errors by using, on average, seven times more labeling corrections than syntactic and phonetic corrections throughout the entire 42 months.

Besides asking questions with embedded lexical information and using mostly semantic corrections during book sharing, parents also seem to naturally modify the text of books to help their young children better comprehend the meaning of texts. In one study, Martin (1998) found that the mothers of three age groups of younger children (6, 12, and 18 month olds) frequently modified the text of books to clearly label the items they discussed. In contrast, mothers of the two groups of older children (24 and 48 month olds) did not modify the texts as frequently. Martin (1998) reasoned that parents intuitively knew that their very young children would have difficulty understanding the text, so they modified it to match their children's comprehension skills. Results of Martin's (1998) study affirmed the conclusions of Ninio and Bruner (1978), Sénéchal et al. (1995), and Vander Woude et al. (2005) that parents' primary focus of early book-sharing conversations is helping children derive meaning from the books' pictures and texts.

Results of studies repeatedly document middle-class parents' finely tuned book-sharing interactions with their young children. The fine-tuning involves adjustments that parents make in their book-sharing conversations as their children increase their language skills over time. Most parents seem to know intuitively the amount and levels of linguistic and cognitive adjustments, such as the amount of labeling, type of questions, and the type of corrections that children need at a particular point in time to be fully engaged in book-sharing conversations. In the next section, we discuss another dimension of meaning that is increasingly introduced by parents from the mainstream culture as their children develop into the later preschool years—engaging children in making inferences about information presented in books.

Inferential Language Use during Book Sharing

The importance of inferential language skills to later higher levels of reading comprehension is being acknowledged more frequently (e.g., Caccamise & Snyder, 2005; Catts & Kamhi, 1999; Kamhi, 2005; Westby, 2004). Comprehending inferential language requires reasoning abilities and/or background knowledge to determine meanings when not all of the needed information is provided in the text or accompanying pictures. In contrast, comprehending literal language requires only that children use information provided directly in the books' texts or the pictures.

To illustrate, discussions at literal levels during book sharing involve asking children to point to specific pictures in the book, to provide labels for objects and characters, or to describe objects, actions, or events directly discussed in the story or directly depicted in an illustration. Some examples of literal questions an adult might ask during book sharing include "Where is the bear?" (with the bear clearly shown in the picture), "What's the bear doing?" (with the bear's action clearly shown in the picture or directly discussed in the text), "What's that?" (with a pointing gesture to an object clearly shown in the picture), or "What color is he?" (with a pointing gesture to a brown bear in the picture). Parents of infants and toddlers usually keep the majority of their linguistic input at the literal level while parents of typically developing 3- to 5-year-old children tend to use more inferential language in book-sharing conversations.

Discussions at inferential levels during book sharing, compared to discussions at literal levels, include questions or comments that rely at least in part on information that cannot be seen directly in the pictures or that is not discussed directly in the text. Some examples include (1) discussing or asking about characters' attitudes, points of view, or motivations; (2) making predictions or identifying causes for events; (3) defining words; or (4) making connections among different texts or between the information in the book and the child's or adult's world knowledge (see van Kleeck, 2006b). Some examples of inferential questions an adult might ask during book sharing include "Why do you think Bird did that? What do you think Bear is going to do next? Do you know what *gentle* means? How do you think Bear feels now?"

One important question regarding the type of adult linguistic input to preschool children pertains to the ratio of literal to inferential linguistic input considered most effective for children's learning. Blank, Rose, and Berlin (1978) recommended that adults engage preschool children in conversations at less challenging literal levels 70% of the time and at more challenging inferential levels about 30% of the time. Results of observational studies indicate that parents seem to intuitively use approximately the same ratio of literal to inferential information in their book-sharing conversations (Hammett & van Kleeck, 2005; Hammett, van Kleeck, & Huberty, 2003; van Kleeck, Gillam, Hamilton, & McGrath, 1997). van Kleeck and her colleagues (1997) proposed that when adults provide most of their storybook discussions at easier levels that their children have already mastered, they create an overall nonthreatening, positive atmosphere for learning in which they can then challenge their children to engage in higher-level, inferential language.

Book Sharing with Children with Language Delays

Children with language delays by definition have poor language skills, and as a result are at high risk for reading difficulties (e.g., Bishop & Adams, 1990; Catts, Fey, & Proctor-Williams, 2000; Catts, Fey, Tomblin, & Zhang, 2002). Not surprisingly, they also have difficulty with language at inferential levels (Bradshaw, Hoffman, & Norris, 1998; Ford & Milosky, 2005; Lehrer & deBernard, 1987), which are important to later higher levels of reading comprehension. Children with language delays tend to participate less in book-sharing interactions, while also needing greater support from and being less challenged by their parents than their typically developing peers (van Kleeck & Vander Woude, 1999; Vander Woude, 1998; Vander Woude & Koole, 2000). They ask fewer questions, initiate fewer new topics, and make fewer comments during book-sharing conversations. Preschool children with both expressive and receptive language delays seem to engage in book-sharing conversations less frequently than do preschool children with expressive-only impairments (Mogford-Bevan & Summersall, 1997; Vander Woude & Koole, 2000).

In comparison to parents of typically developing children, parents of preschool children with language delays talk more frequently than do their children during shared book reading (Evans & Schmidt, 1991; Sigel & McGillicuddy-Delisi, 1984; Sulzby & Kaderavek, 1996). In addition, parents of children with language delays appear to use fewer inferential questions and comments than do the parents of typically developing children (e.g., Armstrong & Pruett, 2000; Evans & Schmidt, 1991; Martin, 1998; Sigel & McGillicuddy-Delisi, 1984). Furthermore, as children with language delays improve their language skills over time, their parents do not appear to correspondingly increase the percentage of inferencing input in their book-sharing conversations as do the parents of children with typically developing language (Vander Woude & Koole, 2000). These tendencies all combine to result in children with language delays generally gaining less experience hearing and using language (both literal and inferential) during book-sharing interactions.

Assessment Strategies
for Book-Sharing Conversations

The research discussed thus far in this chapter highlights the importance of the amount and nature of book sharing for children with and without language delays, and leads rather naturally to recommending interrelated strategies for educational assessments and interventions. Recommended assessments include standardized language and early literacy evaluations, parent interviews about book sharing in the home, and observations of children and parents during book-sharing conversations.

Initially, it is important to establish baseline data for preschool children's language skills in general, such as their understanding of vocabulary, their use of syntax, their use of inferential language, and their development of early literacy skills. Some commonly used standardized tests available for assessing preschool children's language and literacy skills to determine general areas of difficulty relative to their age peers include the Preschool Language Scale–IV (Zimmerman, Steiner, & Pond, 2002), an overall assessment of young children's language skills; the Peabody Picture Vocabulary Test–IV (PPVT-4; Dunn & Dunn, 2007), a test of receptive vocabulary; the Structured Photographic Expressive Language Test–II (SPELT-II; Werner & Kresheck, 1983), a test of expressive syntax; the Preschool Language Assessment Instrument–2 (PLAI-2; Blank, Rose, & Berlin, 2003), an assessment of children's literal and inferential language skills; and the Test of Early Reading Ability–3 (TERA-3; Reid, Hresko, & Hammill, 2001), a general assessment of children's print convention and letter knowledge. Conducting these assessments before recommending intervention strategies provides a general picture of children's overall language skills, while using the following informal assessment strategies and goals provides important information for designing specific intervention strategies parents and other adults can use in book-sharing conversations with children.

Parent Interviews

First, assessment of preschool children's language and early literacy development should include a comprehensive parent interview that includes questions on the book-sharing routines in the family's home (see Boudreau, 2005, for an example of an early literacy questionnaire for parents that includes questions on book-sharing routines). Questions should address the literacy habits of the child's parents and/or other significant adults in the child's life (e.g., "How do the adults in your home read books or magazines?"). Questions should also address how frequently adults in the home specifically read to the child, what types of books are chosen to read to the child, and how much the child enjoys sharing books with adults. Results of the parent interview provide important information about the frequency and type of literacy experiences in the home, in addition to providing possible directions for an intervention.

Observations of Child Book-Sharing Behaviors

In addition to parent interviews, observations of children's and parents' book-sharing conversations provide additional assessment data useful for planning specific interventions. It is important to observe the book-sharing conversations of both the adult and the child while reading books. The results of the developmental research on book sharing described previously in this chapter provide general guidelines for describing parent–child book-sharing behaviors. Three general stages of preschool children's behaviors during book sharing are outlined in Table 2.1: the early, middle, and late stages. It is important to note that these stages are estimates of when typically developing middle-class children learn to use increasingly complex ways of participating in book-sharing conversations; large variations exist in how and when children develop their book-sharing knowledge and skills, particularly among children of diverse socioeconomic and cultural backgrounds. (See Battle, Chapter 6, this volume, and van Kleeck, 2006a, for in-depth discussions of cultural influences on emergent literacy development.)

Early Stage

Initially during the early stage of book-sharing development, usually when children are between the ages of 6 to 18 months, infants learn to recognize pictures and differentiate between pictures and objects (DeLoache et al., 1979). Infants usually display their knowledge of pictures by looking at specific pictures in books when directed to do so by their parents (e.g., when a parent says, "Look! A doggy!" the child looks at the picture to which the parent is pointing). Also

TABLE 2.1. Developmental Stages of Preschool Children's Book-Sharing Knowledge and Skills

Stage	Knowledge and skills
Early (6–18 months)	• Recognize pictured objects in books. • Discriminate between pictures in books and objects. • Focus jointly with an adult on pictures in books. • Treat books as manipulative toys (e.g., opening and closing the book indiscriminately). • Explore the pictures in the book by scratching, grasping, or trying to manipulate the pictures (e.g., hits a picture of a ball in the book or licks a picture of an ice cream cone). • Turn the pages of the book even though the timing may be inappropriate. • Vocalize when looking at the pictures in the books. • Vocalize in response to adult's questions. • Maintain attention for relatively short periods of time.
Middle (18–36 months)	• Answer adult's what-questions about pictures with single words first and with longer utterances later during the middle stage. • Complete adult's sentences with the appropriate words when reading familiar books. • Request book sharing first by bringing favorite books to adults and later by naming specific books. • Point to specific pictures in the book (e.g., Adult asks, "Where is the doggy?" Child points to the picture in the book.); first by both manually exploring and pointing and then later by only pointing. • Turn the pages of the books appropriately when assisted by an adult. • Point to the pictures in the books and ask, "What's that?" • Begin to relate the events in the book to real-life events.
Late (36–60 months)	• Ask "Why?" in response to events and characters' motivations. • Understand increasingly complex story structures. • Learn how to predict events in the story. • Discuss characters' motivations with increasing complexity. • Formulate and request formal definitions of the words in the books. • Retell stories with increasing accuracy and detail. • Talk about letters and print conventions of books.

Note. The stages are general estimates of when typically developing children learn to use increasingly complex ways of participating in book-sharing conversations. There is great individual variation in how and when children develop their book-sharing knowledge and skills.

during the early stage, infants begin exploring or acting upon books by physical movements such as hitting pictures, scratching images in the book, or turning the pages of books, usually inappropriately, throughout the shared book-reading activity (DeLoache & DeMendoza, 1987; DeLoache et al., 1979, 1998, 2000; Murphy, 1978). Infants make specific vocalizations in the early stage of book sharing that are interpreted by their parents as legitimate responses to questions (Ninio & Bruner, 1978; Sénéchal et al., 1995; van Kleeck, Vigil, & Beers, 1998).

Middle Stage

The greatest developmental changes in children's book-sharing behaviors occur during the middle stage, usually when children are between the ages of 18 and 36 months. These developmental changes closely correspond to the children's linguistic and cognitive development. Throughout the middle stage, children gradually increase their attention spans and verbally respond with specific labels more frequently to their parents' questions. Children begin to answer their parents' "Where?" and "What?" questions appropriately and complete the sentences in familiar books. They move from manually exploring pictures to simply pointing to them and vocalizing (Troseth, Pierroutsakos, & DeLoache, 2004). By the middle stage, the children usually demonstrate more focused page-turning behaviors along with pointing to pictures (Bus & van IJzendoorn, 1997; Murphy, 1978; Sénéchal et al., 1995). Moreover, children at the middle stage begin making simple connections to their real-life experiences (e.g., Heath, 1982; Snow & Goldfield, 1983). Children initiate more conversational topics at the end of this stage, often by asking "What's that?" or even using a simplified version of that question (e.g., "Dat?"). In general, children become more responsible for a greater percentage of the book-sharing conversations during the middle stage (Fletcher & Jean-Francious, 1998; Goodsitt, Raitan, & Perlmutter, 1988; Snow & Goldfield, 1983). Finally, by the conclusion of the middle stage, children are beginning to retell the stories of books that they have read repeatedly (Sulzby, 1985; Sulzby & Zecker, 1991).

Late Stage

Most of the book-sharing conversations at the early and middle stages consist of literal, rather than inferential, language (van Kleeck, Alexander, Vigil, & Templeton, 1996). During the late stage of preschool book-sharing development, when children are approximately 36 to 60 months of age, children are able to increasingly understand and use inferential language in book-sharing conversations (De Temple & Snow, 1996; Sigel & McGillicuddy-Delisi, 1984; van Kleeck et al.,

1997). Throughout the later stage, children learn how to predict events in the stories they read with adults. Children's ability to predict what may happen next is related to their increased knowledge of the structures of stories. Their understanding of how one event logically leads to another helps them to reconstruct the plot or central theme of a story. By the end of the late stage, children can retell the stories, sometimes using actual phrases or vocabulary from the book's text with increasing complexity, including details about the setting, the plot, and the characters (e.g., Neuman, 1996). (See Roth, Chapter 5, this volume, for another perspective on children's early story development.)

Children also evaluate characters' motivations and actions, such as asking why a character wants to do a particular action. For example, while reading the children's book *Mooncake* (Asch, 1983), a 4-year-old child asked, "Why does Bear want to go to the moon?" (The example is from transcripts of unreported data from van Kleeck, Vander Woude, & Hammett, 2006.) Furthermore, between the ages of 36 and 60 months, children request and make formal definitions of words. For example, Jason, who was in the late stage, read a book about castles with his mother. While reading about the parts of the castle, he asked "What's a *keep*? Is that a place they keep stuff?" His mother replied, "Yeah, sort of. It's the strongest part of the castle and the lord of the castle usually stays there so he is safe. So the *keep* keeps important people safe." Then later during the same book-sharing conversation, when his mother read the word *keep* again, Jason said, "So that's the strongest part of the castle, right?" (These examples are from transcripts of unreported data from Vander Woude, 1998.)

Initiating discussions about vocabulary in books is an important high-level inferential discourse skill related to later school success. Indeed, children who have larger vocabularies have better reading comprehension skills (e.g., Dole, Sloan, & Trathern, 1995); and later, as adolescents, children are expected to routinely elaborate on and provide more sophisticated definitions for more literate vocabulary (see Nippold, 1998). When children ask for formal definitions of specific words or phrases, they demonstrate a sophisticated understanding of the importance of learning new vocabulary to fully understand the meaning of the text. Furthermore, like Jason's example above, when children use formal definitions during book-sharing conversations, they demonstrate that they know how to display their knowledge during literate activities.

Children in the late stage of preschool book-sharing conversations begin to talk about the letters and discuss print conventions of books. Parents of older preschool children typically talk about letters and their associated sounds only when they read alphabet books; parents of younger children may treat alphabet books as picture books. For example, in a longitudinal book-sharing study of 14 mothers and their children, van Kleeck (1998) found that mothers of 24-month-old children treated alphabet books as picture books, and focused on the meaning of the text rather than on specific letters. In contrast, the mothers of the 36- to 48-month-old children focused mostly on letter knowledge (see van Kleeck, 1998, for a summary report of the data). These findings were replicated in another study with 28 mothers and their children ages 42 to 49 months (see van Kleeck, 1998). When the parents and children read rhyming books and storybooks, no mention was made of letter names or sounds; however, when reading alphabet books, the parents referenced alphabet letters frequently. Thus, a word of caution is necessary here: The genre of the book, especially alphabet books, makes a difference in how frequently parents refer to print. To accommodate genre differences, we recommend video recording at least two book-sharing conversations, one of the parent and child reading a storybook and another with the parent and child reading an alphabet book when observing children in the late stage of preschool book sharing. Also, video recording the conversations allows the speech–language pathologist and other early childhood professionals to first evaluate the child's behaviors and then to view the same book-sharing conversations again to document observations of the parent's conversational content.

Finally, during the late stage, children begin to understand conventions or rules for print. They learn that text presents a unique experience for learning. They understand and use text-related vocabulary, such as *page, read, write, letter*, and *book* (e.g., Lomax & McGee, 1987; Tumner, Herriman, & Nesdale, 1988). They learn about title pages, authors, and illustrators. Some preschool children at this stage even ask quite sophisticated questions such as if the copyright dates are the books' "birthdays" and if the ISBN numbers are the books' phone numbers (van Kleeck, 2004). Preschool children also learn other print conventions: pages have a top and a bottom, text moves from left to right on the page, the text tells the story, and groups of alphabet letters make different words on the page (e.g., Badian, 2000; Clay, 1979; Tumner et al., 1988).

Justice and Ezell (2001b) recommended using a "Written Language Awareness Checklist" when observing parents sharing books with their young children. The list included nine print convention skills, such as distinguishing the differences between print and pictures, that parents and preschool children are likely to use during book sharing and other early literacy events, such as writing or talking about environmental print. Another print convention assessment, the Preschool Word and Print Awareness measure, by Justice and Ezell (2001a), requires adults to share a specific book, *Nine Ducks Nine* (Hayes, 1990), and ask designated print awareness questions while sharing the book (see Justice, Bowles, & Skibbe, 2006, for a copy of the protocol and description of its psychometric properties).

It is important to note, first, that the information provided in Table 2.1 does not necessarily include exhaustive lists of children's book-sharing behaviors; the skills listed are those most commonly addressed in book-sharing research. Additionally, remember that during the later stages preschool children continue to use the knowledge and skills they have learned in the earlier stages. For example, even though children learn to provide verbal labels for "What?" questions as 12 to 18 month olds, they continue to answer "What?" questions throughout the preschool years. Therefore, children's book-sharing behaviors should be understood as cumulative knowledge and skills, rather than discrete behaviors observed only at each specific stage.

Observations of Parent Book-Sharing Behaviors

Observing parent book-sharing behaviors is as important as observing children's development of book-sharing skills over time. We identify four dimensions of book-sharing conversations listed in Table 2.2 as described by van Kleeck (2004): (1) attend to the child's interests and experiences; (2) focus on establishing meaning first and then later separately on print form; (3) frame books increasingly as unique contexts; and (4) use progressively more inferential language. These four dimensions are present in most typical book-sharing conversations.

TABLE 2.2. Content of Parental Book-Sharing Conversations

Type of content	Examples
Attend to the child's interests and experiences.	• Follow the child's lead by naming or discussing pictures the child notices. • Use attentional evocatives to engage the child. • Relate information in books to child's real-life experiences.
Focus on establishing meaning first, then later separately on print form.	• Comment frequently on the pictures and story. • Modify the book's text. • Ask the child to point to specific objects or characters. • Ask the child to label pictures and events. • Describe the characteristics of objects and characters. • Talk about the actions in pictured scenes. • Ask the child to recall events previously presented in the book. • Refer to letter names and associated sounds.
Frame books as unique contexts.	• Use book-related vocabulary. • Refer to pictures as representations of objects and people. • Teach children that books are for reading, not for manipulating like other toys. • Teach children that the topics of book-sharing conversations are the same as the books' topics. • Talk about the books' special features such as title pages, authors, illustrators, copyright dates, or ISBNs.
Use progressively more inferential language.	• Summarize events in the story. • Define the text's vocabulary. • Explain a character's point of view or a motivation for actions. • Identify similarities and difference between the story's characters and objects and the child's real-life experiences. • Make personal judgments about the story's characters or events. • Make predictions about events in the story. • Problem solve situations in the story. • Explain the story's concepts and actions.

Note. Adapted from van Kleeck (2004, p. 192). Copyright 2004 by The Guilford Press. Adapted with permission of the publisher and author.

Attending to Children's Interests

When talking with even very young children during book sharing, parents can increase their children's attention and motivation for sharing books by attending to their children's specific interests and daily experiences. One way of doing this is to observe what young children look at or point to and then name or discuss those pictures (e.g., after the child hits a picture of a ball and says, "Ba!" the parent says, "Oh yes! Ball! That's a ball!"). Parents can also draw their children's attention to particular pictures in the book by using attentional evocatives with enthusiasm (e.g., "Look! A baby! See the baby?"). (These examples are from unreported transcriptions from Vander Woude et al., 2005.) Finally, parents can relate the events and objects in the books to their children's real-life experiences. For example, when Timothy's mother was reading a book about different occupations when he was 4 years old, she read about what a builder does and stated, "Look, a builder. Uncle Tim is a builder. He builds houses. He built Grandma's house." (This example is from unreported transcripts from Vander Woude, 1998.) Looking for these three specific behaviors during book sharing documents shows how a parent attends to his or her child's interests, and ultimately helps the child maintain his or her motivation for participating in early literacy events.

Focusing on Establishing Meaning First and Print Separately Later

Recall that middle-class parents first focus overwhelmingly on helping their children understand the meaning of the text, and then later as their children become older preschoolers, they focus on understanding the form of the text (i.e., letter names and sounds), but typically only when sharing alphabet books. Parents help their children comprehend the meaning of the text and pictures by making comments on specific pictures or events in the book (e.g., "I see an ice cream cone. The boy is getting the newspaper."). (These examples were drawn from unreported transcripts for the study by Vander Woude et al., 2005.) Also, when children are younger than the age of 3 years, parents modify the book's text and substitute vocabulary and simplified sentences that they believe their children will understand. Parents use these modifications intuitively and naturally when sharing stories with their young children (Martin, 1998).

Likewise, parents help children learn new vocabulary or how to display their known vocabulary by asking their children to point to specific objects or characters in the book (e.g., "Where is the ball?" "Where is the prince?"). Parents also ask their children to provide actual labels for pictures and events (e.g., "What's this?" "What is that boy doing?"), and describe characteristics of those objects and characters (e.g., "That boy is wearing a red shirt and blue jeans."). Parents also help children understand the events of a story by talking about specific actions in scenes and asking the child to remember previous events in the book (e.g., "Do you remember where the family was going to go next?"). Finally, when their children are between 3 and 5 years old, parents may refer to the print in books, including the names of the letters and their associated sounds, especially if they are reading alphabet books (e.g., "Look, your name starts with the same letter!"). (These examples were drawn from unreported transcripts from Vander Woude, 1998.)

Framing Books as a Unique Context

When parents have book-sharing conversations, even with their very young children, they introduce their children to specific vocabulary and rules for book sharing. Shared book-reading discussions naturally include vocabulary such as *book, story, page, picture, draw, write,* and *read.* These basic vocabulary words lead to more complex vocabulary when preschool children are older. For example, parents often help their children notice and define special attributes of books such as the authors, illustrators, and dedications that are defined by unique vocabulary.

When parents help their children realize that books have features, children can begin to use this vocabulary competently in their book-sharing conversations (Justice & Ezell, 2000a, 2000b, 2002). Likewise, as infants, children often do not differentiate books from other manipulative toys, so parents teach their children that books are to look at rather than to manipulate like other toys. For instance, parents remind their young preschool children to be gentle with the book, to not put the book in their mouth, and to turn pages carefully. Parents also remind their children that the topics of book-sharing conversations are restricted to the topics of the books they are reading (e.g., Snow & Goldfield, 1983). In addition to teaching children how to use books, parents also provide important prerequisites for helping their children understand how to converse while sharing books. The unique context of book sharing possesses its own vocabulary and rules for participating in the routine, rules that teachers often assume children already know when they begin attending school.

Using Increasingly More Inferential Language

In addition to helping children frame book reading as a unique context, parents also begin to use more inferential language in their book-sharing conversations. Recall that inferential language requires going beyond what is directly represented in the book's pictures or stated in the text. As shown in Table 2.2, using inferential language includes summarizing or discussing past events in the story (e.g., "Little Bird flew south for the winter, didn't he? And then he came back!"), defining vocabulary in the story (e.g., "A wheelbarrow helps you carry lots of tools."), explaining a character's point of view or motivations for actions (e.g., "Do you think the boy did that because he was frustrated?"), and stating opinions about the characters' motives (e.g., "Do you think that was a nice thing to do?").

Parents also identify similarities between the story's characters and objects and children's real-life experiences (e.g., "Doesn't that girl remind you of Katie? She looks just like her."). Additionally, they use higher-level inferential language that teaches their children how to predict events (e.g., "Where do you think Bear is going next?"), problem solve predicaments or events in the plot (e.g., "What do you think Bear should do now? He can't shoot the arrow far enough, can he?"), and explain the story's concepts and actions (e.g., "When the sun moves this way, the Bear's shadow gets longer."). Middle-class parents use inferential language both in their comments and in their questions, and do so much more frequently when their children are 4 to 5 years old. (These examples are from unreported transcripts from van Kleeck et al., 1997.)

Observations of parents' and children's behaviors during book sharing provide important data for developing appropriate interventions for children at risk for language and early literacy delays. Bear in mind that parents' and children's book-sharing behaviors influence one another. For example, parents who ask many questions during book sharing will more than likely have children who talk more during book-sharing conversations (Anderson-Yockel & Haynes, 1994). Likewise, parents who pay attention to their children's interests and enthusiastically praise their contributions are more likely to have children who like participating in book-sharing events (McNeill & Fowler, 1999).

Furthermore, parents and their children tend to match the literal and inferential language levels of each of their contributions to the book-sharing conversations (Danis, Bernard, & Leproux, 2000; Hammett, Bradley, & Huberty, 2002). For instance, if a mother uses higher-level inferential language in her utterance, it is more likely than chance that her child's subsequent utterances will focus on inferential language as well; conversely, if the child uses more inferential language, the mother will match the child's level in her subsequent responses. Consequently, an association usually exists between the content of the children's book-sharing behaviors and the content of the parents' conversations. With such assessment data gathered, corresponding intervention strategies can be developed. In the next section, we describe specific strategies that help parents make the most of book-sharing opportunities.

Intervention Strategies for Shared Book-Reading Conversations

Recommended intervention strategies include encouraging more frequent book sharing with prereaders, beginning in infancy, general interactive discussions about the book, and specific discussions that include inferential and literal discussion of material presented in the book. One relatively straightforward way of providing rich early literacy environments is to encourage more frequent book sharing along with specific strategies for improving the quality of those experiences (e.g., Crain-Thoreson & Dale, 1992; Vivas, 1996; Wells, 1985). Recall that children whose parents begin sharing books with their children as infants have better language skills than do the children of parents who start sharing books later in the preschool years (e.g., Bus, 2003; DeBaryshe, 1993). As such, the first recommendation is to encourage adults to begin sharing books when their children are very young, and to continue sharing books on a routine basis.

Evidence from intervention studies that have used "dialogic reading" suggests that having discussions about the book, rather than simply reading the book without discussion, are associated with accelerated language development, at least for vocabulary learning (Mol et al., 2008). Thus, a second strategy involves teaching adults to use dialogic reading to help their children develop both receptive and expressive vocabulary skills, as well as general language skills. The dialogic reading program focuses on teaching parents and preschool teachers strategies for encouraging their children to become more active participants during shared book reading (see Table 2.3 for a summary of the strategies, and for a review, see Zevenbergen & Whitehurst, 2003). For 2- to 3-year-olds, Whitehurst and colleagues (e.g., Arnold, Lonigan, Whitehurst, & Epstein, 1994; Whitehurst et al., 1988) recommended that adults ask "What?" questions (such as "What is this?"), and then follow children's answers by repeating what the child said and adding related questions (e.g., "Yes, that's a bear. What did the bear do?"). They also recommended that adults prompt preschool children with open-ended questions, such as "What is this?" or "What is he doing now?" rather than "Is this a wheelbarrow?" or "Is he fishing?" In addition to asking open-ended questions, Whitehurst and his colleagues also recommend teaching parents to expand their children's utterances by adding descriptive words or more adult-like syntax to children's previous utterances (e.g., the child says, "Brown bear!" and the adult expands by saying, "Yes, that brown bear is fishing."). Moreover, adults are taught strategies for keeping the book-sharing routine positive by assisting children when they do not know the answers (e.g., if the child answers the parent's question incorrectly, the parent is instructed to say the correct answer and then ask the child to repeat the correct answer), praising and encouraging children's interactive attempts, and following the children's interests in particular parts of the books (e.g., when the child looks at or points to a picture, ask open-ended questions about that picture).

The dialogic reading approach suggests that more challenging kinds of questions should be asked of children between the ages of 4 and 5 years so that children are held to higher levels of account-

---

TABLE 2.3. Parent Interactional Book-Sharing Strategies

- Use imitations and expansions.
- Use semantic extensions.
- Use corrective repairs.
- Request clarification.
- Respond to child's questions.
- Ask questions.
- Scaffold incorrect answers.
- Hold child accountable.
- Provide praise and encouragement.

Note. Adapted from van Kleeck (2004, p. 192). Copyright 2004 by The Guilford Press. Adapted with permission of the publisher and author.

ability in responding. Children at this age are asked, for example, to recall information from the book, to retell the information from a page in their own words, and to relate information in the book to their own real-life experiences. When adults learn these dialogic reading methods, even preschool children with language delays show accelerated growth in their vocabulary skills (e.g., Crain-Thoreson & Dale, 1999; Dale, Crain-Thoreson, Notari-Syverson, & Cole, 1996; Hargrave & Sénéchal, 2000; McNeill & Fowler, 1999; Whitehurst et al., 1988).

Since dialogic reading primarily improves children's literal language abilities (i.e., vocabulary needed to label and describe), a third recommendation is to encourage adults to focus increasingly on inferencing as preschool children mature in order to develop foundational knowledge for later higher-level reading comprehension skills (see van Kleeck, 2008). Explicitly teaching inferencing skills (such as predicting, summarizing, and connecting background information to interpret information in the book) constitutes the bulk of reading comprehension strategy instruction used with older school-age children (see Pressley & Hilden, 2004, for a discussion of comprehension strategies for older school-age children). If we reinterpret research on older school-age children using the lens of literal versus inferential language, such as the studies discussed by Pressley and Hilden (2004), and a study of preschoolers by van Kleeck et al. (1997), we find that many middle-class parents provide their preschool children with a great deal of implicit comprehension strategy instruction via comments and questions that require inferencing. Furthermore, three recent intervention studies have shown that providing deliberate, structured input at both literal and inferential levels can improve the inferential language abilities of preschoolers with language delays (Bradshaw et al., 1998; Horstman & Vander Woude, 2007; van Kleeck, Vander Woude, & Hammett, 2006).

Although more evidence is needed with larger groups of children to support the benefits of using inferential questions with children during book sharing, initial results indicate that purposefully using inferential questions and scaffolding children's incorrect answers to those questions is a promising intervention. One study that focused on improving the inferential language of preschool children with language delays was that of Bradshaw et al.

(1998). Their study, which included two children, was designed to examine the relative effectiveness of two styles of sharing books on the children's inferential language skills. One style was an expansion condition based on a previous study by Yoder, Spruytenburg, Edwards, and Davies (1995). For this condition, children's answers first were expanded to more syntactically correct utterances, and "descriptions" then were requested. Descriptions were utterances that provided more information about the characters and objects in the books. Following descriptions, cloze procedures were used to request "interpretations," which involved talking about the characters' emotional states, motives or plans, and talking about the causes and effects among events. Thus, for the expansion condition, adults helped the children with language delays to move naturally from repeatedly using literal language to using inferential language, while expanding children's utterances, as in the following example adapted from Bradshaw et al. (1998, p. 88):

ADULT: Who is this? (request for label; literal language)

CHILD: A cow

ADULT: That is a cow. (expansion)
And what is she doing? (request to describe an action; literal language)

CHILD: take bath

ADULT: The cow is taking a bath (expansion)
because ... (cloze requesting an interpretation of the cow's motive for taking a bath; inferential language)

CHILD: him dirty

ADULT: because she is dirty. (expansion)

The other condition incorporated literal and inferential content into the questions and modeled answers of the conversations, but did not include syntactic expansions and cloze procedures, as shown in the following example adapted from Bradshaw et al. (1998, p. 88):

ADULT: What's this? (request to label; literal language)

CHILD: caterpillar

ADULT: What's the caterpillar doing? (request to describe an action; literal language)

CHILD: eat rose

ADULT: Why will he eat the rose? (request to interpret inner state; inferential language)

CHILD: [No response]

ADULT: He will eat the rose because he is hungry. (modeled answer)

The findings showed that expansion and cloze procedures were more effective than the questions and modeled answers in increasing the preschool children's use of inferential language during the conversations. In fact, for the expansion condition, the children used 25% more utterances and 77% more interpretations than they did in the question and modeled answer condition.

In another study by van Kleeck, Vander Woude, and Hammett (2006), both of the conditions used in the Bradshaw et al. (1998) study were combined because earlier research by van Kleeck et al. (1997) showed that parents naturally use all of these conversational strategies (expansions, cloze procedures, questioning, and modeling answers) when sharing books with their preschool children who have typical language development. For this study, 30 preschool children between the ages of 3 years, 10 months to 5 years, 0 months with specific language impairments from low-income families were randomly assigned to either a control group that received no book-sharing intervention or to a treatment group that received twice-weekly 15-minute sessions for 8 weeks, in addition to their regularly scheduled speech–language treatment. During the 15-minute sessions, adults asked both literal and inferential questions by using scripts that were embedded throughout the text of the books (see Appendix 2.1 for an example). Two books with three different versions of scripted questions were used for the 8 weeks; additionally, approximately 70% of the questions were at literal levels and approximately 30% of the questions were at inferential levels. Results suggested that adult input at both literal and inferential levels increased the literal and inferential language skills of the children with specific language impairments.

In a small intervention study with children identified as at risk for reading failure (based on their alphabet knowledge), Horstman and Vander Woude (2007) used the same intervention materials as van Kleeck, Vander Woude, and Hammett (2006). Seven children who attended kindergarten in the morning received treatment for

16 weeks, while another seven children who attended in the afternoon received treatment for 8 weeks.

After 8 weeks of treatment, results demonstrated increases that moved children's scores into the average range of functioning on expressive vocabulary using the Expressive One-Word Picture Vocabulary Test (Gardener, 1990) and on early literacy skills measured by the TERA-3 (Reid et al., 2001). For the group that received 16 weeks of treatment, however, no further significant increases were noted at 16 weeks beyond those noted at 8 weeks. On inferential language skills, as measured by the PLAI-2 (Blank et al., 2003), increases in scores did not appear to be associated with the treatment.

Even though we need to learn more about how we can help at-risk children develop language and early literacy skills, research on the frequency of book sharing, dialogic reading, and the use of inferential language input in book-sharing conversations provides an important framework for interventions that use book sharing. Although simply increasing the frequency of book sharing at a very young age ensures that children will be exposed to more literate talk over the preschool years, it is important to also pay attention to how books are shared with young children. Adding dialogic reading provides children with additional practice with vocabulary or literal language development via encouraging them to participate more fully in book-sharing conversations. Using both literal and inferential language in book-sharing conversations provides important exposure to and practice with the type of inferencing strategies important for later reading comprehension. As a whole, these strategies provide a semantically rich and meaningful environment for the knowledge needed for later literacy development.

Case Study

Given the above discussion, in this section we present a case study of a preschool child, Joseph (not his real name), to illustrate early literacy and language assessment and intervention procedures, and the associated benefits of book-sharing activities for young children with language impairments. Joseph represents a typical preschooler with a specific language impairment from a low-income family. As reported by his teachers and his mother, Joseph has a relatively short attention span and does not enjoy engaging in early literacy activities. Given previous research on predictors for literacy achievement, we know that he is at risk for academic failure without early intervention. The following description presents Joseph's background information, the results of his language and literacy assessment, and his growth in language and literacy after 8 weeks of carefully designed shared book-reading sessions.

Background Information

Joseph, a 4-year, 2-month-old White boy whose family speaks only English, was enrolled in a Head Start preschool in a relatively large Midwestern city. Joseph had attended this Head Start preschool for approximately 1 year and had participated as a subject in the book-sharing intervention study conducted by van Kleeck, Vander Woude, and Hammett (2006), as described earlier in this chapter. Joseph had no history of otitis media and he passed a pure tone-hearing screening evaluation. His mother reported that she reads children's books to him and his two younger brothers more than three times a week. His mother also reported that Joseph often does not pay attention long enough to complete one storybook.

Language and Early Literacy Assessment

Before Joseph participated in the book-sharing intervention, assessments of his expressive and receptive language skills, his early literacy skills, and his nonverbal cognitive ability were administered. Results of the initial assessment indicated that Joseph had significant deficits in both expressive and receptive language skills; however, his nonverbal cognition and early literacy skills were within the average range. Specifically, on the Peabody Picture Vocabulary Test–III (PPVT-III; Dunn & Dunn, 1997), a test of receptive vocabulary, his standard score of 42 was almost four standard deviations (SDs) below the mean for his age ($X = 100$; $SD = 15$). Joseph also scored 2.7 SDs below the mean ($X = 100$; $SD = 15$), with only 12% correct, on the Structured Photographic Expressive Language Test–II (SPELT-II; Werner & Kresheck, 1983). For the SPELT-II, children answer the examiner's questions while looking at photographic stimuli designed to elicit specific syntax structures. Selected examples of some of Joseph's responses on the SPELT-II included: "She all gone" for the correct answer "She drank it"; "He go fall the bike" for "She rode the bike"; "He going the tree" for "He wants to climb the tree"; and "He combed them my hair" for "They are combing their hair."

To further assess Joseph's expressive language skills, a conversational language sample was video recorded while Joseph and an adult played with a toy house and barn. Joseph's mean length of utterance in morphemes (MLU) for the 100-utterance language sample was 3.84. From British norms obtained from 65 children who were 4 years, 3 months of age (Joseph was 4 years, 2 months), the average MLU was 3.7, so Joseph's MLU is actually a bit above the mean (Wells, 1985). Miller and Chapman (1981), from data of only five American children, estimated the MLU of a child age 4 years, 3 months to be 4.71, with an *SD* of 1.0. In both cases, Joseph's MLU is within the average range. Although his MLU was normal for his age, an analysis of Joseph's utterances during the play conversation indicated similar errors to those errors identified on the SPELT-II that were indicative of a language impairment, as shown in the following conversational sequences from the language sample:

(a) ADULT: He just fell over, didn't he?

JOSEPH: Make a over.

JOSEPH: Make a new over.

ADULT: Make a new over?

JOSEPH: Make him over.

(b) ADULT: What else do you see in here?

JOSEPH: I see the this, a this.

ADULT: This and this? (*Points to a couch and dresser.*)

JOSEPH: Mhm. (*Agrees.*)

The Preschool Language Assessment Instrument (PLAI; Blank et al., 1978), an assessment of children's literal and inferential language skills, was also administered. The first two levels (Levels I and II) of the PLAI correspond to literal language because they refer to information that is perceptually present and less cognitively challenging. Examples of Levels I and II questions include "Point to your _____," "What is this?," and "What is happening in this picture?" The second two levels (Levels III and IV) of the *PLAI* correspond to inferential language because the questions at this level ask for information about objects, actions, or events that are not directly available from the perceptual scene. Examples include "Tell me what a *car* is," and "What will happen to the man if he closes the umbrella?"

To score the test, each of the 15 items at each of the four levels were scored according to the guidelines in the original PLAI, which gave 3 points for fully adequate, 2 points for acceptable, 1 point for ambiguous, or 0 points for inadequate (i.e., invalid, irrelevant, no response, or child says, "I don't know."). As such, an average score of 3 is the highest possible at each level. Joseph scored in comparison to his age peers, as follows: "moderately strong" for literal language at Level I ($M = 1.5$), "weak" for literal language at Level II ($M = 0.7$), and "weak" for inferential language at Levels III ($M = 0.5$) and IV ($M = 0.5$). Before intervention began, Joseph had 16 answers that were classified as adequate—only seven of those were fully adequate— and 29 of his answers were classified as inadequate—five of those were invalid and 15 of those were irrelevant.

The Test of Early Reading Ability–2 (Reid, Hresko, & Hammill, 1991) was also administered to assess Joseph's general early literacy skills. He achieved a standard score of 92, which placed him in the average range in comparison to his age peers. He was able to accurately identify the McDonald's logo, identify chocolate candy given a picture of the wrapper, identify the word *fork* when presented with both the word and the picture of a fork, say where street signs may be found when presented with pictures of different types, and identify which logo represents Jell-O. Joseph was not able to identify any letters, numbers, or simple words.

Finally, as part of the assessment, a student clinician read the book *Bear Shadow* (Asch, 1985) to Joseph. Two books similar to *Bear Shadow* were used during the intervention; *Mooncake* (Asch, 1983) and *Skyfire* (Asch, 1984). While reading *Bear Shadow* with Joseph, the student clinician asked 20 questions that used literal or inferential language, five at each of four levels. Joseph was able to correctly answer four out of five literal questions at Level I (e.g., "Where's the fish?, "What is Bear's shadow on now?"), but only one out five literal questions at Level II (e.g., "What is Bear doing?"). He was not able to correctly answer any of the five inferential questions at Level III (e.g., "Where did all this dirt come from?") or any of the five inferential questions at Level IV (e.g., "Bear looks like he's thinking. What do you think he's gonna do?"). Joseph also reportedly had difficulty paying attention for the entire book-sharing time, which may have adversely affected his answers to the questions. He asked, "All done?" three times while sharing the book. He also made four comments unrelated to the book's topic.

Book-Sharing Intervention

For the book-sharing intervention, Joseph and a student clinician read one of two books, twice a week for 15 minutes. Following the protocol of the intervention, the clinician asked Joseph questions that were either literal or inferential. If Joseph did not answer a question correctly, the clinician then provided a subsequent question to help him answer the first question correctly or she provided the correct answer (see Appendix 2.1 for examples). Both the questions and the responses were scripted and embedded in the books at exactly the point in the story that the clinician was to ask them, and, if necessary, help the child respond to them. The clinician also expanded and extended any of Joseph's questions or comments that were related to the book's topic; and in an effort to increase Joseph's attention span, the clinician asked Joseph to turn the pages of the book and praised him when he was paying attention or asked "good" questions.

After sharing books twice a week for 8 weeks for 15 minutes, Joseph showed gains in his vocabulary skills, his literal language use, and his early literacy skills in general. He achieved a standard score of 78 on the PPVT-III, which was still below average in comparison to his age peers, being 1.5 SDs below the mean; however, he was able to correctly identify 30 words in comparison to five words 8 weeks earlier. Note that Joseph's standard score improved from $-3.9\ SD$ to $-1.5\ SD$ below the mean, a gain of 2.4 SDs. Given that there were just four total hours of intervention, it is very unlikely that this dramatic score improvement was due to actual leaps and bounds in Joseph's receptive vocabulary abilities. Indeed, we have some evidence that his initial vocabulary may not have been as depressed as a test score of almost 4 SDs below the mean would indicate. This evidence comes from looking at the number of different words (NDW) Joseph produced spontaneously during the half-hour language sample collected before the intervention began. Joseph's NDW in the nontest conversational context was 75. Paradise et al. (2003) found that the mean NDW for 234 children who were 48 months old (Joseph was 51 months old) was 161, with an

SD of 35. This puts Joseph –2.5 *SD*s below these children 3 months younger than him. While this is still very low, it is not nearly as low as Joseph's preintervention score on the standardized test, the PPVT-III. Other factors may have been impacting Joseph's performance on the pretest PPVT-III.

It may be that Joseph's poor preintervention standard score on the PPVT-III was due in part to his short attention span. It is also possible that, as a result of the intervention, Joseph became much more comfortable with the testing context, in which the child's task is to display his or her knowledge to the examiner. van Kleeck (2006a) discusses how many children receive very little practice at home in answering questions adults ask that they know the answer to ("known-information" questions), and are therefore at great disadvantage when they get to school, where such questions abound (e.g., Reid, 2000). In middle-class families, by contrast, known-information questions are common, particularly when children are engaged in book sharing. Having little practice with known-information questions may also be why Joseph's productive language as measured by his MLU obtained during the preintervention language sample was within the average range (at the mean), while his preintervention score on the SPELT-II, a test of expressive syntax, was –2.7 *SD*s below the mean. Children becoming more comfortable with displaying their knowledge for adults may be a "side" benefit of book-sharing interventions for children from nonmainstream backgrounds.

Whatever the case may be, in addition to better receptive vocabulary skills, Joseph demonstrated significantly better literal language use on Levels I and II on the PLAI; he now scored in comparison to his age peers, as follows: "strong" for literal language at Level I (M = 2.0), "moderately strong" for literal language at Level II (M = 1.4), and remained "weak" for inferential language at Levels III (M = 0.7) and IV (M = 0.5). Even so, a comparison of the number of adequate versus inadequate answers revealed substantial progress in the 8 weeks. He now had a total of 20 adequate answers, 13 of which were fully adequate, and a total of 25 inadequate answers, 12 of which were irrelevant answers. When reading *Bear Shadow* (Asch, 1985) with the same clinician again after the 8-week intervention, Joseph was able to answer four of the five Level I literal questions correctly, three of the five Level II literal questions correctly, one of the five Level III inferential questions correctly, and two of the Level IV questions correctly. Most importantly, perhaps, Joseph's behavior during the book sharing improved substantially. Although he still needed to be reminded to stay on task occasionally, after the 8 weeks of book sharing, he was able to pay attention most of the time, seldom asking when he would be finished. He was able to turn the pages of the book appropriately and use unique book vocabulary correctly, such as *story, writing, letters, page, authors*, and *title*. Also, as Joseph became more familiar with the books, he liked retelling the story after they finished reading. When he retold the stories, he would pretend to read the text and would often use the same vocabulary and phrases he had heard previously.

Although Joseph still showed room for improvement, he increased his language skills during the 8 weeks of book-sharing intervention, and he also seemed to become much more comfortable with displaying his knowledge. His receptive vocabulary and use of literal language improved, as well as his ability to answer some questions with inferential language content. After the 8 weeks, it was recommended that Joseph continue to participate in book-sharing conversations twice a week with an increased focus on his inferential language use and a continued focus on his vocabulary skills.

To summarize, Joseph's case study illustrates one method for assessing the needs of and providing intervention for children at risk for later academic failure. The book-sharing intervention described above included controlled, age-appropriate dialogic conversations during repeated book-sharing opportunities that ultimately facilitated growth in Joseph's language and early literacy skills and perhaps more importantly, in his enjoyment of literacy activities and the kinds of "school-like" discourse that accompany such activities (including displaying one's knowledge). If adults can help children truly enjoy early literacy activities, they have begun to make an important difference in their future academic lives.

Summary

Shared book reading is one key early literacy routine for improving young children's literal and inferential language development. In addition, it provides a positive environment for socializing young children in how to participate in literacy activities, an experience that can begin as young as infancy. These early language and literacy skills are important for later literacy achievement, especially in the development of reading comprehension skills. Although much research on the characteristics and short- and long-term benefits of shared book reading has been completed in the past few years, more intervention studies with larger groups of children are needed. Additional research is needed on the early literacy development of infants and toddlers, especially with those identified as being at risk for language delays. Such research may lead to further identification of specific conversational strategies that work best for developing young children's language and early literacy skills at different developmental stages. Finally, although there is a large body of evidence-based interventions that have focused on phonological awareness skills for children, there continues to be a need for studies on young children's inferential language development and its relationship with later reading comprehension development.

Findings of recent longitudinal research suggest that 5–10% of school-age children are known as "poor comprehenders"; that is, children who do not demonstrate decoding deficits, but do show significant reading comprehension deficits later in elementary school (Leach, Scarborough, & Rescorla, 2003; Nation, Clarke, Marshall, & Durand, 2004; Nation & Snowling, 2004; Yuill & Oakhill, 1991). Many of these children meet the diagnostic criteria for significant language delays (Nation et al., 2004), or at least exhibit lower language comprehension skills than their age mates (Catts, Adlof, & Weismer, 2006). As Catts and his colleagues (2006) indicated, there is a need to identify children who have poor language comprehension skills before they begin formal reading instruction and then to teach them the language and strategies needed for successful oral language comprehension and reading comprehension. In this chapter we have reviewed what the evidence to date suggests are the best ways to teach children the language skills they need to become proficient at reading comprehension, and we await further evidence that will help us refine ways of talking and sharing books with young children so that we can offer ever more effective early literacy experiences to young prereaders who are at risk for later reading and academic difficulties.

DISCUSSION QUESTIONS

1. Discuss some of the special properties of sharing books with infants and why sharing books with this age group is important for language and early literacy development.

2. Why should adults include inferential language in book-sharing conversations?

3. Describe the differences between sharing books with preschool children with language delays and preschool children with typical language development.

4. Discuss two strategies for assessing book-sharing conversations. Why are these methods of assessment important?

EXERCISES

1. Choose three different narrative books for the early, middle, and late stages of preschool book-sharing behaviors. Develop appropriate questions and comments for at least three of the pages in each book.

2. Interview parents of 3- or 4-year-old children with language delays. Use the interview prompts in Table 2.1 as a guide. How do they perceive the importance of book sharing with their children? What does their child enjoy or dislike about book sharing? What suggestions for improving the book-sharing conversations would be helpful for them?

3. Video record several different children who are approximately the same age, as they share an alphabet book and a storybook with a parent. Code the children and the parent's book-sharing behaviors as outlined in Tables 2.2 and 2.3. What behaviors were you able to observe? Describe the similarities and differences in how each of the parents and children shared the two different genres of books.

References

Anderson-Yockel, J., & Haynes, W. (1994). Joint picture-book reading strategies by working class African American and white mother–toddler dyads. *Journal of Speech, Language, and Hearing Research, 37,* 583–593.

Armstrong, M., & Pruett, A. (2000). *Shared reading: A comparison of children with language impairment and normal language abilities.* Paper presented at the American Speech–Language–Hearing Association Convention, Washington, DC.

Arnold, D. H., Lonigan, C. J., Whitehurst, G. J., & Epstein, J. N. (1994). Accelerating language development through picture-book reading: Replication and extension to a videotape training format. *Journal of Educational Psychology, 86,* 235–243.

Asch, F. (1983). *Mooncake.* Englewood Cliffs, NJ: Prentice-Hall.

Asch, F. (1984). *Skyfire.* Englewood Cliffs, NJ: Prentice-Hall.

Asch, F. (1985). *Bear shadow.* Englewood Cliffs, NJ: Prentice-Hall.

Badian, N. A. (2000). Do preschool orthographic skills contribute to prediction of reading? In N. A. Bathian (Ed.), *Prediction and prevention of reading failure* (pp. 31–56). Timonium, MD: York Press.

Bishop, D. V. M., & Adams, C. (1990). A prospective study of the relationship between specific language impairment, phonological disorders, and reading retardation. *Journal of Child Psychology and Psychiatry, 21,* 1027–1050.

Blank, M., Rose, S. A., & Berlin, L. J. (1978). *The language of learning: The preschool years.* New York: Grune & Stratton.

Blank, M., Rose, S. A., & Berlin, L. J. (2003). *Preschool language assessment instrument* (2nd ed.). Austin, TX: PRO-ED.

Block, C. C., & Pressley, M. (2002). *Comprehension instruction: Research-based best practices.* New York: Guilford Press.

Boudreau, D. (2005). Use of a parent questionnaire in emergent and early literacy assessment of preschool children. *Language, Speech, and Hearing Services in Schools, 36,* 33–47.

Bradshaw, M. L., Hoffman, P. R., & Norris, J. A. (1998). Efficacy of expansions and cloze procedures in the development of interpretations by preschool children exhibiting delayed language development. *Language, Speech, and Hearing Services in Schools, 29,* 85–95.

Bus, A. G. (2003). Social-emotional requisites for learning to read. In A. van Kleeck & S. A. Stahl (Eds.), *On reading books to children: Parents and teachers* (pp. 3–15). Mahwah, NJ: Erlbaum.

Bus, A. G., & van IJzendoorn, M. (1997). Affective dimension of mother–infant picture-book reading. *Journal of School Psychology, 35,* 47–60.

Caccamise, D., & Snyder, L. (2005). Theory and pedagogical practices of text comprehension. *Topics in Language Disorders, 25,* 5–20.

Catts, H. W., Adlof, S. M., & Weismer, S. E. (2006). Language deficits in poor comprehenders: A case for the simple view of reading. *Journal of Speech, Language, and Hearing Research, 49*(2), 265–277.

Catts, H. W., Fey, M. E., & Proctor-Williams, K. (2000). The relationship between language and reading: Preliminary results from a longitudinal investigation. *Logopedics, Phoniatrics, Vocology, 25,* 38–58.

Catts, H. W., Fey, M. E., Tomblin, J. B., & Zhang, X. (2002). A longitudinal investigation of reading outcomes in children with language impairments. *Journal of Speech, Language, and Hearing Research, 45,* 1142–1157.

Catts, H. W., & Kamhi, A. G. (1999). *Language and reading disabilities.* Boston: Allyn & Bacon.

Clay, M. M. (1979). *The early detection of reading difficulties: A diagnostic survey with recovery procedures*. Exeter, NH: Heinemann.

Crain-Thoreson, C., & Dale, P. S. (1992). Do early talkers become early readers? Linguistic precocity, preschool language, and emergent literacy. *Developmental Psychology, 28*, 421–429.

Crain-Thoreson, C., & Dale, P. S. (1999). Enhancing linguistic performance: Parents and teachers as book-reading partners for children with language delays. *Topics in Early Childhood Special Education, 19*, 28–39.

Dale, P. S., Crain-Thoreson, C., Notari-Syverson, A., & Cole, K. (1996). Parent–child book reading as an intervention technique for young children with language delays. *Topics in Early Childhood Special Education, 16*, 213–235.

Danis, A., Bernard, J. M., & Leproux, C. (2000). Shared picture-book reading: A sequential analysis of adult–child interactions. *British Journal of Developmental Psychology, 18*, 369–388.

DeBaryshe, B. D. (1993). Joint picture-book reading correlates of early oral language skill. *Journal of Child Language, 20*(2), 455–461.

DeLoache, J. S., & DeMendoza, O. A. (1987). Joint picture-book interactions of mothers and 1-year-old children. *British Journal of Developmental Psychology, 5*(2), 111–123.

DeLoache, J. S., Pierroutsakos, S. L., Uttal, D. H., Rosengren, K. S., & Gottlieb, A. (1998). Grasping the nature of pictures. *Psychological Science, 9*(3), 205–210.

DeLoache, J. S., Strauss, M. S., & Maynard, J. (1979). Picture perception in infancy. *Infant Behavior and Development, 2*(1), 77–89.

DeLoache, J. S., Uttal, D. H., & Pierroutsakos, S. L. (2000). What's up: The development of an orientation preference for picture books. *Journal of Cognition and Development, 1*(1), 81–95.

De Temple, J., & Snow, C. E. (1996). Styles of parent–child book reading as related to mothers' views of literacy and children's literacy outcomes. In J. Shimron (Ed.), *Literacy and education: Essays in honor of Dina Feitelson* (pp. 49–68). Cresskill, NJ: Hampton Press.

Dickinson, D. K., & McCabe, A. (2001). Bringing it all together: The multiple origins, skills, and environmental supports of early literacy. *Learning Disabilities Research and Practice, 16*(4), 186–202.

Dole, J., Sloan, C., & Trathern, W. (1995). Teaching vocabulary within the context of literature. *Journal of Reading, 38*, 452–460.

Dunn, L. M., & Dunn, L. M. (1997). *Peabody Picture Vocabulary Test—Third edition*. Circle Pines, MN: American Guidance Service.

Dunn, L. M., & Dunn, L. M. (2007). *Peabody Picture Vocabulary Test—Fourth edition*. Minneapolis, MN: Pearson.

Evans, M. A., & Schmidt, F. (1991). Repeated maternal book reading with two children: Language-normal and language impaired. *First Language, 11*, 269–287.

Fletcher, K. L., & Jean-Francious, B. (1998). Spontaneous responses to repeated reading in young children from at-risk backgrounds. *Early Childhood Development and Care, 146*, 53–68.

Ford, J., & Milosky, L. (2005). *The time course of emotion inferencing: Difference in children with LI.* Paper presented at the 26th Annual Symposium on Research in Child Language Disorders, Madison, WI.

Gardener, M. F. (1990). *Expressive One-Word Picture Vocabulary Test—Revised.* Novato, CA: Academic Therapy Publications.

Goodsitt, J., Raitan, J. G., & Perlmutter, M. (1988). Interaction between mothers and preschool children when reading a novel and familiar book. *International Journal of Behavioral Development, 11*(4), 489–505.

Hammett, L. A., Bradley, B., & Huberty, C. (2002). *Dynamic interactions between parents and preschoolers during book sharing: A twin case study.* Paper presented at the American Speech–Language–Hearing Association Convention, Atlanta, GA.

Hammett, L. A., & van Kleeck, A. (2005). *Patterns of parents' talk during book sharing with preschool children: A comparison between storybook and expository book conditions.* Paper presented at the National Reading Conference, Miami, FL.

Hammett, L. A., van Kleeck, A., & Huberty, C. (2003). Clusters of parent interaction behaviors during book sharing with preschool children. *Reading Research Quarterly, 38*, 442–468.

Hargrave, A. C., & Sénéchal, M. (2000). A book-reading intervention with preschool children who have limited vocabularies: The benefits of regular reading and dialogic reading. *Early Childhood Research Quarterly, 15*, 75–90.

Hayes, S. (1990). *Nine ducks nine.* Cambridge, MA: Candlewick Press.

Heath, S. B. (1982). What no bedtime story means: Narrative skills at home and school. *Language and Society, 2*, 49–76.

Horstman, A., & Vander Woude, J. (2007). *Response-to-intervention program for accelerating language and literacy development.* Paper presented at the American Speech–Language–Hearing Association Convention, Boston, MA.

Justice, L. M., Bowles, R. P., & Skibbe, L. E. (2006). Measuring preschool attainment of print-concept knowledge: A study of typical and at-risk 3- to 5-year-old children using item-response theory. *Language, Speech, and Hearing Services in the Schools, 37*(3), 224–235.

Justice, L. M., & Ezell, H. K. (2000a). Enhancing children's print and word awareness through home-based parent intervention. *American Journal of Speech–Language Pathology, 9*, 257–269.

Justice, L. M., & Ezell, H. K. (2000b). Increasing the print focus of adult–child shared book reading through observation learning. *American Journal of Speech–Language Pathology, 9*, 36–47.

Justice, L. M., & Ezell, H. K. (2001a). Word and print awareness in 4-year-old children. *Child Language Teaching and Therapy, 17*, 207–226.

Justice, L. M., & Ezell, H. K. (2001b). Written language awareness in preschool children from low-income households: A descriptive analysis. *Communication Disorders Quarterly, 22*(3), 123–134.

Justice, L. M., & Ezell, H. K. (2002). Use of storybook reading to increase print awareness in at-risk children. *American Journal of Speech–Language Pathology, 11*, 17–29.

Kamhi, A. G. (2005). Finding beauty in the ugly facts about reading comprehension. In H. W. Catts & A. G. Kamhi (Eds.), *The connections between language and reading disabilities* (pp. 201–212). Mahwah, NJ: Erlbaum.

Karrass, J., & Braungart-Rieker, J. M. (2005). Effects of shared parent–infant book reading on early language acquisition. *Journal of Applied Developmental Psychology, 26*(2), 133–148.

Leach, J. M., Scarborough, H. S., & Rescorla, L. (2003). Late-emerging reading disabilities. *Journal of Educational Psychology, 95*, 211–224.

Lehrer, R., & deBernard, A. (1987). Language of learning and language of computing: The perceptual–language model. *Journal of Educational Psychology, 79*, 41–48.

Lomax, R. G., & McGee, L. M. (1987). Young children's concepts about print and meaning: Toward a model of word-reading acquisition. *Reading Research Quarterly, 22*, 237–256.

Martin, L. E. (1998). Early book reading: How mothers deviate from printed text for young children. *Reading Research and Instruction, 37*(2), 137–160.

McNeill, J. H., & Fowler, S. A. (1999). Let's talk: Encouraging mother–child conversations during story reading. *Journal of Early Intervention, 22*, 51–69.

Miller, J. F., & Chapman R. S. (1981). The relation between age and mean length of utterance in morphemes. *Journal of Speech and Hearing Research, 24*, 154–161.

Mogford-Bevan, K. P., & Summersall, J. (1997). Emerging literacy in children with delayed speech and language development: Assessment and intervention. *Child Language Teaching and Therapy, 13*, 143–159.

Mol, S. E., Bus, A. G., de Jong, M. T., & Smeets, D. J. H. (2008). Added value of dialogic parent–child book readings: A meta-analysis. *Early Education and Development, 19*(1), 7–26.

Murphy, C. M. (1978). Pointing in the context of a shared activity. *Child Development, 49*, 371–390.

Nation, K., Clarke, P., Marshall, C. M., & Durand, M. (2004). Hidden language impairments in children: Parallels between poor reading comprehension and specific language impairment? *Journal of Speech, Language, and Hearing Research, 47*, 199–221.

Nation, K., & Snowling, M. J. (2004). Beyond phonological skills: Broader language skills contribute to the development of reading. *Journal of Research in Reading, 27*(4), 342–356.

Neuman, S. B. (1996). Children engaging in storybook reading: The influence of access to print resources, opportunity, and parental interaction. *Early Child Research Quarterly, 11*, 495–514.

Ninio, A., & Bruner, J. (1978). The achievement and antecedents of labeling. *Journal of Child Language, 5*(1), 1–15.

Nippold, M. (1998). *Later language development: The school-age and adolescent years.* Austin: TX: PRO-ED.

Paradise, J. L., Dollaghan, C. A., Campbell, T. F., Feldman, H. M., Bernard, B. S., Colborn, D. K., et al. (2003). Developmental outcomes at the age of 4 years. *Pediatrics, 112,* 265–277.

Pressley, M., & Hilden, K. (2004). Toward more ambitious comprehension instruction. In E. Silliman & L. Wilkinson (Eds.), *Language and literacy learning in schools* (pp. 151–174). New York: Guilford Press.

Raikes, H., Pan, B. A., Luze, G., Tamis-LeMonda, C. S., Brooks-Gunn, J., Constantine, J., et al. (2006). Mother–child book reading in low-income families: Correlates and outcomes during the first three years of life. *Child Development, 77,* 924–953.

Reid, D. K. (2000). Discourse in classrooms. In K. Fahey & D. K. Reid (Eds.), *Language development, differences, and disorders* (pp. 3–38). Austin, TX: PRO-ED.

Reid, D. K., Hresko, W., & Hammill, D. D. (1991). *Test of Early Reading Ability–2.* Austin, TX: PRO-ED.

Reid, D. K., Hresko, W. P., & Hammill, D. D. (2001). *Test of Early Reading Ability–3.* Austin TX: PRO-ED.

Richman, W. A., & Colombo, J. (2007). Joint book reading in the second year and vocabulary outcomes. *Journal of Research in Childhood Education, 21,* 242–253.

Rogoff, B., Malkin, C., & Gilbride, K. (1984). Interaction with babies as guidance in development. In B. Rogoff & J. Wertsch (Eds.), *Children's learning in the zone of proximal development* (pp. 31–44). San Francisco: Jossey-Bass.

Sénéchal, M., Cornell, E. H., & Broda, L. S. (1995). Age-related differences in the organization of parent–infant interactions during picture-book reading. *Early Childhood Research Quarterly, 10*(3), 317–337.

Sigel, I. E., & McGillicuddy-Delisi, A. V. (1984). Parents as teachers of their children: A distancing behavior model. In A. Pelligrini & T. Yawkey (Eds.), *The development of oral and written language in social contexts* (pp. 71–92). Norwood, NJ: Ablex.

Snow, C. E., & Goldfield, B. A. (1983). Turn the page please: Situation-specific language acquisition. *Journal of Child Language, 10,* 551–569.

Sulzby, E. (1985). Children's emergent reading of favorite storybooks: A developmental study. *Reading Research Quarterly, 20,* 458–481.

Sulzby, E., & Kaderavek, J. (1996). Parent–child language during storybook reading and toy play contexts: Case studies of normally developing and specific language-impaired (SLI) children. *National Reading Conference Yearbook, 37,* 95–106.

Sulzby, E., & Zecker, L. B. (1991). The oral monologue as a form of emergent reading. In A. McCabe & C. Peterson (Eds.), *Developing narrative structure* (pp. 175–213). Mahwah, NJ: Erlbaum.

Troseth, G. L., Pierroutsakos, S. L., & DeLoache, J. S. (2004). From the innocent to the intelligent eye: The early development of pictorial competence. In R. V. Kail (Ed.), *Advances in child development and behavior, Vol. 32* (pp. 1–35). San Diego, CA: Elsevier Academic Press.

Tumner, W. E., Herriman, M. L., & Nesdale, A. R. (1988). Metalinguistic abilities and beginning reading. *Reading Research Quarterly, 22,* 134–158.

Vander Woude, J. (1998). *Coconstruction of discourse between parents and their young children with specific language impairments.* Unpublished doctoral dissertation, Wayne State University, Detroit, MI.

Vander Woude, J., & Koole, H. (2000). *"Why they do thats?" Abstract language in shared book reading.* Paper presented at the American Speech–Language–Hearing Association Convention, Washington, DC.

Vander Woude, J., van Kleeck, A., & Bormann, A. (2005). *Development of maternal specialized corrective repairs during book sharing.* Paper presented at the X International Congress for the Study of Child Language, Berlin, Germany.

van Kleeck, A. (1998). Preliteracy domains and stages: Laying the foundations for beginning reading. *Journal of Children's Communication Development, 20,* 33–51.

van Kleeck, A. (2004). Fostering preliteracy development via storybook-sharing interactions: The cultural context of mainstream family practices. In C. A. Stone, E. Silliman, B. Ehren, & K. Apel (Eds.), *Handbook of language and literacy* (pp. 175–208). New York: Guilford Press.

van Kleeck, A. (2006a). Cultural issues in promoting dialogic book sharing in the families of preschoolers. In A. van Kleeck (Ed.), *Sharing books and stories to promote language and literacy* (pp. 179–230). San Diego, CA: Plural.

van Kleeck, A. (2006b). Fostering inferential language during book sharing with prereaders: A foundation for later text comprehension strategies. In A. van Kleeck (Ed.), *Sharing books and stories to promote language and literacy* (pp. 269–318). San Diego, CA: Plural.

van Kleeck, A. (2008). Providing preschool foundations for later reading comprehension: The importance of and ideas for targeting inferencing in book-sharing interventions. *Psychology in the Schools, 45*(6), 1–17.

van Kleeck, A., Alexander, E. I., Vigil, A., & Templeton, K. E. (1996). Verbally modeling thinking for infants: Middle-class mothers' presentation of information structures during book sharing. *Journal of Research in Childhood Education, 10*(2), 101–113.

van Kleeck, A., Gillam, R. B., Hamilton, L., & McGrath, C. (1997). The relationship between middle-class parents' book-sharing discussion and their preschooler's abstract language development. *Journal of Speech, Language, and Hearing Research, 40,* 1261–1271.

van Kleeck, A., & Vander Woude, J. (1999). *Conversations between parents and children with delayed language during book sharing.* Paper presented at the American Speech–Language–Hearing Association Convention, San Francisco, CA.

van Kleeck, A., Vander Woude, J., & Hammett, L. (2006). Fostering literal and inferential language skills in Head Start preschoolers with language impairment using scripted book-sharing discussions. *American Journal of Speech–Language Pathology, 15,* 85–95.

van Kleeck, A., Vander Woude, J., & McDonald, E. (2006). *A longitudinal investigation of mothers' labeling routines during book sharing with children aged 6 to 24 months.* Unpublished manuscript, University of Texas, Dallas.

van Kleeck, A., Vigil, A., & Beers, N. (1998). *A longitudinal study of maternal book-sharing emphasis on print form and print meaning with preschoolers.* Paper presented at the American Speech–Language–Hearing Association Convention, San Antonio, TX.

Vivas, E. (1996). Effects of story reading on language. *Language Learning, 46,* 189–216.

Wells, G. (1985). Preschool literacy-related activities and success in school. In D. R. Olson, N. Torrance, & A. Hilyard (Eds.), *Literacy, language, and learning: The nature and consequences of reading and writing* (pp. 229–255). New York: Cambridge University Press.

Werner, E. O., & Kresheck, J. D. (1983). *Structured Photographic Expressive Language Test II.* DeKalb, IL: Janelle.

Westby, C. (2004). Twenty-first-century literacy for a diverse world. *Folia phoniatrica et logopeadica, 56,* 254–271.

Whitehurst, G. J., Falco, F. L., Lonigan, C. J., Fischel, J. E., DeBarysche, N. D., Valdez-Menchacha, M. C., et al. (1988). Accelerating language development through picture-book reading. *Developmental Psychology, 24,* 552–559.

Whitehurst, G. J., & Lonigan, C. J. (2001). Emergent literacy: Development from prereaders to readers. In S. B. Neuman & D. K. Dickinson (Eds.), *Handbook of early literacy research* (pp. 11–29). New York: Guilford Press.

Yoder, P. J., Spruytenburg, H., Edwards, A., & Davies, B. (1995). Effect of verbal routine contexts and expansions on gains in the mean length of utterance in children with developmental delays. *Language, Speech, and Hearing Services in Schools, 26*(1), 21–32.

Yuill, N., & Oakhill, J. (1991). *Children's problems in text comprehension: An experimental investigation.* New York: Cambridge University Press.

Zevenbergen, A. A., & Whitehurst, G. J. (2003). Dialogic reading: A shared picture-book reading intervention for preschoolers. In A. van Kleeck, S. A. Stahl, & E. B. Bauer (Eds.), *On reading books to children: Parents and teachers* (pp. 177–200). Mahwah, NJ: Erlbaum.

Zimmerman, I., Steiner, V., & Pond, R. (2002). *Preschool Language Scale–IV.* San Antonio, TX: Psychological Corporation.

APPENDIX 2.1. Example of Scripted Questions and Book Sharing

Excerpt of text: "Bear thought for a moment. Then he went inside and got his bow and arrow. With a piece of string, he attached a spoon to the arrow" (Asch, 1983, p. 4). The scripted questions and scaffolds for this text and accompanying picture are listed below.

Language levels	Adult's questions	Child's possible responses	Adult's scaffolds
Literal language	What's this? (point to the house)	1. A house. 2. A building. 3. Inappropriate response, no response, I don't know.	1. Yeah, it's a pretty, brick house, isn't it? 2. Yeah, it's a building. Maybe the building is Bear's house. 3. Do you think maybe that's Bear's house? I think it might be. Looks like a house made out of brick to me.

Literal language	What's this part of the house called?	1. Window
		2. Inappropriate response, no response, I don't know.
		  a. "-dow"
		  b. Inappropriate response, no response, I don't know.
			1. Yeah, it's a window.
			2. I think that's a win _____.
			  a. Yes, that's a window.
			  b. It's a window.

Literal language	What's Bear doing here?	1. Putting the spoon on there (on the arrow).
		2. Inappropriate response, no response, I don't know.
		  a. String
		  b. Inappropriate response, no response, I don't know.
			1. Yeah, he's attaching the spoon on the arrow with a string, isn't he?
			2. He's attaching the spoon on the arrow with the (pointing to the string) _____.
			  a. Yeah, he's attaching the spoon on the arrow with a string, isn't he?
			  b. String. He's attaching the spoon on the arrow with the string, isn't he?

Inferential language	What do you think Bear could use to attach the spoon onto the arrow?	1. Maybe glue, tape, or a rubber band. 2. Inappropriate response. 3. No response, I don't know.	1. Yes, he could maybe use (fill in child's response, if appropriate), couldn't he? 2. Well, I'm not sure that would work, but maybe he could use glue or tape or something like that. 3. Maybe he could use glue or tape. Do you think that might work?

CHAPTER THREE

Metaphonological Awareness
ENHANCING LITERACY SKILLS

Elizabeth Hester
Barbara W. Hodson

When Isabelle Liberman (1973) showed that an awareness of the sound structure or phonology of language was closely tied with learning to read, the tide began to turn in reading research. The connection of phonological awareness with reading has come to be regarded as the most important discovery in the field in our time (Stanovich, 2000; Vellutino & Scanlon, 1991), leaving, for all but a few (see Paris, 2005), only questions on measuring and tracking the development of phonological abilities. What does it mean to be *aware*? How do we become aware and remain aware? Does awareness imply consciousness? The question of consciousness seems to be at the very heart of what it means to be human. Are animals conscious? Can machines be programmed to be conscious? The race to answer these questions is driving research today in philosophy, biology, the computational sciences (Dennett, 1991, 1998; Morin, 2006), and, yes, speech and language. We do not have clear answers and must proceed with all due scientific caution in approaching and applying a concept as deep and enticing as awareness.

Most of the time, we give little thought to the sound structure of language. As speaker and listener, we focus on the communication—the meaning of the message. But deep in our evolutionary history, sensitivity to slight differences in sound permitted us as a species to develop a complex communication system that contributed to our survival (Hester, 2005; Lieberman, 1991). The phonological systems of languages are made up of subtle contrasts in sounds embedded in words. The child must discover the contrasts that are meaningful in the surrounding sea of speech sounds in order to use language to communicate efficiently. The typical 2-year-old understands that giving him or her a *pat* is not the same as giving him or her a *bat*. To use written language, an awareness of these contrasts is necessary for breaking this continuous stream into discrete units and mapping them onto printed symbols. Speech developed at least 30,000 years before written language (Moats, 1998). The phonological awareness that is needed to use written language successfully is necessarily more highly developed than that required for speech (Treiman & Zukowski, 1991). In this chapter, we explore the development of this relationship: how a child's phonology develops in tandem with the other components of language, specifically the lexical and syntactic components, and how the child maintains an awareness of the connection between sound and meaning. But first we must look more closely at the terms involved and the concepts implied.

What's in a Name: Metaphonological or Phonological? Sensitivity or Awareness?

Terminology

The term "awareness" is broad, complex, and, ultimately, ambiguous. At what point does subtle attention become conscious awareness? This question leads to additional questions regarding the nature of attention. Stanovich (2000) suggested using the term "phonological sensitivity" in place of "phonological awareness" because of the connection of the notion of awareness with the more problematic concepts of consciousness and attention. He acknowledged, however, that the term "phonological awareness" is now deeply entrenched in both writing about and thinking about the speech sound system and reading, and that it is difficult to discuss the literature without using this term (see Kaderavek, Cabell, &

Justice, Chapter 4, this volume, for an in-depth discussion of early writing development).

Metaphonology, metaphonological skill, and metaphonological awareness may be more appropriate terms than sensitivity or awareness. The *meta-* prefix ironically has an established role in the description of consciousness in such terms as "metacognition," "metaknowledge," and "metalinguistics" (Dennett, 1991). *Meta-* means beyond or behind (Merriam-Webster, 2006), as in standing behind or above phonology or cognition and examining it. Cognition, knowledge, and linguistics, in common with phonology, are the very tools we use to think and talk. The *meta-* perspective connotes an observational stance of sorts. So, metaphonological awareness, then, is the sensitivity to the speech-sound structure of a language in order to analyze, store, and manipulate it when acquiring a lexicon or mapping to written symbols.

The term "metaphonology" also implies an analytic, as opposed to holistic, processing stance (Byrne, 1998; Stanovich, 2000). Metaphonological skill or phonological awareness involves the ability to identify and isolate the subunits that make up words and sentences. It is a metalinguistic skill that goes beyond the ability to hear or auditorily discriminate the differences among sounds and requires an explicit analysis of the sound structure of words (Brady, 1991). The analysis from larger to smaller sound units appears to follow a developmental pattern; that is, awareness of smaller units of speech sound with more complex and precise analysis tends to become more prominent as children progress through the preschool and early school years. We next discuss these levels of analysis in more detail when we look at development of metaphonology but first we must consider the bigger picture.

The analytic stance required for developing sufficient metaphonological awareness in order to decode print and access meaning comes naturally and easily for only a small percentage of children. Most children require specific guidance; some find decoding to be extremely difficult. Weaknesses in metaphonology have been shown to be closely tied to deficits in other aspects of language, particularly those related to the organization and representation of the lexicon (Edwards & Lahey, 1998). We next examine the progression toward full metaphonological awareness in light of phonological development and its role in the acquisition of a lexicon.

From Whole to Part to Whole: Language Development, Phonology, and Metaphonology

Children do not develop phonology or metaphonology in a vacuum. They acquire the sound system of a language while learning to understand and use words. Phonology is the vehicle or form that carries meaning of a language. Language form, grounded in speech sounds, and its content or meaning are inextricably bound. Extensive research (Edwards, Beckman, & Munson, 2004; Luce, 2000; Luce & Lyons, 1999) recently has focused on understanding the relationship of words and their component sounds to the organization, representation, and acquisition of the lexicon.

Much of the research on the lexicon stemmed from Jusczyk's (2000) pioneering work with infants. Jusczyk's work starts with the challenging two-sided dilemma: How do infants learn words without familiarity with the sounds of a language and how do they learn the sounds, or the phonology, of a language without knowing the words? He and others (see Vihman, 1996, for a summary) found that infants appear to track phonological patterns with the aid of the prosody of infant-directed speech. The exaggerated fluctuations in pitch and timing in speech directed toward infants help focus their attention on sentence boundaries, clauses, phrases, words, and even parts of words. The infant acts as an observant scientist and an obsessive statistician who carefully notes sounds and sound combinations (see the discussion of phonotactics below) and keeps track of where these sounds occur in an utterance (Gopnik, Meltzoff, & Kuhl, 1999; Kuhl, 2000; Saffran, Werker, & Werner, 2006). The infant attends to vowel differences, common word stress patterns (i.e., strong–weak and weak–strong), and specific features of consonants (e.g., stop versus continuant) during the first 6 months of life and begins to connect sound with meaning in the second half of the first year. A landmark in the development of that sound-meaning association comes with the recognition of the sound pattern that is the child's own name, which occurs around the age of 4½ months (Jusczyk, 2000). The 9-month-old infant has accrued an extensive store of data that will enable him or her to predict that a particular sound sequence indicates the end as opposed to the beginning of a word (Saffran et al., 2006). In English, for example, the likelihood that the sound sequence *nts* signals the beginning of the word is just about nil (i.e., zero). The infant uses such phonotactic cues to attend to meaningfully recurring sound sequences or words. The child's developing vocabulary and phonological systems are closely intertwined.

Vocabulary Growth and the Developing Phonological Representation

When Waterson (1971) first suggested that very young children do not necessarily represent speech sounds cognitively in the same way adults do, the idea seemed radical. It indeed ran counter to the prevailing notion that children's representations matched those of the adult speakers around them (Vihman, 2004). Research since that time has supported Waterson's (1971) idea. Young children grasp the prosodic framework of whole utterances. Short, frequent phrases such as "All gone," "Bad dog," or "Don't touch that," are represented as whole units at this point. The phonological representation is the mental information an individual holds about speech sounds and their organization in words (Scarborough & Brady, 2002). This information is intimately linked with a child's vocabulary growth.

Development of Phonological Awareness

As the child gains experience with language and opportunities for linking sounds with meaning increase, the child's phonological representation becomes increasingly segmental (Brady 1991; Treiman & Zukowski, 1991; Walley, 1993). Phonological representation in typically developing children appears to move generally from larger units, such as phrases and words, to smaller units including syllables and, eventually, phonemes. This progression is evident in their performance on tasks probing levels of phonological awareness. The relationship of phonological awareness to phonological representation is that of process to product: Awareness is the process of attending to aspects of the representation. Tasks probing phonological awareness, which we describe in more detail in the section "Assessing and Enhancing Metaphonological Skills," include identifying and producing rhyming words and words that start with the same sounds (alliteration), and counting words and syllables.

The development of phonological awareness is not simplistic, quick, or unilateral. Very young infants appear to actually have more global or open-ended linguistic perceptual abilities than older infants. They are better able than their older peers to detect subtle phonetic contrasts, such as dental and retroflex alveolar stops and aspiration variations, which are not meaningful in their own language (see Vihman, 1996, for a summary). With increased exposure to a particular language, they begin to map the phonemic boundaries of that language and lose the ability to distinguish other subtle differences. The development of a segmental phonological representation is protracted (Walley, 1993); that is, it does not occur all at once in a single child nor does it happen evenly across all children. The variation in the development of segmental phonological representation is thought to be due to the child's individual experience with words and the types of relations among the words that are noticed by that child. Bloom and Lahey (1978) classically described this as the linking of linguistic form and experience. This linking at first may be overly narrow, as when a child regards only his or her own pet as a "dog," or it may be applied too widely, as when the term "dog" is applied to all four-legged animals.

Phonological Awareness and Vocabulary Development

It is theorized that pressure to develop a more phonemic level of phonological organization, at least at an implicit level, begins with the word spurt, the burst of vocabulary growth that typically is seen in children around the age of 2 years (Walley, 1993). Children who maintain the infantile holistic representation and do not begin the transition toward segmentation are at grave risk for delayed language acquisition, affecting further vocabulary growth as well as syntactic development both receptively and expressively (Edwards & Lahey, 1998; Scarborough, 1990).

Even very young children (between 1 and 2 years of age), however, understand and use as many as six different words that differ by only one sound (Dollaghan, 1994; Fisher, Hunt, Chambers, & Church, 2001). The word *be*, for example, has at least eight other close neighbors familiar to young children, including *he, key, me, knee, see, she, tea*, and *we* (Dollaghan, 1994). It would thus seem that phonological organization and some level of speech-sound sensitivity are important in lexical acquisition from the earliest stages. The development of a child's phonological representation in relation to vocabulary growth has been tracked by examining word frequency, neighborhood density, and phonotactic probability

(Charles-Luce & Luce, 1990). Word frequency refers to how commonly a word occurs in the lexicon. The neighborhood density is a calculation of the number of words in the lexicon that differ from a given word, most simply a word with a consonant–vowel–consonant (CVC) structure, by only one sound. So, as in the case of the word *be*, there are many neighbors, but the word *work* would have few neighbors. Phonotactic probability is a measure of the likelihood that certain sounds will occur together and is more of a sound-based or phonological measure than a lexical measure. In English, it is likely that the common blends or clusters, such as *bl-*, *pl-*, *br-*, *tr-*, *st-*, *sp-*, and *-ts* and *-ps* occur together, but unlikely that combinations such as *bk*, *ln*, or *tb* will occur together unless they meet at word or syllable boundaries. The concepts upon which the terms "word frequency," "neighborhood density," and "phonotactic probability" are based are somewhat problematic or relative because they all depend on the lexicon in question (Dollaghan, 1994). Even among adults, there is a big difference between describing the "lexicon" as including the contents of a dictionary and calling it a list of the words in spoken conversation.

The changes in the lexicon and in phonological representation are reciprocal for both children and adults. In learning new words and new sound sequences, the robustness of the phonological representation is enhanced. The meaningful differences or phonemic contrasts between the sounds that make up words are strengthened and become ever more important as more words are acquired. The growing lexicon also flourishes if there is an awareness of these sound differences. If children are aware that, for example, *pit* and *bit* sound subtly different but mean something very different, they will more likely understand and use these words correctly, and they will more easily acquire other phonological neighbors such as *hit*, *mitt*, *knit*, and so on. This reciprocal development of the lexicon and phonological representation is the basis of the metaphonological skill needed to develop fluent reading decoding. Next, we look briefly at the development of this skill.

The Development of Metaphonological Skills

The emergence of language in the growing child has held the fascination of philosophers and scientists as well as fathers and mothers.

Despite differences in individual experiences, most of us learn to communicate with each other. And most of us, with guidance, can develop intricate skills in both oral and written language—skills we use to tell a story, to deceive, and to dream. It should begin to be clear from the preceding discussion that the linguistic skill that surrounds the development of metaphonological awareness is complex. Not all people develop this awareness in the same way or in the exact same stages, but certain trends are apparent.

Origins of Metaphonological Awareness

The Tacit Level of Metaphonological Awareness

At the earliest or most simplistic level, "awareness" is quite subtle and may truly be more like sensitivity. Stackhouse (1997) regarded this basic level of awareness as one end of a continuum (see Figure 3.1) from tacit (or unspoken) to explicit awareness. Fully developed, explicit awareness emerges through the accumulation of sensory experience with the phonological system: by hearing the sounds, by seeing or "lip-reading" how the sounds look when other people produce them, and by writing the symbols linked to the sounds. Syl-

FEEDBACK	Auditory	Articulatory	Orthographic
		Lip-reading	
LEVEL OF ANALYSIS	Syllable Segmentation		
	Rhyme		
		Blending	
		Sound Segmentation	
			Sound Manipulation
			Cluster Segmentation
LEVEL OF AWARENESS	Tacit ⟶		Explicit

FIGURE 3.1. Metaphonological skill and level of awareness. From Stackhouse (1997, p. 161). Copyright by Joy Stackhouse. Reprinted by permission.

lable segmentation and rhyming reflect a tacit level, whereas sound segmentation and manipulation indicate an explicit level of awareness. Preschool children without knowledge of the alphabet can reliably match syllable counts and can identify and sometimes produce rhymes. The tacit level of awareness reflects a dawning understanding of the form of words as distinct from their meaning. This is evident even in 2- and 3-year-old children. The child may comment on rhyming words as being "the same" or on long words or funny sounding words. The 2-year-old child of a friend chimed in with "Minnehaha" when long words were mentioned in her presence. The fact that the child comments on speech form reflects metalinguistic abilities and indicates a level of analysis beyond mere discrimination of the differences in sounds.

Transition to More Sophisticated Metaphonological Awareness

The ability to detect and produce rhyming sequences develops during the preschool years. Consistent performance on phonological awareness tasks such as syllable segmentation and rhyme and alliteration identification is evident after 4 years of age (Gillon, 2004). Four-year-olds have an affinity for word-form jokes or puns, and both 4- and 5-year-old children spontaneously produce rhymes in play. Names are the particular object of rhyming (e.g., *Charlie–farlie*, *Lizzie–dizzie*), and the penchant for puns is seen in the endless variations of knock–knock jokes, the humor of which is often lost on adults. Table 3.1 provides a summary of metaphonological

TABLE 3.1. Typical Metaphonological Development

3–5 years	5–7 years
Rhyming	Onset and rime blending
Alliteration	
Words/syllables	Phonemes
Segmentation	Segmentation
Blending	Blending
Manipulation	Manipulation
Grapheme–phoneme awareness	Grapheme–phoneme correspondence

Note. From Hodson (2005, p. 23). Copyright 2005 by the American Speech–Language–Hearing Association. Reprinted by permission.

development in typically developing children between the ages of 3 and 7 years.

More Explicit Metaphonological Awareness

As a child gains experience with the alphabetic principle—the notion that letters or graphemes stand for speech sounds—metaphonological awareness becomes more explicit. Phoneme awareness allows the child to break down a word into its component sounds, or phonemes, and move or change these sounds while holding the original word in memory. Given the word *bat*, for example, the child is asked to change the /b/ to /k/, resulting in the new word, *cat*. It generally requires familiarity with the alphabet and the reading decoding process (Gillon, 2004). But mere familiarity does not guarantee a phonological representation robust enough for fluent sound manipulation or reading decoding (Hester & Hodson, 2004). Young children, especially children with speech and language delays, benefit from repeated and explicit instruction in metaphonological awareness (Cunningham, 1990; Rvachew, Nowak, & Cloutier, 2004). Explicit instruction in metaphonological awareness does not mean all other aspects of language should be neglected. Instruction should take place within the context of meaningful language and literature that are rich with stimulating vocabulary and interesting sentence and narrative structure.

Metaphonological Awareness Beyond the Preschool Years

The development of metaphonological awareness continues well beyond the preschool years. The nature of phonological representation in adults is not fully understood. With the move from a tacit to explicit level of awareness, the phonological representation does not simply move from an unanalyzable whole to an alphabet soup of loose pieces. The fluent, mature language user most likely holds representations at multiple levels simultaneously and uses the one that is most efficient as needed (Storkel & Morrisette, 2002; Velleman & Vihman, 2002; Vihman, 1996). For fluent reading and for comprehension of a spoken sentence, adults and older children may use a more holistic representation rather than relying on sound-by-sound decoding (Levelt, 1998; Torgesen, 2003). So, when decoding a string of familiar words within a sentence, the skilled reader relies on lexical orthographic representations—essentially, sight words (Torgesen, 2003), which are closely linked to the visual representations also drawn on in spelling—only new or less familiar words must be analyzed phonetically or sounded out. The skilled reader may also draw on strategies that fall between these two extremes, such as decoding by analogy (referring to a word that rhymes with or looks very similar to the target) or by derivation (using morphologic knowledge of word roots and endings). For the adult or the skilled reader, these words to be sounded out often include the names of people or places or technical terms, such as those encountered in a neuroanatomy class. (Indeed, transcription of neuroanatomy terms such as "suprachiasmatic nucleus" or "brachium conjunctivum" is a challenging exercise for advanced students of phonetics that requires strong metaphonological skills.) The level of segmental representation needed to be a fluent reader is not fully understood. It is clear that not all adults attain and maintain a high level of segmental awareness. This is evident to both the teacher and student in an entry level college phonetics class; some "sail right through" and truly enjoy phonetic transcription whereas others study and struggle and are glad when the course is over (see Moran & Fitch, 2001).

The Biology of Metaphonological Awareness and Emergent Literacy

Reading is a complex skill that involves genes, the brain, and behavior at multiple levels. It is a skill unique to humans that can only be learned from others in a social context and yet it has deep biological roots (Grigorenko, 2003). These roots or biologically based aptitudes, for the most part, are common to the various linguistic systems and to the learning process in general. The neurophysiological systems recruited to comprehend language and produce spoken utterances form the biological basis of reading (Grigorenko, 2003). It is thus difficult, if not inappropriate, to look for a gene for reading, although both reading and language disorders commonly seem to run in families.

The relationship of reading and language disorders is complex and is at the core of the controversy surrounding the concept of dyslexia. Most simply, dyslexia is a serious reading difficulty in the absence of other evident deficits in sensory, motor, cognitive, or socioeconomic development (Berninger, 2001; Vellutino, Fletcher, Snowling, & Scanlon, 2004). The controversy stems from the interpretation of the *reading*, which may be broken down into multiple subskills including decoding, comprehension, and inferencing. Decoding alone encompasses more basic skills including the full phonological awareness continuum (as described above) and sound–symbol association; that is, the linking of visual and auditory images represented by the printed letters or graphemes. Researchers in the investigations described below strive to isolate these various components of reading in order to document the breakdown that occurs in the individual with dyslexia.

Genetic Investigations

Both dyslexia and spoken language disorder are studied using the same techniques, which involve a combination of cytogenetics and family and population genetics (Gilger, Ho, Whipple, & Spitz, 2001; Grigorenko, 2003; Plomin & DeFries, 1998). Several chromosomes and genes have been implicated within the family groups studied, but cautions remain on broader interpretation. The identified genes may actually be related to broader areas of language learning and learning in general. This notion is supported by the high degree of comorbidity with other neuropsychological deficits in reading, including weaknesses in spoken language, writing, math, and attention (Grigorenko, 2003).

Neuroimaging Investigations

Attempts to locate the neurobiological basis of reading also must deal with the complex nature of the skill. This is done by fractionating the process into components, including visual, semantic, lexical, and sublexical phonetic and phonological encoding. Activity in the nervous system is assessed using positron emission tomography (PET), functional magnetic resonance imaging (fMRI), and to a lesser extent, event-related potentials (ERPs) and magnetoencephalography (MEG). At the level of lexical phonology, which typically is measured by rhyme judgments, activity has been reported in many cortical regions but most commonly in the posterior superior temporal gyrus, left insula, and the inferior frontal cortex (Joseph, Noble, & Eden, 2001; Shaywitz, 2003).

Sublexical phonology, which primarily involves the phonemic level, is further removed from semantic processing (this becomes less certain when strings of sounds or syllables that begin to sound word-like are assessed). Activation is evident in the left inferior frontal area, the premotor cortex, and the left orbital frontal area. In addition to areas implicated in lexical activity, sublexical tasks also involve the insula, the middle temporal gyri of the occipitotemporal junction, and extensive lateral and medial frontal lobe activation (Joseph et al., 2001). Individuals with dyslexia show relatively reduced activation in posterior regions including Wernicke's area, the angular gyrus, and the striate cortex, with increased anterior activation in the inferior frontal gyrus (Shaywitz, 2003; Shaywitz et al., 1998).

Some argue that the components of reading can never be fractionated or separated entirely from other environmental factors (see Gilger et al., 2001), and thus, all attempts to measure activity associated with a particular task may be unrealistic. Although this argument is part of a larger debate on the nature of language itself, the study of reading using neuroimaging continues to contribute to both our understanding of the reading process and of the neurobiology of language. As research on the neurobiological basis of language and reading proceeds, it is hoped that the fruits of this inquiry can be used to further inform the assessment and enhancement of metaphonological skills in young children.

Assessing and Enhancing Metaphonological Skills

Metaphonological assessment typically involves evaluating a child's knowledge and skills in one or more of the following: (1) rhyming, (2) alliteration or onset, (3) segmenting, (4) blending, and (5) manipulation. The term "onset" refers to the consonant(s) preceding the rime in a syllable (e.g., *sl* in *sleep*), whereas alliteration refers to the first sound (e.g., *s* in *sleep*). Thus, onset can be a consonant cluster as well as an initial consonant. The rime, which is obligatory, consists of a vocalic element and refers to the part of the syllable/ word from the vowel to the end. The tasks that are used commonly to assess rhyming and alliteration/onset include (1) judgment, (2) matching, (3) oddity, (4) supply/generation, and (5) categorization. Tasks assessing the segmental level include segmentation, blending, and manipulation.

Assessment of Emerging Metaphonological Awareness

Judgment and Matching

Judgment, which involves a "yes" or "no" type of response regarding whether the words rhyme or begin with the same sound, is the least satisfactory of the tasks because of the "chance" factor. That is, a child could guess "yes" or "no" and have a 50% chance of scoring correctly. Matching, which involves determining whether words rhyme with (or begin with the same sound as) the designated word, can be used with preschool children if pictures of the words are provided. Matching is generally a more satisfactory assessment measure than judgment because the simple 50–50 chance factor is reduced, and it provides the examiner with an opportunity to observe how the child is reasoning (e.g., are the child's choices phonologically or semantically related to the target or do they appear to be random guesses?).

Oddity

Oddity tasks, which were the mainstay of studies by Bradley and Bryant (1983) in England, are more difficult than matching tasks. The child must decide which word is different (e.g., "Which beginning sound is not like the others for *dog, boy, bat, ball?*"). Oddity tasks seem to place more demand on working memory.

Generation of Words

The fourth major type of task, in which the child is asked to supply words that rhyme with (or that begin with) the same sound as the specified word, has been found to be the most difficult for preschool children (Keller, 2000). To supply a rhyming word on demand requires word retrieval that is supported only by the context of the target word. This is often particularly challenging for children with phonologically weak lexical representations, as we described in the earlier section on language development, phonology, and metaphonology.

Categorization

The fifth type of task, categorization, involves both matching and oddity. Children typically sort the pictures of words that match and place the matching words in one pile and the nonmatching word(s) in a separate place. It is especially helpful to use manipulatives for preschool children (e.g., two or three blocks of the same color for pictures of words that match, with a block of a different color for the nonmatching words).

Segmentation and Blending

Segmentation and blending tasks should involve larger units before smaller units. Most preschool children can segment and blend at the word/syllable level (e.g., "How many parts are in *ice cream cone?*"). Segmenting and blending at the phoneme level is considerably more difficult. Typically developing children are not able to segment and blend phonemes until the age of 5 or 6 years. Two intermediary levels for segmentation and blending include (1) onset and rime (e.g., *sh + eep*) and (2) body and coda (e.g., *shee + p*).

Manipulation

These tasks include (1) deletion (e.g., take /m/ away from *mice*), (2) addition (e.g., add /m/ to *ice*), (3) substitution (e.g., substitute /b/ for /m/ in *mat*), and (4) transposition (e.g., switch /t/ and /p/ in *pat*). Preschool children enjoy manipulating phonemes in songs (e.g., "Apples and Bananas"), and syllable/word-level units are appropriate tasks for preschool children (e.g., *cowboy*, take away *cow*, what is left?). It should be noted, however, that phoneme manipulation tasks generally require some experience in reading.

Performance on phoneme manipulation tasks has been found to be highly correlated with literacy scores. Hester and Hodson (2004) found that performances of third graders on pig Latin tasks (e.g., *silly* → "illy-sa") predicted reading scores, and Strattman and Hodson (2005) found that scores of second graders on spoonerism tasks (e.g., switching the beginning sounds of *bow* and *coy* to obtain *cowboy*) were highly predictive of their reading and spelling abilities (see Kaderavek et al., Chapter 4, this volume, for an in-depth discussion of early spelling development).

Enhancing Metaphonological Skills in Preliterate Children

All of the tasks mentioned in the preceding section on assessment can also be used as instructional tasks. Findings from treatment research studies (e.g., Hatcher, Hulme, & Ellis, 1994) indicate, however, that results are improved when the tasks are "linked to literacy." Another major finding has been that the instruction needs to be direct, explicit, and systematic (Lyon & Moats, 1997), but also "fun" (Torgesen & Mathes, 2000). Additionally, graphemes need to be incorporated (Ball & Blachman, 1988), and our clinical experience has shown that it is useful to explain and demonstrate articulatory characteristics (e.g., place and manner of production for consonants).

Task Complexity

Levels of task complexity also need to be considered. For example, it is easier for a preschool child to begin with identification (e.g., point to a picture) rather than production (i.e., naming). Word/syllable-level tasks (e.g., "How many words/syllables are in *hotdog*?") are easier than onset and rime tasks (e.g., "What's the first sound in *dog*?"), which, in turn, are easier than phoneme tasks (e.g., "How many sounds are in *dog*?" or "What are the sounds in *dog*?"). In terms of numbers, incorporating two items, that is, two syllables or sounds as the case may be, is easier than three, and three would be easier than four, and so on. Continuous phonemes (e.g., /f/) are usually easier for children to identify than stops (e.g., /p/). Another consideration is that children typically are able to identify word-initial sounds before word-ending phonemes and word endings before word-medial sounds.

Generally, metaphonological awareness activities for preschool children may include any number of word play variations (i.e., activities that focus on the form rather than the meaning of a word), but these all should enhance "foundation" skills (e.g., rhyming, syllable segmentation). Although there has been some controversy regarding the importance of rhyming (see Muter, Hulme, Snowling, & Taylor, 1997), the consensus seems to be that rhyming and word play appear to "set the stage" for later phonemic awareness skill development. In addition, awareness of letter–sound relationships should be facilitated at the preschool level.

Sample Programs for Enhancing Metaphonological Awareness Skills

A number of publications are available, including computer software (e.g., *Earobics*, Wasowicz, 1997), that can be used to enhance metaphonological skills of preschool and kindergarten children. Three programs that have been developed for use with kindergarten children are discussed in this section to provide information about methods and activities that can be used in the learning environment.

Road to the Code

Road to the Code: A Phonological Awareness Program for Young Children (Blachman, Ball, Black, & Tangel, 2000) provides 44 lessons that are to be taught in 20-minute sessions to small groups of children in kindergarten. The program includes a "Say-It-and-Move-It" activity, in which children move tiles to boxes from left to right under a picture as they pronounce each sound. The "Letter Name and Sound Instruction" activity involves teaching names and sounds of six consonants and two short vowels. The third component, "Phonological Awareness Practice," involves activities that vary from rhyming words to comparing words with similar beginning sounds and blending sounds to make words. Blachman et al. (2000) found that children who participated in this program in kindergarten were better readers in grades 1 and 2 than their peers who did not receive the instruction. Blachman and Tangel published "follow-up" lessons in Road to Reading: A Program for Preventing and Remediating Reading Difficulties (Blachman & Tangel, 2008) for students in grades 1 to 3.

Gillon Phonological Awareness Tracking Programme

The Gillon Phonological Awareness Training Programme (Gillon, 2000) involves direct, systematic phonological awareness instruction in the context of positive language interactions (Gillon, 2004). The kit contains activities for (1) rhyming, (2) phoneme analysis and manipulation, (3) phoneme identity, (4) phoneme segmentation, (5) phoneme blending, (6) sound–symbol associations, and (7) tracking speech sounds (first without letters and then with letters). Treatment study results indicated that performances of children with expressive phonological impairment between the ages of 5 and 7 years who participated in this program for 20 hours were significantly better than control groups on measures of reading accuracy, reading comprehension, and nonword decoding ability (Gillon, 2000).

Animated Literacy

Animated Literacy (Stone, 2004) is a comprehensive multisensory language-based early literacy classroom program that includes (1) pattern songs for phoneme manipulation (e.g., "Bay a Bay"); (2) phoneme stories, characters, and gestures (e.g., Polly Panda painting purple *P*'s); (3) a guided drawing–writing component (e.g., instructions and demonstration for drawing *pup* and then writing the word). The lessons focus on prediction, comprehension, association with prior knowledge, and the enjoyment of language. Forty-three "Animated Alphabet" stories, characters, gestures, and songs are included to introduce phonemes and graphemes.

Whiting (2006) provided several types of treatment to two groups of children who were enrolled in a Head Start program. One class received large-group phonological awareness and small-group alphabet knowledge instruction (e.g., Road to the Code, Animated Literacy) biweekly for 15 weeks. A second group participated in small-group shared book-reading activities for equivalent amounts of time. A control group participated in the regular Head Start program curriculum activities, but received no specialized intervention. Analysis of variance results indicated that posttreatment scores on the Assessment of Primary Literacy Skills (Hodson, 2006) for the first group were significantly better than those of the other two groups ($p = .005$) on overall primary literacy measures and for the phonological awareness component but not for alphabet knowledge. Differences between the shared book-reading group and the control group were not significant for any measures.

Depending on their comfort level with metaphonology and their clinical resources, speech–language pathologists may choose to follow a single program fairly closely, or they may decide to integrate parts of various programs within the larger framework of their remediation plans. This is what was done in the case we describe next.

Case Study

The following case study is included to illustrate how the information presented in this chapter on assessing and enhancing metaphonological awareness can be applied with a child with a phonological disorder. The case study demonstrates the use of various activities within the context of individual and group settings.

The child reported in this section, Michael (not his real name), entered our university phonology clinic at the age of 3 years, 6 months because his speech was extremely difficult for others to understand (Hodson, 1994, 1997). His medical history reports indicated that he had recurrent episodes of otitis media, accompanied by fluctuating hearing loss. Michael attended the university phonology clinic for six terms, including one summer session. Treatment for his intelligibility difficulties was based on the Cycles Phonological Remediation Approach (Hodson, 2007; Hodson & Paden, 1991). His early phonological production target patterns included "syllableness," final consonants, /s/ clusters, velars, and liquids.

We had become aware that children with highly unintelligible speech often experience difficulties in the domain of phonological awareness (e.g., Webster & Plante, 1992) and ultimately literacy. Michael's metaphonological awareness skills were generally poor, with rhyming skills particularly being deficient. We began incorporating metaphonological awareness tasks for a few minutes during each treatment session. For example, four-line rhymes (e.g., "Jack and Jill"), which were printed on file folders, were read to Michael at the end of each session and then sent home for his parents to read to him each night. They were instructed that they were to pause after a couple of readings and let Michael "fill in" the appropriate rhyme word. New rhyme folders were exchanged for prior folders every 2 or 3 weeks.

During the semester prior to entering kindergarten, Michael participated in a research project involving 11 individual 30-minute instructional sessions (Domnick, Hodson, Coffman, & Wynne, 1993). Nursery rhymes and Dr. Seuss books were used to develop awareness of beginning sounds and rhymes, which were pointed out and discussed. In addition, matching tasks incorporating pictures were used for both rhyming and alliteration (e.g., "Which two words begin with the same sound: *bat, car, boy*?"). Segmentation skills were enhanced by having Michael jump for each syllable.

Michael also was taught to identify the first and last sounds in words with three phonemes. Plastic letters were incorporated during this identification activity for graphemes (e.g., *c ... a ... t*) followed by discussion of the names of the letters and identification of the beginning and ending sounds.

During his final semester at the university phonology clinic (his spring semester of kindergarten), Michael participated in a second metaphonological skill-enhancement research project (Hodson, Buckendorf, Conrad, & Swanson, 1994) along with four other kindergarten children for six 2-hour sessions. Michael's mother had reported during the fall semester that his kindergarten teacher had expressed concern regarding his early literacy skills, stating that he was performing at the bottom of his class on preliteracy tasks. Stories, gestures, and songs from *Animated Alphabet* (Stone, 1992) were incorporated for 18 phonemes. Blending was emphasized, first at the onset and rime level and then at the phoneme level. Phoneme manipulation was taught via songs (e.g., "Apples and Bananas," "Eeples and Baneenas"). Activities from Stone's drawing/writing book were presented during the last three sessions. Each child drew a *top*, a *mop*, and a *jet* and then printed the word above the picture. Michael evidenced substantial gains on clinician-generated posttreatment measures of metaphonological skills. In addition, his kindergarten teacher reported during the year-end parent conference that Michael had shown considerable improvement; she indicated that during the final month of his kindergarten year he was performing in the middle of his class.

The case study shows the interrelationship among language, phonology, and metaphonology in a young child and that intervention that addresses these skill areas effectively facilitated Michael's development in language and emergent literacy. The involvement of his parents in the intervention ensured the generalization of the gains that Michael made in language in emergent literacy to the home and school settings.

Summary

Two major challenges in a young person's life are learning to communicate verbally and unlocking the mystery of printed language. Both of these skills are closely connected with metaphonological awareness, the ability to attend to and analyze the sound structure of language. This analysis of the phonological representation is initially gross or holistic and gradually becomes more fine-grained or segmental. Metalinguistic skill develops as the child grows and gains experience with language. During the early school years, this segmental phonological representation is further developed when the child learns the alphabet. All individuals do not acquire this phonological foundation in the same way or with equal robustness. Many require explicit instruction in order to develop a level of awareness necessary for fluent reading and further language growth.

A series of tasks involving breaking words into their constituent sounds, putting these sounds together, and manipulating the parts of these words is used to assess metaphonological awareness. Programs to enhance this skill focus on fortifying the individual's phonological representation and making it salient and accessible (that is, easily accessed in fluent reading decoding) to the would-be reader. The goal of metaphonological awareness instruction is to strengthen the link between the speech-sound system and printed symbols in order to lead ultimately to fluent reading.

Recognition of the bond between awareness of the phonological system and reading was a milestone in the study of language acquisition and in the teaching of decoding. We can use this analytic approach to reading to break down the process and to try to trace its activity in the nervous system in both skilled and less skilled readers. We then come full circle, using reading in a metacognitive way to teach us more about the way we think and the way we process language. We have come a long way in recent years; the road ahead beckons with further understanding of the links among language, literacy, and our neurobiology, and the application of this knowledge to the development of optimal methods of instruction.

DISCUSSION QUESTIONS

1. What does the term "metaphonological awareness" mean? How does it compare with the terms "phonological sensitivity" and "phonological awareness"?

2. Describe the relationship of phonological representation to literacy.

3. What brain areas have been associated most closely with reading in general and metaphonology in particular?

4. Describe typical metaphonological development in the preschool years.

5. Describe metaphonological assessment tasks and note age expectations.

EXERCISES

1. Develop a rhyme-matching task for a preschool child. Include six target words. Be sure to list your alternate nonmatches and describe your stimuli.

2. Briefly describe two appropriate phonological awareness tasks for third graders. Be sure to cite justification for your selection.

3. Suppose that you are working in a large urban school district. Your superintendent is concerned about the number of kindergarten children at risk for delays in literacy development. She asks you to design a suitable program. What tasks would you choose and how would you justify your selection?

References

Ball, E., & Blachman, B. (1988). Phoneme segmentation training: Effect on reading readiness. *Annals of Dyslexia, 38*, 208–225.

Berninger, V. W. (2001). Understanding the "lexia" in dyslexia: A multidisciplinary team approach to learning disabilities. *Annals of Dyslexia, 51*, 23–48.

Blachman, B. A., Ball, E. W., Black, R., & Tangel, D. M. (2000). *Road to the code: A phonological awareness program for young children.* Baltimore: Brookes.

Blachman, B. A., & Tangel, D. M. (2008). *Road to reading: A program for preventing and remediating reading difficulties.* Baltimore: Brookes.

Bloom, L., & Lahey, M. (1978). *Language development and language disorders.* Sommerset, NJ: Wiley.

Bradley, L., & Bryant, P. (1983). Categorizing sounds and learning to read: A causal connection. *Nature, 30*, 419–421.

Brady, S. A. (1991). The role of working memory in reading disability. In S. A. Brady & D. P. Shankweiler (Eds.), *Phonological processes in literacy* (pp. 129–151). Hillsdale, NJ: Erlbaum.

Byrne, B. (1998). *The foundation of literacy: The child's acquisition of the alphabetic principle.* Hove East Sussex, England: Psychology Press.

Charles-Luce, J., & Luce, P. (1990). Similarity neighborhoods of words in young children's lexicons. *Journal of Child Language, 17*, 205–215.

Cunningham, A. E. (1990). Explicit versus implicit instruction in phonemic awareness. *Journal of Experimental Child Psychology, 50*, 429–444.

Dennett, D. C. (1991). *Consciousness explained.* Boston: Little Brown.

Dennett, D. C. (1998). *Brainchildren: Essays on designing minds.* Cambridge, MA: MIT Press.

Dollaghan, C. A. (1994). Children's phonological neighborhoods: Half empty or half full? *Journal of Child Language, 21*, 257–271.

Domnick, M., Hodson, B., Coffman, G., & Wynne, M. (1993). *Metaphonological awareness performance and training: Highly unintelligible prereaders.* Poster presentation at the annual convention of the American Speech–Language–Hearing Association, Anaheim, CA.

Edwards, J., Beckman, M. E., & Munson, B. (2004). The interaction between vocabulary and phonotactic probability effects on children's production accuracy and fluency in nonword repetition. *Journal of Speech, Language, and Hearing Research, 47*, 421–436.

Edwards, J., & Lahey, M. (1998). Nonword repetition of children with specific language impairment: Exploration of some explanations for their inaccuracies. *Applied Psycholinguistics, 19*, 279–309.

Fisher, C., Hunt, C., Chambers, K., & Church, B. (2001). Abstraction and specificity in preschoolers' representations of novel spoken words. *Journal of Memory and Language, 45*, 665–687.

Gilger, J. W., Ho, H., Whipple, A. D., & Spitz, R. (2001). Genotype–environment correlations for language-related abilities: Implications for typical and atypical learners. *Journal of Learning Disabilities, 34*(6), 492–502.

Gillon, G. (2000). *The Gillon phonological awareness training programme.* Christchurch, New Zealand: Canterprise, University of Canterbury.

Gillon, G. T. (2004). *Phonological awareness: From research to practice.* New York: Guilford Press.

Gopnik, A., Meltzoff, A. N., & Kuhl, P. K. (1999). *The scientist in the crib: Minds, brains, and how children learn.* New York: Morrow.

Grigorenko, E. L. (2003). The first candidate gene for dyslexia: Turning the page of a new chapter of research. *Proceedings of the National Academy of Sciences of the USA, 100*(20), 11190–11192.

Hatcher, P., Hulme, C., & Ellis, A. (1994). Ameliorating early reading failure by integrating the teaching of reading and phonological skills: The phonological linkage hypothesis. *Child Development, 65*, 41–57.

Hester, E. (2005). The evolution of the auditory system: A tutorial. *Contemporary Issues in Communication Science and Disorders, 32*, 5–10.

Hester, E., & Hodson, B. (2004). The role of phonological representation in decoding skills of young readers. *Child Language Teaching and Therapy, 20*(2), 115–133.

Hodson, B. (1994). Determining intervention priorities for preschoolers with disordered phonologies: Expediting intelligibility gains. In *Children's phonology disorders: Pathways and patterns* (pp. 65–87). Rockville, MD: American Speech–Language–Hearing Association.

Hodson, B. (1997). Disordered phonologies: What have we learned about assessment and treatment? In B. Hodson & M. Edwards (Eds.), *Perspectives in applied phonology* (pp. 197–224). Gaithersburg, MD: Aspen.

Hodson, B. (2005). *Enhancing phonological and metaphonological skills of children with highly unintelligible speech.* Rockville, MD: ASHA.

Hodson, B. (2006). *Assessment of primary literacy skills: Metaphonological awareness and alphabetic principle.* Unpublished manuscript, Wichita State University at Wichita, KS.

Hodson, B. (2007). *Evaluating and enhancing children's phonological systems: Research and theory to practice.* Greenville, SC: Thinking Publications University.

Hodson, B., Buckendorf, R., Conrad, R., & Swanson, T. (1994). *Enhancing metaphonological skills of highly unintelligible 6-year-olds.* Poster presentation at the annual convention of the American Speech–Language–Hearing Association, New Orleans, LA.

Hodson, B., & Paden, E. (1991). *Targeting intelligible speech: A phonological approach to remediation.* Austin, TX: PRO-ED.

Joseph, J., Noble, K., & Eden, G. (2001). The neurobiological basis of reading. *Journal of Learning Disabilities, 34*(6), 566–579.

Jusczyk, P. W. (2000). *The discovery of spoken language.* Cambridge, MA: MIT Press.

Keller, K. (2000). *Phonological awareness skills of typically developing children entering kindergarten.* Unpublished master's thesis, Wichita State University at Wichita, KS.

Kuhl, P. (2000). A new view of language acquisition. *Proceedings of the National Academy of Science, 97*(22), 11850–11857.

Levelt, W. J. M. (1998). *Speaking: From intention to articulation.* Cambridge, MA: MIT Press.

Liberman, I. (1973). Segmentation of the spoken word and reading acquisition. *Bulletin of the Orton Society, 23*, 65–77.

Lieberman, P. (1991). *Uniquely human: The evolution of speech, thought, and selfless behavior.* Cambridge, MA: Harvard.

Luce, P. (2000). *Accessing spoken words in the mental lexicon.* Presentation at the annual convention of the American Speech–Language–Hearing Association, Washington, DC.

Luce, P. A., & Lyons, E. A. (1999). Processing lexically embedded words. *Journal of Experimental Psychology: Human Perception and Performance, 25*(1), 174–183.

Lyon, R., & Moats, L. (1997). Critical conceptual and methodological considerations in reading-intervention research. *Journal of Learning Disabilities, 30*, 578–588.

Merriam-Webster. (2006). In *Merriam-Webster* online. Retrieved May 31, 2006, from *www.m-w.com/dictionary.*

Moats, L. C. (1998). Teaching decoding. *American Educator, 22*, 42–49.

Moran, M. J., & Fitch, J. L. (2001). Phonological awareness skills of university students: Implications for teaching phonetics. *Contemporary Issues in Communication Science and Disorders, 28*, 85–90.

Morin, A. (2006). Levels of consciousness and self-awareness: A comparison and integration of various neurocognitive views. *Consciousness and Cognition, 15*, 358–371.

Muter, V., Hulme, C., Snowling, M., & Taylor, S. (1997). Segmentation, not rhyming, predicts early progress in learning to read. *Journal of Experimental Child Psychology, 64*, 370–396.

Paris, S. G. (2005). Reinterpreting the development of reading skills. *Reading Research Quarterly, 40*(2), 184–202.

Plomin, R., & DeFries, J. C. (1998, May). The genetics of cognitive abilities and disabilities. *Scientific American*, pp. 62–69.

Rvachew, S., Nowak, M., & Cloutier, G. (2004). Effect of phonemic perception training on the speech production and phonological awareness skills of children with expressive phonological delay. *American Journal of Speech–Language Pathology, 13*, 250–263.

Saffran, J. R., Werker, J. F., & Werner, L. A. (2006). The infant's auditory world: Hearing, speech, and the beginnings of language. In R. Siegler & D. Kuhn (Eds.), *Handbook of child development* (pp. 58–108). New York: Wiley.

Scarborough, H. S. (1990). Very early language deficits in dyslexic children. *Child Development, 61*, 1728–1743.

Scarborough, H. S., & Brady, S. A. (2002). Toward a common terminology for talking about speech and reading: A glossary of the "phon" words and some related terms. *Journal of Literacy Research, 34*(3), 299–336.

Shaywitz, S. E. (2003). *Overcoming dyslexia: A new and complete science-based program for reading problems at any level.* New York: Knopf.

Shaywitz, S. E., Shaywitz, B. A., Pugh, K. R., Fulbright, R. K., Constable, R. T., Menck, W. E., et al. (1998). Functional disruption in the organization of the brain from reading in dyslexia. *Proceedings of the National Academy of Sciences of the USA, 95*, 2636–2641.

Stackhouse, J. (1997). Phonological awareness: Connecting speech and literacy problems. In B. W. Hodson & M. L. Edwards (Eds.), *Perspectives in applied phonology* (pp. 157–196). Gaithersburg, MD: Aspen.

Stanovich, K. E. (2000). *Progress in understanding reading: Scientific foundations and new frontiers.* New York: Guilford Press.

Stone, J. (1992). *Animated alphabet.* LaMesa, CA: Stone Creations.

Stone, J. (2004). *Animated literacy.* LaMesa, CA: Stone Creations.

Storkel, H. L., & Morrisette, M. L. (2002). The lexicon and phonology: Interactions in language acquisition. *Language, Speech, and Hearing Services in Schools, 33*, 24–37.

Strattman, K., & Hodson, B. (2005). Predictors of second-graders' reading and spelling scores. *Child Language Therapy and Teaching, 21*, 165–190.

Torgesen, J. (2003). *Reading fluency.* Paper presented at the meeting of the American Speech–Language–Hearing Association, Chicago, IL.

Torgesen, J., & Mathes, P. (2000). *A basic guide to understanding, assessing, and teaching phonological awareness.* Austin, TX: PRO-ED.

Treiman, R., & Zukowski, A. (1991). Levels of phonological awareness. In S. A. Brady & D. P. Shankweiler (Eds.), *Phonological processes in literacy* (pp. 67–83). Hillsdale, NJ: Erlbaum.

Velleman, S. L., & Vihman, M. M. (2002). Whole-word phonology and templates: Trap, bootstrap, or some of each? *Language, Speech, and Hearing Services in Schools, 33*, 9–23.

Vellutino, F. R., Fletcher, J. M., Snowling, M. J., & Scanlon, D. M. (2004). Specific reading disability (dyslexia): What have we learned in the past four decades? *Journal of Child Psychology and Psychiatry, 45*, 2–40.

Vellutino, F. R., & Scanlon, D. M. (1991). The preeminence of phonologically based skills in learning to read. In S. A. Brady & D. P. Shankweiler (Eds.), *Phonological processes in literacy* (pp. 237–252). Hillsdale, NJ: Erlbaum.

Vihman, M. M. (1996). *Phonological development: The origins of language in the child*. Cambridge, MA: Blackwell.

Vihman, M. M. (2004). Early phonological development. In J. E. Bernthal & N. W. Bankson (Eds.), *Articulation and phonological disorders* (pp. 63–104). Boston: Allyn & Bacon.

Walley, A. (1993). The role of vocabulary development in children's spoken word recognition and segmentation ability. *Developmental Review, 13*(3), 286–350.

Wasowicz, J. (1997). *Earobics*. Evanston, IL: Cognitive Concepts.

Waterson, N. (1971). Child phonology: A prosodic view. *Journal of Linguistics, 7*, 179–211.

Webster, P., & Plante, A. (1992). Effects of phonological impairment on word, syllable, and phoneme segmentation and reading. *Language, Speech, and Hearing Services in Schools, 23*, 176–182.

Whiting, E. (2006). *Enhancing Head Start children's early literacy skills: An investigation of intervention outcomes*. Unpublished doctoral dissertation, Wichita State University at Wichita, KS.

CHAPTER FOUR

Early Writing and Spelling Development

Joan N. Kaderavek
Sonia Q. Cabell
Laura M. Justice

The bidirectional relationship between oral language and written language development has been discussed frequently in the literature on early reading development (e.g., Berninger et al., 2006; Fey, Catts, & Larrivee, 1995; Scott, 2005; Sulzby, 1985; Tannen, 1982). Oral language plays a unique and special role in children's writing development; reciprocally, early writing development may also enhance children's oral language achievements. Children's earliest writing efforts typically are translated for others within the context of oral discourse as children interpret and explain their writing to others, as demonstrated in the following example of 3-year-old Abby, showing her mother a paper with scribbling on it:

> ABBY: Look, Mommy, I wrote a letter to Grandma.
>
> MOTHER: What does it say?
>
> ABBY: It says "I love you very much."

Children's early scribbles and apparently random marks on paper may appear unsophisticated (and even uninterpretable) to the naive adult. Such early experiences in children's attempts to write words, letters, and other symbols provide a foundation for later developments in writing (Casbergue & Plauché, 2005), including spelling and writing for communication or composition.

In this chapter, we discuss the early foundations of writing development, which have been viewed historically as a major accomplishment of elementary language arts instruction. Research of the last several decades has shown, however, that writing development starts well before elementary school and for many children emerges without formal instruction. As speech–language pathologists (SLPs) and other early childhood professionals (e.g., teachers, psychologists, and day care providers) become increasingly aware of the importance of literacy development to support oral language achievements, and vice versa, they recognize the need to incorporate writing and reading activities into their interventions with young children. These early childhood specialists can foster children's development as writers through the use of a variety of contextually relevant, meaningful, child-focused interventions that provide a set of tools to improve children's emergent literacy and oral language achievements simultaneously.

Writing Development: Preschool to Second Grade

Children's writing development is a multidimensional construct that includes spelling, composition, and handwriting. *Spelling development* refers to children's increasingly complex knowledge of the sound, pattern, and meaning layers of the writing system (Bear, Invernizzi, Templeton, & Johnston, 2008). That is, children draw upon their knowledge of phonology, orthography, and morphology when spelling words and these processes work in increasing synchrony as children's spelling develops (Cassar & Treiman, 2004). *Composition development* refers to children's representation of linguistic meaning through their writing; it draws upon their language skills in pragmatics, syntax, and semantics (Berninger et al., 2006). *Handwriting development* refers to children's increasing abilities to navigate the motoric aspects of writing, and corresponds to the concept of "penmanship" (Berninger et al., 2006; Mäki, Voeten, Vauras, & Poskiparta, 2001). While spelling, composition, and handwriting represent key elements of writing development, they are best considered as separate constructs that emerge concurrently. Of particular relevance to the early childhood specialist is the fact that development in both spelling and composition also correlate with other aspects of the child's literacy development, such as phonological awareness, reading ability, and oral language, including syntax and vocabulary (see Hester and Hodson, Chapter 3, this volume, for a discussion of the relationship between phonological awareness and emergent literacy development).

Like many other areas of language and literacy development, children's achievements in writing appear to follow a general developmental trajectory of increasingly sophisticated accomplishments. This trajectory is best viewed as quasi-linear rather than strictly linear. A linear model describes development whereupon children master a skill at one level prior to moving on to subsequent levels. A quasi-linear trajectory, in contrast, describes developmental phenomenon whereupon children's skills are developing simultaneously so that children refine skills of varying complexity concurrently rather than sequentially (Anthony, Lonigan, Driscoll, Phillips, & Burgess, 2003). Thus, within the quasi-linear trajectory model, professionals need not be concerned that a child has mastered a particular skill or competency in writing development (e.g., representing the initial sounds of words when writing) before moving on to seemingly more difficult tasks (e.g., composing a letter to a friend).

In the next sections, we present four levels corresponding to children's early developments as writers. Table 4.1 includes a summary of the levels of writing development. It is important to note that the levels presented in this chapter are intended to assist intervention efforts and do not imply that development is strictly linear or stage-like; readers should recognize that although each level builds on the previous one, achievements in each level may overlap with achievements in other levels. With regard to the spelling levels presented, even the researchers who developed the framework acknowledge the overlap among sound, pattern, and meaning layers, implying a quasi-linear nature of spelling development (Bear et al., 2008). Furthermore, it is likely that the mechanism underlying spelling development changes as children's spellings grow in sophistication and that children use multiple sources of linguistic information at all levels, with children relying more heavily on certain types of knowledge during different levels (Pollo, Treiman, &

Kessler, 2008; Treiman, 2000). We also encourage readers to recognize that the age and grade levels provided here are only general yardsticks, as children's development as writers is strongly associated with their direct and mediated experiences with books and other forms of writing.

Level 1

Level I characteristics are typically seen in preschool children up to 4 years of age (Bear et al., 2008; Nicholls et al., 1989). Children learn that (1) writing consists of marks arranged horizontally on paper from left to right and from top to bottom on a page; (2) writing is made up of discrete symbols consisting of "words" and "letters"; (3) there is a finite set of symbols that reoccur in writing; the symbols are formed in a particular fashion and have specific names; and (4) symbols can be grouped together to form words that can be held in memory and reproduced as needed (Nicholls et al., 1989; Schickedanz & Casbergue, 2004). Children's writing at Level I may include scribbles, seemingly random marks, letter-like forms, drawing with or without the inclusion of letters, letter strings and numbers, and inclusion of environmental print (Bear et al., 2008; Pollo et al., 2008). Children's spelling at this stage does not mirror conventional writing in that they may use letter-like forms and strings of letters but are not yet producing words that look "adult-like" in any conventional sense. For this reason, children are often called *emergent spellers* at this level (Bear et al., 2008). Children who have considerable exposure to print at an early age have been observed to begin to make scribble marks as early as 12 to 18 months of age (Sulzby, 1990).

One of the watershed events of Level I occurs when children come to differentiate writing from drawings, reflecting their awareness of the functionality of the written form (Treiman, 2000). For some children, such awareness occurs well before the third birthday. The ability to differentiate writing from drawing is an important event, as experts contend that children learn the function of print before they can come to understand the symbolic use of print form, such that form follows function (Bromley, 2003; Justice & Ezell, 2004; Martlew & Sorsby, 1995). With an awareness of print function, children begin to differentiate their writing from their drawings. Before this awareness emerges, a child's writing and pic-

TABLE 4.1. Levels of Writing Development

Level	Kinds of writing produced	Child learns (concepts)	Child learns (production)	Spelling	Oral language–reading connections
Level I (preschool)	Scribble with or without drawing; mock linear; letter-like forms; letter strings	• How writing differs from drawing • Print carries meaning • Concept of "letter"	• Pays attention to print • Controls a writing implement • "Writes" across the page from left to right • Produces some letter-like shapes	Emergent (writing bears no letter–sound correspondence)	• Uses no letter–sound correspondence to "read" (prealphabetic phase of reading development) • Oral language often guides drawing (i.e., narrative action in drawings); early letter attempts may be less associated with oral language productions • Knows 1,800 root words • Recognizes environmental print • Keeps a topic in discourse • Pretends to read • Points to pictures in book and helps tell stories
Level II (late preschool–midkindergarten)	Writing that the child can "read" (including conventional letters)	• To choose own words to make a written text • Concept of "word in text" • To recognize name with distractor • To recognize own name and others	• Recognizes most letter names • Forms and orients many letters • Begins to control letter size • Uses letters to make words • Begins to leave spaces between words	Early letter name (represents salient sounds; represents initial and final sounds in words)	• Uses partial cues (i.e., beginning and ending sounds) to read words (partial alphabetic phase of reading development) • Knows 2,400 root words • Can rhyme and segment syllables; can complete sound alliteration tasks

Level	Texts	Goals	Writing	Spelling stage	Literacy behaviors
Level III (midkindergarten–mid-first grade)	Simple texts that can be at least partially read by others; writing is dysfluent and labored	• To produce messages that others can read • Concept of "sentence" and "story"	• Writes name fluently • Organizes words into sentences • Uses punctuation • Recognizes all letter names • Knows most letter sounds • Distinguishes between upper and lower case letters in writing	• Knows some letter sounds Late letter name (represents all or most sounds in words)	• Reads with more complete letter–sound connections (full alphabetic phase of reading development) • Can tell an episodic oral narrative • Builds a store of sight words • Knows 3,000 root words • Can complete onset–rime blending and segmenting • Manipulates words at the phoneme level • Decodes simple words • Reads preprimer- and primer-level texts
Level IV (late first grade–second grade)	Writing in phrases with greater fluency	• To write extended and coherent text • To study long-vowel patterns in single-syllable words	• Links sentences • Monitors and alters text • Writes phrases with fluency • Writes simple paragraphs • Applies writing process	Within word pattern (represents most short vowels correctly, using but confusing long-vowel patterns)	• Uses word chunks to read and increases oral reading fluency (consolidated alphabetic phase of reading development) • Uses complex grammar and specialized vocabulary • Begins to read silently • Reads first- to second-grade-level texts

Note. Data from Bear et al. (2008); Biemiller and Slonim (2001); Dyson (2001); Ehri (2005); Nicholls et al. (1989); and Vygotsky (1978).

tures are intertwined and undifferentiated; once a child represents the unique nature of print, he or she will differentiate print from pictures, for instance, by "signing" his or her name to a picture with the signature clearly separated from the illustration. By differentiating their writing from their drawings, children are demonstrating an awareness of print function. As adults, we assume that we write to say something; however, this is not necessarily true for young children. Children may not associate any specific meaning with the written form initially, but when they do come to do so, they have reached an important writing milestone (Nicholls et al., 1989).

Children's early writing experiences typically occur within meaningful situations that take place in the home, classroom, and community (Ritchie, James-Szanton, & Howes, 2003). Especially important to writing development is children's writing discoveries during play, in which they begin to explore the symbolic uses of literacy that they see every day. Within their play, children may practice making lists, writing and sending cards, writing directions, and "reading" books; these activities illustrate everyday use of written language that children see around them, and helps them to recognize and represent the myriad purposes of print (Morrow, 2005).

Children's achievements within Level I are fostered by adult mediation as adults help children connect meaning with their print. At first, children may not be interested in explaining or emergently reading their writing (Sulzby, 1986, 1990). Through exposure to parents and teachers who are interested in what they have to say, children begin to link meaning to their written forms. With mediated support, children begin to link their drawings to oral language accounts and to be more specific in their written language intentions. Children have been observed to use oral language to narrate a drawing as it "unfolds" or, after the fact, to explain and describe their illustration (Dyson, 2001).

Toward the end of Level I some children will produce mock words—words that look like real words but have no correspondence to letter–sound relationships. It has been noted that some children repeatedly use the familiar letters in their names or copy letters from the classroom environment (Treiman, Kessler, & Bourassa, 2001). This is the *nonphonemic* letter string produced by a child in the *prealphabetic phase* of development (Ehri, 2005). Indeed, this seemingly random string of letters is likely not random, as children employ orthographic knowledge by using meaningful patterns to which they have been exposed (Pollo et al., 2008). *Orthographic knowledge* includes children's understandings of the conventions of written language (e.g., knowledge of valid letter sequences, spaces, capitalization of letters; Cassar & Treiman, 2004). In this way, children are testing their hypotheses about how writing works and revising their hypotheses as their knowledge of orthography grows.

Children's name writing is of particular importance in writing development and is often the first stable letter sequence seen in emergent writing (Ferreiro, 1986; Sulzby, 1986). Name production and letter knowledge appear to be closely intertwined, with children first writing the letters in their names even prior to letter–sound awareness (Bloodgood, 1996). Evidence suggests that children do not use a phonological strategy when writing their names, rather they remember their names as a logogram and use their orthographic knowledge (Cabell, Justice, Zucker, & McGinty, 2009; Welsch, Sullivan, & Justice, 2003). Thus, they are often able to write their names at a higher level than other words (Levin, Both-De Vries, Aram, & Bus, 2005).

Associated Areas of Development

Children's fine motor skills at Level I develop to the point that a child is able to hold a pencil or crayon and make marks on paper. Progressively, children are able to make more purposeful marks to make circles or lines and then, ultimately, make some letter-like shapes. Drawing is an activity that integrates the motor, cognitive, and social purposes of emergent writing. The child must use eye–hand coordination and fine motor skills to at first scribble, but later visually represent important objects and events (Craig, Kermis, & Digdon, 2001).

Children's fine motor development is demonstrated simultaneously in other developmental domains. For example, at 1 to 2 years old, children are able to pull off their shoes and socks and turn the pages of a book. Between 2 and 3 years of age, children learn to open simple containers, fold paper, and snip with scissors. Between 4 and 6 years of age, children's fine motor skills are such that they can manipulate clay by rolling balls and snakes, cut on line continuously, and dress themselves without assistance (Lerner, Lowenthal, & Egan, 2003). Handwriting development corresponds to these more general motor achievements in that a child who has difficulty using scissors, zipping, and buttoning is likely to need more support to develop penmanship skills.

Level II

Level II encompasses late preschool to midkindergarten, between 4 and 5 years of age. At Level II and beyond, children come to use widely different writing forms to communicate meaning. Some children may use many different forms of writing at one time (e.g., scribble, drawing, letter strings, invented spelling) while other children will demonstrate only one or two forms of writing (Sulzby, 1990). An interesting component of Level II is that children will move between writing forms depending on the goal or purpose of writing. For example, children may continue to use scribble during dramatic play when they sense the writing form "doesn't matter" but may use more conventional writing when generating a wish list of birthday gifts (Schickedanz & Casbergue, 2004).

In the kindergarten year, children learn to write for real audiences and for real purposes (Hansen, 1998). Children's writing is advanced by their desire to solve problems; they want to express what they think and know. However, different children solve problems in varying ways. One child may "write a letter" by copying familiar words from classroom print. His or her words are spelled correctly but he or she is nonchalant about the letter's meaning. Another child appears interested in communicating meaning in his or her letter; the child carefully draws a picture and accompanies his or her illustration with one or two words using invented spelling.

A critical juncture in writing development is children's awareness of the nonrandom connection between words as they are pronounced and the letters used to represent these sounds. Children begin to rely heavily on phonological knowledge to spell. *Phonological knowledge* involves the awareness of the sound structure of language that helps children to grasp the alphabetic principle, which is the understanding that spoken and written language correspond in a systematic way. They begin to represent these connections at Level II, during which they move from no representation of sounds in their writings to representation of salient sounds. It is clear that children are not simply memorizing the way a word looks and reproducing it; rather they are relying on phonological information to represent spoken language (Treiman, 2000). For example, these *late emergent* spellers may write VN for *The End* (Bear et al., 2008). When children begin to consistently represent sounds in words and demonstrate an understanding of the concept of word in text, they are called *early-letter name* spellers. Children at this stage typically will not represent all phonemes in a word (e.g., spelling *tip* as TP or *back* as BK; see Bear et al., 2008).

The importance of children's transition to letter-name spelling is an important milestone in developmental spelling. Read's (1971, 1975) seminal work on *invented spelling* instituted a dramatic shift in the evaluation of children's beginning writing (Richgels, 2001). Rather than seeing early writing efforts as "misspellings," educators recognized children's efforts at constructing letter–sound relationships and came to view Level II achievements as an important, if not critical, stage in spelling development. Through these early spelling attempts, children actively try to make sense of the spelling system, relying heavily on the names of the letters. Treiman (1994) found that young children wrote the nonwords *zef* and *gar* as F and R, respectively. As children's understanding grows, they may write the same nonwords as ZF and GR, respectively (Cassar & Treiman, 2004). Children's reliance on letter names may help them to more readily learn letter sounds, thus aiding their reading development (Justice, Pence, Bowles, & Wiggins, 2006; Treiman, Tincoff, & Richmond-Welty, 1996). It is important to note that children's spelling patterns may not be completely consistent during a level; for instance some letter-name spellings are more prevalent than others due to the phonological properties inherent to the letter names. A child may spell *beet* as BET while continuing to spell *car* as CR, because the sound /ar/ is phonologically difficult to separate (see Treiman, 2000).

Often, at this stage, only beginning and final sounds are included (e.g., KT for *cat*), or children may use the first letter as a representation of the entire word (e.g., T for *team*). Children's attention to phonology is increasingly evident in this level, as they attempt to produce letters corresponding to the sounds they hear. For example, a child may write *jam* as DN. The choice of D instead of J corresponds to phonological aspects of the initial sound in *jam*. The child substitutes N for M as the final letter because of phonological similarities between /m/ and /n/ (i.e., both sounds are nasals). Children represent the sounds that they are able to most capture via spoken language. Consequently, very few vowels will be produced at Level II. Children at Level II may write *cup* as CP and *light* as LT. Consonants are more likely to be salient than vowels and therefore, will be used predominately at this level (Schickedanz & Casbergue, 2004).

As the child begins to explore letter–sound relationships at Level II, his or her efforts often will be written as isolated words rather than in connected text (Sulzby, 1990). In other words, children are more likely to practice writing a series of words rather than attempting to produce composition. Children may ask an adult, however, for help in writing simple messages, as in "I love mommy," in which they represent the letters that are dictated to them. Their writing, even with help, looks anything but conventional: they may omit the spaces between words and they may continue a long word from the end of a line to the start of the next line:

It is interesting that at Level II, children's left-to-right print orientation may change as they attempt to problem solve complex tasks associated with spelling and writing (Sulzby, 1986). A Level I reader/ writer easily may readily demonstrate a Level II left-to-right finger sweep when emergently reading a book. Now, as a Level II writer, the child is faced with a more challenging task as he or she attempts to follow these conventions with his or her own writing. Focusing on the letter–sound relationships, and running out of room on the page for his or her writing, letters may be placed above or below his or her starting point.

Writing development is characterized by a series of cognitive "leaps" and an active problem-solving process. When faced with a writing challenge, children may creatively solve a problem in a way that is inconsistent with their perceived ability (Bus et al., 2001). For example, one preschool child consistently was observed to write left to right using invented spelling. Then, on one occasion, she asked for help from her father to write a date on a picture she had just created. As her father dictated, she wrote the date right to left. When her father commented that she was writing the date backwards, she said that she wanted it backwards and continued writing right to left. As Figure 4.1 shows, this "mirror-image writing" is as intact as if she had written from left to right and seemed to require no additional effort on her part (I. Mykel, personal communication, August 15, 2006). This is an example of the quasi-linear trajectory, in which children's achievements overlap and recycle in varying iterations as they refine and develop writing skill. It should be noted that although the writing sample in Figure 4.1 is presented as an example of left-to-right confusion (frequently occurring at Level II),

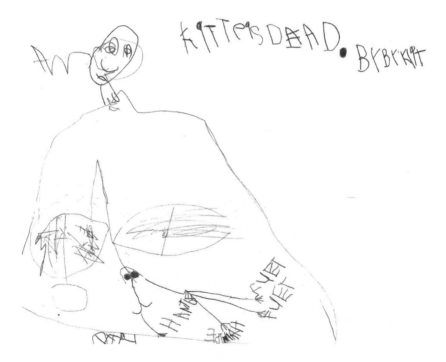

FIGURE 4.1. Example of a 3-year-old child's writing of "Kitty is dead, Bye-bye Kitty" with mirror writing of date (August 14, 2006).

overall it is an example of Level III writing because most or all of the sounds are represented.

Associated Areas of Development

Children's phonological development is strongly linked to their writing and spelling development at Level II. Learning to spell helps children learn to segment and blend the sounds in words, both of which are important achievements in phonological awareness. Conversely, as children's phonological awareness abilities develop and they become increasingly sensitive to the phonological segments of spoken language (e.g., the initial and final sounds in words), the phonological segments become well represented in their spelling. Importantly, both phonological awareness and spelling development support children's simultaneous achievements in decoding (Lonigan, 2006). Ehri (2005) refers to Level II as the *partial alphabetic phase*, because children are unable to segment words fully into their phonemes and therefore, rely on partial letter–sound cues to decode words. For example, children at Level II may read the word *brother* as *beaver*, using the first and last letters as cues (Ehri, 1997).

Whereas Level I writing attempts are often accompanied by oral language discourse, at Level II children may experiment with letter forms completely divorced from discourse in which they explain or explore their own writings. In other words, children at this level begin to write on their own. Children copy letters they observe in the environment or label pictures with salient sounds. With a heightened attention to exploring and analyzing their own writing, children may seem less concerned with the meaning of what they write than at earlier developmental levels (Schickedanz & Casbergue, 2004).

Level III

Level III describes children in midkindergarten to mid-first grade. During Level III, children begin to clearly demonstrate an understanding of how to represent speech in a form able to be read by others, and increasingly refine their skills in composition and expression of meaning. These Level III skills are often evidenced by children's use of captioning to explain a drawing and their preparation of short written personal or fictional narratives (see Roth, Chapter 5, this volume, for a discussion on the development of early stories and expository discourse). At this level, children will attempt to make their sentences more complex and descriptive (Nicholls et al., 1989) and demonstrate an awareness of the mechanics of the writing task. For instance, the child at Level III may slow down the rate of speech while dictating to an adult who is writing down the child's words (Sulzby, 1990).

Children's *print concepts* should be well developed by Level III. Print concepts include children's awareness of the vocabulary used to talk about sound and print, such as *word, letter, rhyme*, and *beginning/ending sound*. It also includes children's knowledge of literacy conventions such as "we read and write print from left to right," "we start writing and reading from the top of the page," and their understanding of words such as *title* and *author*. Print concept learning begins very early in literacy development (see Table 4.1), and by Level III, sophisticated knowledge of print concepts enable the writer to organize words into sentences, to leave spaces between the words, and to write for a variety of different genres (e.g., making lists, writing stories).

Children's spellings during Level III show a number of developmental errors in which they "use but confuse" some patterns (Invernizzi, Abouzeid, & Gill, 1994). For example, a Level III writer might spell *float* as FLOT and *bright* as BRIT. Children at this level are moving through the *mid-to-late letter-name* stage (Bear et al., 2008). Spellers will begin to incorporate vowels more regularly into their written words, typically using short vowels in simple CVC (consonant–vowel–consonant) words. Thus, a major accomplishment for those in the letter-name stage is representation of vowels. However, children make logical substitutions (e.g., *a* for short *e, e* for short *i, i* for short *o*) by using the letter name closest in articulation to the short vowel they are trying to represent. Although children in Level III primarily use phonological knowledge, orthographic knowledge continues to influence spellings; this can be seen when a child writes PTE for *pot*. From exposure, the child knows a word contains a vowel, but he or she does not know which one or where to place it (Treiman, 2000). In addition, kindergarteners and first graders are beginning to distinguish between unacceptable and acceptable letter sequences (e.g., *ckun* vs. *nuck*; *nnus* vs. *nuss*), and their spelling errors often mirror the rules of English orthography (e.g., not beginning a word with *ck*; Cassar & Treiman, 1997; Treiman, 1993).

As the letter-name stage progresses, children will begin to identify blends (e.g., *fl, gr, sn*), digraphs (e.g., *sh, th*), and preconsonantal nasals (e.g., *bump, went*; Bear et al., 2008). Although Level III writers are continuing to figure out precise orthographic patterns for spelling an increasing array of complicated words, they do have a core written vocabulary of grammatical functional words (e.g., *a, the, to, on, is*) and sight words (e.g., their own names, names of parents and friends).

Associated Areas of Development

Children's decoding ability at Level III aligns with their writing and spelling abilities. Children decode in a word-by-word fashion, slowly sounding out each word. This dysfluent reading mirrors their labored writing; children often vocalize during both their decoding and encoding attempts. Children at Level III are able to fully segment words into phonemes and become *full alphabetic phase* readers (Ehri, 2005). Repeated encounters with words in written text help children develop phonological connections between a word and its conventional spelling pattern and pronunciation, which in turn supports children's development of a corpus of sight words (i.e., words read automatically) (Lombardino, Bedford, Fortier, Carter, & Brandi, 1997). As children gain exposure to words, connections among phonology, orthography, and morphology are increasingly unified and solidified in memory (Ehri, 2005).

Another important associated area of development at Level III is the beginning reader's/writer's ability to comprehend and produce oral and written narratives. Children begin to produce more elaborate narratives at this time, which include an initiating event, a consequence, and a resolution of the event. Narrative story structure can be elicited by asking children to tell personal or fictional narratives; younger children and children with language impairment tend to tell more complete personal narratives as compared to fictional narratives (McCabe, Bliss, Barra, & Bennett, 2008). During a personal narrative, a child relays a past experience; when telling a fictional narrative the child recalls a previously heard or read story. (As children's narrative development emerges in oral language, a corresponding accomplishment is the ability to produce more complex narratives in writing.)

Narratives require that children use literate-like language forms (Curenton & Justice, 2004). During narrative production, children must supply the supporting context and not rely on clarifying questions from the listener. *Literate language* involves using language in a deliberate and metacognitive fashion to reflect on experiences, reason about, plan, and predict experiences (Westby, 1985). Literate language deficits negatively impact academic achievement (Greenhalgh & Strong, 2001; Lyon, 1999). Children who have difficulty in the narrative oral genre also are likely to have difficulty in written narrative production (Fey, Catts, Proctor-Williams, Tomblin, & Zhang, 2004; McFadden & Gillam, 1996). Facilitating children's proficiency in oral narrative production can be a useful foundation for facilitating written narrative development.

An additional associated area of development for children at Level III is increased sensitivity to various text genres (Nicholls et al., 1989). For example, children at Level III demonstrate beginning understandings of the varying writing styles needed for a *story* compared to a *report*. Awareness of text genre is a high-level skill developing from early stages of print awareness. At Level I, children have learned that print is used to make lists and can be observed in environmental print. At Level II, children develop awareness of several more genres (e.g., producing a simple story), and at Level III, children begin to experiment with writing different genres. They learn to use writing to share experiences (i.e., the personal narrative), to demonstrate and share knowledge (i.e., the report, newspapers), and to organize and prepare for larger or more complex writing tasks (i.e., semantic maps, journal writing). Writing for varying purposes facilitates connections between writing, reading, knowledge seeking, and the sharing of personal perspectives.

Level IV

Level IV describes children in late first grade to second grade. At Level IV, young writers are increasingly sophisticated in their independent writing and ability to express their thoughts and feelings through writing. Consequently, Level IV writing still is heavily dependent upon a child's oral language abilities, such as his or her use of cohesive devices for organizing written narratives. Children at this level may write many sentences beginning with *and* because it is difficult to break oral language into independent sentences.

As children progress in Level IV, they develop an awareness of "within-word" orthographic patterns, such as representing the silent *e* at the end of words (e.g., *cake*). Spellers at this stage are referred to as *within-word pattern* spellers (Bear et al., 2008) as they begin to represent long-vowel patterns, diphthongs, and consonant-influenced vowels. Importantly, during Level IV, children are better able to differentiate different written vowel patterns. For example, vowel combinations (e.g., C<u>A</u>K<u>E</u>, S<u>OA</u>P) are used to represent long-vowel patterns, while one vowel in isolation is used to represent short-vowel sounds (e.g., S<u>U</u>N, C<u>A</u>T). However, Level IV writers continue to make a number of consistent spelling errors as they sort out the many ways in which phonology is represented in print (e.g., they may spell *seat* as S<u>E</u>T<u>E</u>, and *rope* as R<u>OA</u>P; see Bear et al., 2008).

Although children at this level rely primarily on phonological (sound) and orthographic (pattern) knowledge, it is important to note that young children also exhibit morphological (meaning) understandings in relation to spelling. For instance, children are more likely to spell *brand* as BRAD than *rained* as RAD, despite the similar phonological information (i.e., preconsonantal nasal). In addition, children may use morphological information to spell the word *dirty* correctly rather than writing DIRDY (i.e., representing the flap with the letter D; see Cassar & Treiman, 2004; Treiman, 2000).

Associated Areas of Development

As children's writing continues to develop, so do their phonemic awareness and decoding abilities. Examination of first- and second-graders' writing skills, particularly their spelling, can illuminate their word-attack strategies, internalized rules for spelling words, and other phonological awareness and decoding abilities. For example, a child with an understanding of onset–rime patterns will problem solve word spelling based on familiar patterns. The child is likely to write the words *here, tier, cheer,* and *year* with similar spelling constructions. Later, with vocabulary development and well-developed "sight word" proficiency, the writer can begin to employ an orthographic strategy rather than relying solely on phonological awareness. Reading, writing, and spelling opportunities reciprocally influence children's decoding and encoding problem solving. Children in Level IV have entered the *consolidated alphabetic phase* of reading development (Ehri, 2005). They are able to consolidate the individual grapheme–phoneme connections into larger chunks (e.g., rimes) and therefore read with greater ease and fluency.

An interesting area of associated development is children's use of technology and computers as tools for writing. Early literacy instruction and exposure is impacted by the use of technology and computers. It has been suggested that children are now exposed to *multiple literacies* (Gee, 2000; Karchmer, Mallette, & Leu, 2003). Rather than assume that computer software is just another avenue to learn traditional literacy, educators should consider that technology requires an elaborate set of skills, problem-solving strategies, and modes of literacy. Now as independent literacy users, children must learn to choose linked data on a Web page. In addition to reading written text, children must select between hyperlinks, graphic, audio, and video information. Educators should encourage exploration of the linkages between literacy and technology and provide multiple opportunities for children to use technology as another literacy tool to present and elaborate their written productions.

Writing Assessment

Early in this chapter, we indicated that writing is a multidimensional construct that includes spelling, composition, and handwriting. For children who show clear deficits in handwriting performance (e.g., difficulty with holding a pencil), the occupational therapist typically conducts the assessment and intervention. In contrast, assessment and intervention for the spelling and composition aspects of writing, as important factors in literacy and language growth, are within the professional roles and responsibilities of the SLP and other early childhood specialists who work with children who have difficulties in spelling and composition.

Assessment typically is used to identify specific ways to promote children's skills in spelling and composition; that is, to identify intervention targets and approaches. Rather than focus on assessments used to diagnose problems in spelling and composition, we discuss specific tools that can provide information regarding intervention targets and approaches with a given child. Thus, in using any of these or other writing assessments, it is important to consider the purposes of the writing and spelling assessments.

Although assessment might be viewed as simply evaluative (i.e., measuring an outcome against a preset benchmark for the purpose of problem identification), the most important reason to examine a young child's writing and spelling is to determine areas in which to provide appropriate instruction. Ongoing assessments help monitor each child's progress and ensure that instruction targets are appropriate.

Assessment of Spelling

A variety of spelling inventories are available to evaluate children's progress in developmental spelling. The goal of these inventories is to determine children's developmental levels in spelling by examining orthographic patterns and error types present in their spelling attempts (Bear et al., 2008; Gankse, 2000). Spelling analysis is similar to conducting a phonological analysis of children's expressive phonology to identify the types of errors present (e.g., final consonant deletion, cluster reduction). As early childhood professionals are well aware, analysis of error patterns using developmental assessments is important for identifying not only a child's current level of development, but also for determining appropriate intervention targets and approaches.

For young writers, a simple five-item spelling inventory can provide useful information about children's early spellings. The Spelling task of the Phonological Awareness Literacy Screening: Kindergarten (Invernizzi, Juel, Swank, & Meier, 2004) consists of five simple words, following the consonant–vowel–consonant (CVC) pattern (e.g., *cat, nut, pit, mop, bet*). The examiner models the sample word, *mat*, for children by saying the word slowly, stretching out the sounds, and writing the word. Next, the examiner dictates the five words, without elongating the sounds, for the children to write down. The children are encouraged to use an alphabet strip located at the top of their papers and to write down all the sounds they hear in each word. Children receive a point for each letter spelled conventionally or for each phonetically acceptable letter. For example, for the *e* in *bet*, children receive a point for *e, a,* or *i*, because these are acceptable letter–sound matches for this level. Children receive an additional bonus point for each word spelled conventionally, for a total of 20 points possible. Professionals can use this spelling inventory as one piece of a broader profile to determine whether children are representing initial sounds, initial and final sounds, or all phonemes in a simple word. The measure demonstrates adequate inter-rater reliability, test–retest reliability, and internal consistency ($r = .99$, $r = .89$, $> .90$, respectively; Invernizzi, Justice, Landrum, & Booker, 2004).

The Developmental Spelling Analysis (DSA; Ganske, 1999) involves presenting children with a list of words that are organized in their orthographic complexity. Typically, an overall screening is conducted first that presents children with a relatively small list of words to spell. The words are ordered for orthographic complexity, based on developments in emergent spelling, letter-name spelling, within-word spelling, and so on. The spelling screening first identifies a general level for a child (e.g., letter-name spelling). A more comprehensive analysis, called a Feature Inventory, is then conducted using specific word lists that correspond to the child's identified stage. For instance, Ganske's DSA (1999) includes two alternate forms, and each form includes four separate lists corresponding to the different stages of spelling development. The list for children at the letter-name spelling level examines children's use of five different spelling features acquired in this level, including (1) use of initial and final consonants, (2) use of initial consonant blends and digraphs, (3) use of short vowels, (4) use of affricates, and (5) use of final consonant blends and digraphs. Analysis of how the child spells each word on the list is conducted to determine those features that are present, those that are used but confused (i.e., not quite stable), and those that are absent. The DSA has demonstrated adequate inter-rater reliability ($r = .97–.99$), test–retest reliability ($r = .94$), and internal consistency (alpha $= .91$). In addition, concurrent and predictive validity has been established with standardized measures of spelling and reading skill. Importantly, teachers using the DSA have rated the tool as easy to use, raising their awareness of children's abilities and helping to guide instruction (Ganske, 1999).

Similar to Ganske's (2000) DSA published in the text *Word Journeys: Assessment-Guided Phonics, Spelling, and Vocabulary Instruction* are the spelling inventories provided in *Words Their Way: Word Study for Phonics, Vocabulary, and Spelling Instruction* (Bear et al., 2008). This practical text provides a number of key tools for the educator, including a qualitative spelling checklist that provides a quick analysis of the features contained in children's spelling; five separate inventories that examine spelling features from emergent to advanced levels; and Spanish versions of spelling inventories. For the SLP or other professionals who might have little background in spelling analysis, both works not only provide practical and usable guides to the theories behind spelling analysis and explicit guidance in using DSA, but also carefully link children's spelling outcomes to specific intervention approaches that can be used to foster ongoing spelling growth. (It is important to note that these assessments tend to overlook certain aspects of orthographic knowledge, in that conventions of writing are not measured [e.g., spaces between words, orientation of writing, acceptable vs. unacceptable letter patterns in words].)

Assessment of Composition

Children's composition can be assessed in much the same way that their spoken language is assessed; that is, through language sample analysis. Rather than analyzing an *oral language sample*, assessment of composition uses a *written language sample*. Written language samples can be collected from the classroom teacher, drawing upon authentic artifacts developed by the child in the classroom, or elicited directly during the assessment. A combination of both is desirable, in that classroom work samples provide a curriculum-relevant tool for analysis, whereas elicited samples allow for control over the length, topic, and demands of the task (Nelson, Bahr, & Van Meter, 2004).

A number of tools are available to analyze a child's composition skill, ranging from standardized norm-referenced tests (e.g., the Oral and Written Language Scales; Carrow-Woolfolk, 1996) to informal checklists and rubrics (e.g., Nelson et al., 2004). Informal checklists and rubrics can be particularly desirable for an in-depth examination of various aspects of composition, including discourse-level analysis, productivity, narrative macrostructure, narrative microstructure, word choice, and writing process (Nelson et al., 2004). *Discourse-level analysis* examines the overall "gestalt" of the work, including whether the sample makes sense, is interesting, and meets the intended goals. *Productivity analysis* examines the overall length of the sample and includes the total number of words and sentences that the child produces in a narrative. *Narrative macrostructure analysis* considers the complexity and coherence of the sample; macrostructure analysis typically documents the number of traditional story grammar components that are included in a narrative (e.g., setting, characters, complicating event, and resolution). In contrast, *narrative microstructure analysis* examines the internal grammatical structure of the sample, such as clause density, conjunction use, sentence types, and verb tenses. *Word choice analysis* examines both the number of different words contained in a narrative as well as the sophistication of word choices. For instance, the word choice analysis may consider whether the sample contains any second-tier words (Beck, McKeown, & Kucan, 2002). Second-tier words reflect words that may not be used in daily conversation but are used by mature language users when they read and write (Pearson, Hiebert, & Kamil, 2007). Second-tier words are differentiated from first-tier words; first-tier words are used with high frequency and typically do not need to be taught to children developing typically (e.g., *happy, house, drive*). In contrast, third-tier words reflect vocabulary that refers to particular domains (e.g., *velopharyngeal*). Beck, McKeown, and Kucan (2008) suggest that vocabulary instruction should focus on second-tier words. *Writing process analysis* considers the process children go through as they write, including planning strategies and revising strategies. The Writing Process and Product Worksheet available in *The Writing Lab Approach* (Nelson et al., 2004) provides an example of a comprehensive tool for examining written composition. (This tool may be most useful for children performing in Levels III and above.)

Writing Intervention

To support early writing development, Morrow (2005) suggests the following principles: (1) maximize children's exposure to many types of print, (2) facilitate print and writing as a source of pleasure and engagement, (3) provide opportunities for children to observe adults reading and writing for work and leisure, (4) provide many different opportunities and materials for writing, and (5) respond to children's writing with interest and mediated adult support regardless of the child's level of writing. A variety of activities are described that may be used to support writers across the various levels of development. Table 4.2 provides an overview of specific goals that link to each of the four levels of development. The activities presented can help to address the goals.

TABLE 4.2. Goals for Writing by Developmental Level

Level	Area of writing development	Goals
I	Spelling	1. Use scribbles with some marks (e.g., letter-like forms, random symbols, some letters) to "write" when working independently; writing is differentiated from pictures 2. Copy some letters and simple words 3. Write own name (albeit not always correctly) in isolation and on works (e.g., drawings) 4. Hold writing utensil independently
	Composition	1. Use a variety of writing materials (e.g., crayons, markers, colored pencils) 2. Use writing for different purposes (e.g., to make a list during dramatic play, to sign name to art works) 3. Read own writing and attempt to explain one's writing to others 4. Write/scribble with a left-to-right directionality
II	Spelling	1. Know many letter names and some letter sounds 2. Write all uppercase letters independently 3. Write own name correctly and independently 4. Use letters for attempting to write novel or less-familiar words using uppercase letters or interchanging uppercase and lowercase letters 5. Use invented spelling, although words may omit all but most salient sounds (e.g., DN for *down*) 6. Use appropriate spacing between words; develop a rudimentary concept of word in text 7. Have a small store of words that can write independently (e.g., *and, mom*, etc.) 8. Use some lowercase letters in writing 9. Form uppercase and lowercase letters legibly
	Composition	1. Write for a variety of different purposes (e.g., a personal story, instructions to others, letters to others) 2. Use some punctuation units—periods, exclamation points, commas—albeit not consistently or not always correctly 3. Read for others what has been written 4. Have own ideas for what to write 5. Follow models to write (e.g., copying sentences and short stories from books or posters) 6. Dictate stories to others 7. Collaborate with others in writing activities (e.g., teachers, specialists, peers)
III	Spelling	1. Know all letter names and letter sounds 2. Independently produce all lowercase and uppercase letters in writing 3. Use invented spelling for novel or less-familiar words

(cont.)

TABLE 4.2. *(cont.)*

Level	Area of writing development	Goals
		4. Represent most salient consonant and vowel sounds in words, albeit with some errors in vowel patterns (e.g., BIN for *been*) and consonant clusters/digraphs (e.g., SPAT for *splat*; DAT for *that*) 5. Place spaces between words consistently 6. Use capital letters appropriately in words (e.g., at start of new sentences, proper names)
	Composition	1. Plan before writing 2. Revise writing with feedback 3. Use writing for several different genres (e.g., story, poem, exposition) 4. Use several different sentence types (e.g., simple and compound sentences; declarative and interrogative sentences)
IV	Spelling	1. Write CVC and other simple word patterns with high levels of accuracy 2. Use long-vowel patterns with increasing accuracy (e.g., silent *e, ee, ea*) 3. Differentiate between some homophones (e.g., *bear* and *bare*) when writing
	Composition	1. Use a variety of sentence patterns to include sentence types (e.g., simple, complex, compound) and modalities (e.g., declarative, interrogative) 2. Use organizers to plan for writing 3. Revise writing with feedback: add text, delete text, rearrange text 4. Understand difference between revising and editing own writing 5. Proofread writing for accuracy 6. Use writing for many different genres (e.g., news story, play, fictional story, personal experience, poetry, songs, book report) 7. Use writing aids when composing (e.g., word walls, dictionary) 8. Review and correct own writing 9. Edit structural aspects of composition, such as errors in spelling, capitalization, grammar 10. Write stories that contain major story grammar units: setting, characters, and plot (i.e., initiating event, complication, resolution) 11. Write expository texts of different structures: compare/contrast, sequence, cause and effect, description 12. Use connectives (i.e., conjunctions, adverbs) to link together sentences in fictional and expository writing

Note. Data from Bear et al. (2008); Fiderer (1993); Morrow (2005); and Stiggins (1997).

Many of the activities presented overlap across levels and are easily adapted for use with other levels. The level of support and expectations for each task will depend on the children's abilities. For example, journals are appropriate at any level. Level I children might be scribbling, developing the understanding that print carries meaning. Level II and Level III children might be using invented spelling, sounding out each word carefully, and practicing letter–sound correspondences. Level IV children might be working on developing coherent stories. Similarly, word study, a powerful approach to spelling instruction, is appropriate across levels (Bear et al., 2008). The features studied increase in complexity as children progress in their writing development.

An additional point that warrants note is that some children are much more concerned with correct spelling than are others. A common question is "How do you spell _____?" When working with children who are overly concerned with correct spelling, professionals may not know how to respond to such a question. For instance, should they tell the child to "sound it out" or should they dictate the correct spelling to the child? As a general rule of thumb, professionals should recognize that providing the spelling of every word for children to copy probably will not be helpful in the long-term, as it does not actively recruit a child to problem solve through the writing task. When young children write, they engage in a powerful phoneme segmentation activity, trying to invent spellings based on their existing orthographic knowledge. For this reason, professionals should encourage invented spelling and children should feel safe as they take the risk of spelling words their own way. The professional's responsibility is to help children take the next step in their knowledge of the writing system, gradually moving children toward more conventional spelling.

Principles and Practices: Level I

At Level I, children experiment with the forms and functions of print through their early writings. Although they do not yet represent letter–sound correspondences, their writings are windows into their understandings of print knowledge and symbolic representations. As children develop their writing during Level I, they are able to explore a variety of print concepts, including the functions of print and the various units of print (e.g., letters, words, numbers). Thus, encouraging children's writing development from toddlerhood through the preschool years is important for supporting emergent literacy development.

Dramatic Play

Play is likely one of the most important tools for supporting emergent literacy development. Through dramatic play, children naturally explore their environments, thus, simply enriching an existing play environment (e.g., office, library, restaurant) with literacy objects can have a dramatic increase on the amount of spontaneous engagement in writing for preschool children (Neuman & Roskos, 1992). Literacy objects include but are not limited to pens, pencils, stationary, notepads, calendars, notebooks, and appointment books. SLPs can work closely with classroom teachers to infuse literacy objects into each play area that will facilitate authentic writing experiences. Additionally, rotating dramatic play themes (e.g., post office, library, grocery store, doctor's office) and the literacy props associated with them may motivate children to not only engage in literacy-enriched play but to explore a broader range of writing functions and conventions.

Adult mediation during play enriches literacy learning for children, including their ability to read environmental print and interact with literacy tools (Neuman & Roskos, 1993). Adults provide an important scaffold to children's writing development when they join into the play situation and help children to incorporate writing into their play (Roskos, Christie, & Richgels, 2003; Roskos, Tabors, & Lenhart, 2004). To provide structure to dramatic play, SLPs and teachers can use a "before, during, and after" sequence. Before guided play, professionals determine literacy goals, consider play situations related to the goals, and invite students to plan the play setting. During play, professionals join in and scaffold learning through responsive interaction. After play, small-group activities explicitly connect the objectives with the play situation (Roskos et al., 2004). For example, the teacher or SLP can encourage writing in a restaurant center by playing the role of a waitperson and writing down an order. After this is modeled for children, the ownership of the task is gradually relinquished to the children. Other ideas of ways to encourage writing in dramatic play centers include writing a prescription (doctor theme), making a list (shopping theme), and taking a telephone message (office theme) (Neuman & Roskos, 1993).

Name Writing

Names hold special importance for children and are often the first words children attempt to write. During Level I, the use of names may be an important motivational tool to encourage children's writing of the specific letters. Indeed, children's names could have a powerful effect on the initial learning of letter sounds, helping children to grasp the beginnings of the alphabetic principle (Bloodgood, 1996). Before children are able to form letters, they should be encouraged to "write" using letter tiles. Children can match uppercase letter tiles to the letters in their name. After mastering an uppercase match to uppercase letters, children can move to lowercase letters, and finally match uppercase and lowercase letters (Johnston, Invernizzi, & Juel, 1998).

Sign-in procedures for attendance also encourage children to write their names, whether the writing is a scribble, letter-like forms, or random letters. This approach can be used as part of an emergent literacy intervention for preschool children with language impairments (Justice, Chow, Capellini, Flanigan, & Colton, 2003). Some SLPs and teachers may prefer children to trace their names by providing dots for children to follow with a pencil, thus reinforcing correct letter formation and fine motor skills (Ritchie et al., 2003). To make this procedure more difficult (for more advanced levels), children can write a sentence after their names. In addition to daily sign in, children can sign their names on notes sent home to parents (Roskos et al., 2004). Making their "mark" on paper helps children to recognize writing as a means of communication, distinct from drawings.

Journal Writing

Many practitioners do not consider journal writing for children at Level I because their writings bear no letter–sound correspondences. However, journal writing is appropriate for these emergent writers because it is a place for experimentation with the concepts and functions of print. Through journal writing, children express their ideas freely on paper in the form of pictures, scribbles, and strings of letters (Invernizzi, Sullivan, Meier, & Swank, 2004). Children who are comfortable telling stories orally should be encouraged to scribble–write their stories. After writing, children then share their stories with classmates, perhaps "reading" the story differently each time it is shared (Klein, 1985). Why encourage children to write before they use letter–sound correspondences? These types of activities potentially help students understand that writing is a valuable way to communicate with others.

Story Dictation

Writing down children's dictated words is an important way for children to make the connection that writing, at the very basic level, consists of spoken words written down. Using the Language–Experience Approach (LEA; Stauffer, 1970), children have a shared experience, such as a field trip or activity. The SLP or teacher writes down the children's words just as they are spoken to create a story about the shared experience. The professional models reading the story for the children, pointing to each word while reading aloud. The text then is made available for students to "reread." Through this approach, children understand that their ideas can be written down and shared with others through print. Because oral language facilitates the transition into written language (Klein, 1985), LEA is a powerful method for reinforcing the relationship between oral and written language.

Principles and Practices: Level II

At Level II, children begin to represent speech sounds in their writing. At first, children may represent a word by writing only the first letter of the word. Writing often lacks spaces between words, sometimes making sentences difficult for the adult to translate (e.g., ILJS for *I like juice*). Bear and colleagues (2008) classify these children as late emergent spellers. As children become aware of word boundaries, they develop the ability to match spoken words to written words while "reading" memorized text. Their writing demonstrates awareness of the concept of word in text with spaces between words and beginning and ending sounds of words represented. These children are in the early letter-name stage of spelling development (Bear et al., 2008). Concept of word in text (i.e., the child's metalinguistic understanding that spoken words are represented by individual units in text) is an important attainment as it likely facilitates the child's ability to segment words into individual phonemes (Morris, Bloodgood, Lomax, & Perney, 2003).

Fingerpointing Text

Fingerpointing to short memorized stories or poems helps emergent writers develop an understanding of concept of word in text, which enables them to represent words as distinct units in their writing. Professionals can point to each word on a sentence strip depicting a short story or poem, and then cut up the sentence strip as each word is said aloud. Children practice matching each cut-up word to an intact sentence strip or recreate a line of text without the support of the original text (Bear et al., 2008). This activity also can be used with songs and chants. SLPs and teachers can introduce children to a song while writing the words to the song on sentence strips, saying each word aloud as it is written. Children then can practice pointing to each word while singing and reassembling the song line by line or word by word (Roskos et al., 2004).

Story Dictation

At Level II, late emergent writers also benefit from the Language–Experience Approach (Stauffer, 1970). Now that children are writing down salient sounds, professionals can call attention to the beginning and ending sounds in words when writing down children's dictated stories. Reinforcing the concept of word in text, the professional points to each word as it is read. When children recognize word boundaries through beginning and ending sounds, they are able to freeze-frame the word in their minds to examine the internal structure of the word, particularly the vowels that are included in the word. After reading the story, children can explore the written characteristics of a story, for instance, by circling all of the B's in the story or by underlining specific words (Roskos et al., 2004). A teacher or SLP can easily adapt the LEA for working with children individually (Morris, 2005). A child first attempts to write a sentence on his or her own. As the child writes, he or she audibly says each word slowly to hear the sound and feel the point of articulation. The child is encouraged to write initial sounds of words. If the child is comfortably writing initial sounds, the teacher or SLP may probe for final sounds. Similarly, if the child is writing initial and final sounds, inclusion of the vowel sound should be encouraged. The professional then rewrites the child's sentence on a sentence strip using standard spelling. The sentence strip can be cut up and reassembled by the child to promote concept of word in text development.

Word Sorts

Given the strong correspondence between phonological awareness and orthographic awareness, supporting children's phonological awareness can also support writing development. Picture sorting is a powerful method for improving children's phonological awareness (Bear et al., 2008). In a picture sort of initial sounds, children sort pictures of words based on their beginning sounds, such as *b* and *m* words. With modeling and guidance, children place pictures under one of two columns (B and M). The professional supplies the category headers (i.e., target features) and exemplars (i.e., key words). For example, a picture of a *boat* is placed under the B and a picture of a *mouse* is placed under the M. After children independently sort pictures under the appropriate columns, they glue the sorted pictures onto paper and write down the picture names. Late emergent spellers most likely will label initial sounds only. The professional can guide the students into stretching out the sounds in a word, such as *boat*. If the child writes B for *boat*, the professional can lead him or her toward the final sound in the word by emphasizing the /t/ sound. BT is an acceptable spelling for boat for late emergent or early letter-name spellers. If a child is already representing initial and final sounds of words, he or she most likely would no longer need to sort pictures of initial sounds. Rather, early word sorts call their attention to the need for a vowel in the medial position. The study of same-vowel word families uses the phonological awareness skill of onset and rime to provide a way to help children understand the necessity of a medial sound. Initially children may study only one word family, such as the -*at* family (e.g., *cat, mat, hat*), matching each picture with a word. Not only does this serve as a review of initial consonants, it also reinforces the idea that rhyming words often look the same at the end (Johnston, 1999). Push It Say It is also an effective technique for reinforcing beginning sounds in word families (Johnston et al., 1998). The onsets (e.g., *c, m, h*) are written on letter cards and the rime (e.g., -*at*) is written on another card. Children form a word by pushing the appropriate letter cards while saying the sounds /c/ and /at/. The initial sound is changed to make new words.

After children are comfortable with one word family, they can begin to contrast two families with the same vowel sound (e.g., -*at* versus -*an*). Pictures as well as words are sorted into these categories. The contrast of same-vowel word families directs attention to the ending sounds in words. It should be noted that same-vowel word families are not designed for instruction in vowel sounds. Rather, word families are useful because the vowel sound is consistent within a family. The short *a* sound is effective to use as the starting point because that vowel is least often confused with other vowels (Johnston, 1999). Gluing and labeling is also appropriate with the pictures used in word family sorts.

Word Boxes

To help children become aware of the existence of medial vowels, word boxes are useful. Word boxes help children visualize the number of sounds in a word (Clay, 1993). On a paper, children see a rectangular box divided into sections (e.g., three sections for the word *cat*). Children then move blank tokens into each box, saying one sound at a time (e.g., /c/ ... /a/ ... /t/). The children then replace each token by writing a letter into the box. To adapt this activity, professionals can simply use words with different numbers of phonemes.

Interactive Writing

Interactive writing is similar to the LEA (Stauffer, 1970), with a few important exceptions. In interactive writing (Boroski, 2004), children share the pen with the professional and therefore, actively engage with the creation of the text. In addition, the professional and children negotiate each sentence instead of the professional acting solely as a scribe. The professional may even choose the topic, thus having greater control over the highlighted skills. For example, if the professional wants to reinforce how to write a friendly letter, he or she can choose this as the joint writing topic. The steps that are followed in an interactive writing session (Boroski, 2004) are (1) deciding on a sentence to write, (2) counting the number of words in the sentence before writing, (3) stretching out the sounds in the first word, (4) sharing the pen with the students, (5) reading the word as it is written, and (6) recalling the sentence and starting the process over with the next word. During interactive writing, professionals scaffold children's work by providing enough support to make the task successful. For example, to reinforce the concept of word in text, professionals may want to draw a line to represent each word. If a student makes a mistake, white correction tape easily allows the child to try again. To further actively involve students, children can copy the text onto whiteboards as each word is written (Morrow, 2005).

Writing for Sounds

Writing for sounds is a method that gives practitioners even more control over the skills reinforced (Johnston et al., 1998). Professionals connect this method with the phonics and spelling features explicitly taught and encourage students to write down all the sounds they hear and feel. For example, if students are studying the short-vowel word families -*at* and -*an*, the adult may dictate the following sentence for a child to write: "The man can pat the cat." To reinforce the concept of word in text, children can be instructed to place a finger between words when writing (Casbergue & Plauché, 2005). A *sound board* with letter names paired with pictures of beginning sounds is an appropriate support for children (Bear et al., 2008). For example, if a child forgets which letter makes the /p/ sound, he or she can look for the picture of the *pig* coupled with the letter *p*. The purpose of writing for sounds is to practice the phonics and spelling features under study. Writing for sounds takes approximately 5 minutes and works well as part of a one-on-one tutorial.

Principles and Practices: Level III

At Level III, children usually represent most of the sounds they hear in words and are in the mid-to-late stage of letter-name spelling (Bear et al., 2008). Instead of representing beginning and ending sounds of words only, they include medial vowels in their invented spelling. However, the medial vowels may be confused (e.g., MAT for *met*, SEK for *sick*). Using a linear strategy for matching letter–sound correspondences, phonetic spellers rely on letter names to spell (e.g., BOT for *boat*, MIT for *might*), and therefore do not yet realize the conventional method for representing long vowels. Their writing, which is similar to their reading at this level, remains dysfluent because they are sounding out each word; however, they are improving their ability to produce connected discourse to relay their thoughts and ideas through writing.

Word Sorts

There are many variations on word sorting. At Level II, we discussed the *closed sort*, in which the professional directed the sort and introduced the category headers and key words. In addition to closed sorts, children in Level III are likely to benefit from an *open sort*. During an open sort, the SLP does not provide category headers and children are encouraged to create their own categories. Open sorts are only appropriate once children have had much practice sorting words and comparing features. Word bank words (i.e., words that are targeted and practiced so as to become instantly recognizable sight words) are an ideal source for words for an open sort. A *no-peeking sort* encourages students to attend to the sounds in words. In this type of paired sorting activity, two children place only the headers and key words. Then, one partner reads a word aloud, without showing it to the second child. The second child points to the category under which the word should be sorted. The first child displays the word and the two children then decide if the correct decision has been made. A no-peeking sort is an appropriate activity after children have worked with their target features for several days. Appropriate word sorts at this level should contrast medial-vowel sounds, beginning with word families with mixed vowels (e.g., *-ip*, *-ap*, *-op*) and moving toward different short-vowel words not in families (Bear et al., 2008).

After children have had practice sorting the words into the appropriate columns, they then write the sort into appropriate columns, referred to as a *writing sort* (Bear et al., 2008). A *no-peeking writing sort* is the same as a writing sort with one exception. In a no-peeking writing sort, the child does not view the word when it is read. The child divides his or her paper into the appropriate number of columns (i.e., the number of contrasted features), the professional reads a word aloud, and the student decides where to write the word. The no-peeking writing sort is an appropriate assessment tool for a spelling check at the end of the week for Levels III and IV. Professionals award one point for correct spelling and one point for correct placement.

Patterned Writing

Children at Level III benefit from patterned writing activities (Bear & Barone, 1998). Due to the labored nature of their writing at this level, providing children with a patterned story is an appropriate scaffold. For example, children use a familiar book such as *Brown Bear, Brown Bear, What Do You See?* (Martin & Carle, 1996) and create their own books. Instead of copying from the book, children may substitute their own words and create a new book based on the same pattern. Instead of writing "Brown bear, brown bear, what do you see?" children may write "Little girl, little girl, what do you smell?" Other simple predictable or rhyming books may inspire children to create books of their own and increase their writing production. Professionals can lead students through the writing process (see Level IV practices) from prewriting to publication. In addition to individual books, professionals should encourage class books based on patterns, where each child writes a page for the book. Professionals often place class-created books in a reading center for children to reread. Not surprisingly, these are popular choices as children are motivated to reread their own work and that of their peers. The patterned writing activity can easily be adapted to meet the needs of Level II and IV learners. For Level II, children may benefit from a more structured, sentence-frame writing activity, in which they need only to fill in a blank (e.g., "I see _____ looking at me."). With Level IV children, professionals could easily incorporate more difficult patterned text, such as poetry.

Classroom Writing Center

A classroom writing center is very important for the early writer and is appropriate at any level. The center should be an attractive and comfortable space for writing, with supports such as an alphabet chart and a list of children's names in the class (Morrow, 2005). The center should contain a portfolio for each child in the classroom that he or she can regularly access. It should also provide a variety of written models, such as sample letters (e.g., "To Grandma") and pictures with printed words on them for children to copy if they wish. For Level III writers, professionals should encourage children to engage in a variety of writing tasks in the writing center, such as creating picture stories with captions (Klein, 1985). Professionals may want to provide a comic-strip template with blank word balloons over the characters. Children can also create the comic strips by using animal stickers. These activities help children with dysfluent writing skills engage in the writing of a larger story. Children should also be encouraged to create their own stories, little books, and illustrations. There is clearly a multitude of options for tasks and materials within a writing center. However, amidst the sea of activities, it is crucial for professionals to remember that in order for the writing center to be effective for students, professionals must first model tasks with students and allow for guided practice before placing tasks at a writing center. Students should be able to complete center tasks independently, devoting their attention to honing their writing skills. While classroom management is outside the scope of this chapter, it is important to note that a good management plan must be in place for a writing center to be effective.

Classroom Mailboxes

A mailbox area encourages children to write to their peers for real purposes. In addition to a variety of tasks, materials can include assorted paper, envelopes, note cards, a variety of writing tools, mailboxes for each student, files for works in progress, displays of student work, and clipboards (Vukelich & Christie, 2004). Many classrooms, even those containing primarily Level I and II writers, have successfully incorporated mailboxes so that children can regularly write to one another. As children progress in their writing skills, their letters to one another mirror their development and become more sophisticated. SLPs and classroom teachers can provide regular time for children to write to their classmates and can also provide prompts for specific writing topics.

Principles and Practices: Level IV

Children at Level IV are typically within-word pattern spellers (Bear et al., 2008). They have progressed beyond the linear sound-by-sound spelling attempts and begin to realize that long vowels are marked in a special way. They begin using but confusing long-vowel patterns (e.g., ROEP for *rope*, COTE for *coat*). Note that this is different from letter-name spellers, who do not mark the long vowels (e.g., ROP for *rope*, COT for *coat*). The word-study sequence for children in the within-word pattern stage consists of the study of patterns within single-syllable words: (1) long-vowel patterns (e.g., silent *e, ee, ea*), (2) *r*-controlled vowels (e.g., *ar, ir, or*), (3) complex consonant clusters (e.g., *shr, thr, scr*), and (4) diphthongs and other vowels (e.g., *oy, oi, aw, au*).

Word Sorts

As children sort words at Level IV, they are contrasting the known with the unknown. For example, they have mastered short-vowel patterns but are now comparing these mastered patterns with long-vowel patterns (e.g., short *a* CVC vs. *a*Ce). In this way, word sorts are recursive, as children revisit previously studied concepts and examine them in new ways. For example, when examining short *e* (CVC) versus long *e* (*ee, ea*) children first sort the words into two columns based on two basic patterns: short *e* versus long *e*. The students then separate the long *e* column by pattern, sorting the words into words spelled with *ee* and words spelled with *ea*. A comprehensive list of word-sorting activities appropriate for children at this level is provided in Bear et al. (2008).

Composition Processes

The educational task at Level IV in terms of writing composition is to help children develop a conscious awareness of the planning, organizing, and editing steps required for good writing. Many classrooms adopt the Writer's Workshop (Graves, 1983) to build children's independence and peer collaboration in the writing process. During the writing process, children practice planning their stories in advance, writing and reading stories to a peer audience, and then editing and modifying their stories in response to feedback. Writing for interested audiences for real purposes is a fundamental principle at this level.

The Writer's Workshop (Graves, 1983) typically consists of three components: (1) a whole-group mini-lesson from the professional (teacher or SLP), (2) independent writing time and adult–student conferences, and (3) sharing time. These components can be readily adapted for intervention. The mini-lesson allows the professional to focus on particular skills pertaining to most of the students. For example, if the professional notices that students are not using question marks correctly in their writing, he or she can teach a brief 10-minute lesson about the use of question marks, perhaps having children choose which unpunctuated sentences need question marks. Through a "think-aloud" professionals make their thought processes available to the children. A think-aloud is a metacognitive strategy frequently used in Writer's Workshop lessons (Graves, 1983). The professional verbalizes the problem-solving strategy to heighten students' meta-awareness of underlying literacy skill.

During the independent writing time, children work on individual writing pieces. Ideas for the pieces may be generated through expanding journal entries or through brainstorming lists of topics. While children are writing, professionals can conference individually with students, rereading the children's writing aloud to them to focus on meaning (Nicholls et al., 1989). To help children revise their work, the professional may ask questions such as, "Is this what you meant to say?" or "Are there any important points you left out?" Professionals use the conference to scaffold children's learning and help them take the next appropriate step. Children should also be encouraged to collaborate with peers, helping with the revision and editing of each other's work. Children place work "in progress" in an editing box; peers read other students' papers and comment on others' written work. Finally, during a short sharing time, children may share works in progress or finished products with their peers. It is important to note that sharing should be encouraged but voluntary. Most children enjoy taking the "author's chair," reading their finished work and answering questions about their compositions.

During the Writer's Workshop (Graves, 1983), children work on individual pieces and are at different points in the writing process. The writing process consists of five steps: prewriting, writing, revising, editing, and publishing (Bear & Barone, 1998). These steps mirror the authentic processes of adult authors. During prewriting, children actively plan what they will write through activities such as webbing. During webbing, the children graphically organize their thoughts, creating what is often called a "semantic map" or "semantic web" (Norris & Huffman, 1993). As they begin the second step, writing, students compose their first draft. The third step, revising, is often the most difficult part of the process, and therefore the focus of most conferences between the professional and the child. During the editing process, children identify and correct misspellings and incorporate other mechanics such as punctuation. Finally, a finished draft is published and shared with the class. Handwriting practice can easily be incorporated as part of the publishing process. A child's written work, in its finished form, needs to be written neatly to be read by others. It is important to note that even within a level, a range of development exists. While some children will quickly advance as independent writers, others will need many collaborative and mediated writing experiences to develop as writers.

Journals

Journals continue to play an important role with Level IV children. A dialogue journal is a way for professionals and students to have an ongoing written conversation (Klein, 1985). The professional's responses should focus on responding to the content of the writing rather than the mechanics (i.e., spelling). Since children at Level IV are reading increasingly complex texts, including early chapter books, reading-response journals are appropriate tools to encourage children to respond to their independent reading (Bear & Barone, 1998). Students may respond to a prompt, write a summary, or provide an independent response. These journals can also be used with Level III children.

Computers

Most educators feel that children's use of independent time spent on the computer should not supplant interactive reading and writing because mediated writing experiences facilitate children's literacy abilities (Aram & Biron, 2004). In addition, the motor activity of forming letters by hand has been found to solidify children's early mental representation of letters (Longcamp, Zerbato-Poudou, & Velay, 2005). Longcamp and colleagues (2005) found that 4- and 5-year-old children who were trained to copy letters by hand learned to visually discriminate among forms more accurately than those who learned by typing the letters. Educators and SLPs who suggest more interactive writing opportunities may run counter to parents who may view children's participation in computer programs very positively. Rather than discounting computer activities, educators may want to encourage parents to seek a balance between book reading and writing interactions along with computer activities, and to interact with their children when they are using the computer at the early stages of writing development (Schickedanz & Casbergue, 2004). An appropriate use of the computer for Level IV writers is at the publishing stage of the writing process. After editing their work, children can be encouraged to use a word processing program to display the writing in its final form.

Case Study

The following case study is included to illustrate the application of the information presented in this chapter on early writing and spelling in assessment and intervention for a preschool child with a language delay. The case study demonstrates the use of the assessment results in planning and implementing an intervention plan that addressed the child's needs in early writing and spelling using various activities and instructional strategies.

Colton (4 years, 6 months) resides in a small, rural community situated deep within the Appalachian Mountains. Characteristic of many families in the community, Colton lives in a home that is lower socioeconomic status, with an annual household income of $14,000 for a family of four. Colton's father works full-time as a coal miner and his mother works half-time at a local convenience store. Both parents completed high school but did not complete any additional schooling.

Colton was a late talker—producing his first word at 22 months and producing two-word combinations at 31 months—and received early intervention from 24 to 36 months in the home environment. Early intervention focused solely on communication development and quality of parent–child interaction. With intervention, Colton's family began to expect and wait for Colton to communicate and provide more language expansion and scaffolding. However, Colton's language development continued to lag behind his peers.

At 3 years, Colton began to attend the local Head Start program 4 days weekly for 6-hour days, and he is now in his second year of the program. At the time of enrollment in preschool, his standard score for expressive language was 80 and his receptive language standard score was 85 on the Clinical Evaluation of Language Fundamentals: Preschool (Wiig, Secord, & Semel, 2004); confirming a mild–moderate language delay. He qualified for speech–language therapy in the classroom two times per week in small groups (four children) for a total of 60 minutes weekly.

Development of emergent literacy skills, including writing and prereading, is an increasing focus in Colton's Head Start program, as the program recently received an Early Reading First (ERF) grant. ERF is a federally funded program providing money to establish model preschool sites throughout the United States. ERF-funded programs (1) provide extended teacher training in theory and research aimed at facilitating children's language and literacy development, and (2) must include explicit instructional opportunities for language and literacy development embedded within a literacy-rich classroom environment. As part of these grant activities, Colton was screened for four areas of emergent literacy skill in the fall of the year, including rhyme awareness, alphabet knowledge, print concepts, and name writing. The measure the program used for screening was the Phonological Awareness Literacy Screening: Pre-Kindergarten (PALS-PreK; Invernizzi et al., 2004). Colton received low scores on all aspects of the screening: He received a score of 0 on the rhyming task, a score of 2 on the alphabet task (corresponding to knowledge of 2 of 26 uppercase letters), a score of 1 on the print concepts task (corresponding to knowledge of the front vs. the back of a book), and a score of 0 on the name-writing task. For the final task, when asked to draw a picture of himself and "sign" it with his name, Colton drew a fairly detailed portrait of himself, but when asked where his name was located on the picture, he pointed to the portrait and said, "Right there."

With these results in hand, the classroom teacher, teaching assistant, and SLP developed a comprehensive intervention plan to improve Colton's emergent literacy skills in all areas examined. Following the principles of embedded–explicit emergent literacy intervention (Justice & Kaderavek, 2004; Kaderavek & Justice, 2004), the team decided to target these literacy areas across the day in a variety of child-centered activities (an embedded approach) and within two structured adult-led small-group sessions each week (an explicit approach). The team would work collaboratively to implement the embedded approach, and the SLP would deliver the small-group sessions. The small-group sessions would supplement rather than replace Colton's language intervention.

In the embedded approach, the team first structured the classroom environment to improve children's regular, incidental interactions with print. A sign-in procedure was implemented for all children, in which they signed their names on sign-in cards and placed the cards in pockets on a poster each morning. The team developed a writing center that contained a variety of writing utensils (e.g., crayons, markers, colored pencils), numerous writing media (e.g., construction paper, typing paper, sentence strips), samples of writing (e.g., list of alphabet letters, list of common sight words), and a journal for each child in the classroom. A range of literacy materials was incorporated into the dramatic play center to correspond to the weekly theme, and print-related displays were placed throughout the classroom. The team worked together to ensure that Colton, as well as his peers, signed in and participated in the writing and dramatic play centers each day. Members of the team also worked individually with him during the center activities to model writing and to scaffold his own attempts.

In the explicit approach, the SLP led two small-group literacy sessions each week in the afternoon for 20 minutes. Colton and four other children in the classroom (only one of whom also had a speech–language Individualized Education Plan) participated. The SLP used the following protocol for lesson planning (see Justice et al., 2003):

1. Name-writing activity: children sign in to the session by writing their name with support by the SLP.
2. Phonological awareness activity: activity focused on rhyme or beginning sound awareness.
3. Storybook reading: SLP reads a storybook, pointing out specific words and letters; after the reading, the children dictate the story to the SLP who writes it on sentence strips. Each child then receives one sentence strip and the children retell the story from print.
4. Alphabet activity: activity focused on alphabet letters.

At the end of the year, Colton's emergent literacy skills were reexamined using PALS-PreK. His performance was quite different from the fall: he received a score of 9/10 on the rhyming task, a score of 11 on the alphabet task (corresponding to knowledge of 11 of 26 uppercase letters), a score of 7/10 on the print concepts task, and a score of 7/7 on the name-writing task. When asked to draw a picture of himself and sign his name, Colton drew his portrait and then wrote his name legibly with all six letters right next to it! When asked by the examiner to point to his name, Colton proudly pointed to his name and said, "It's right there! C-O-L-T-O-N, Colton!" In addition to his development in early literacy skills, Colton's language development also continued to improve. His receptive and expressive language was at the low–average level of performance at the end of the school year.

Because of Colton's slower-than-typical early development and socioeconomic risk factor, he is likely to need continued support to maintain his reading development as he enters kindergarten and primary grades. However, at this early stage, focused language/literacy intervention has set Colton on the right path for success.

This case study shows the importance of the collaborative efforts of the classroom teacher, teaching assistant, and SLP in addressing Colton's needs in oral and written language using embedded and explicit intervention within an educational setting. Communication among the professionals and his parents ensured the meaningful incorporation of Colton's intervention goals within a literacy-rich classroom environment.

DISCUSSION QUESTIONS

1. Describe the four levels of writing development. For each level, discuss the associated areas (e.g., fine motor development, reading, oral language). How should this knowledge impact classroom instruction? How would you use this knowledge to differentiate instruction for children?

2. Discuss the purposes of various writing assessments. Compare/ contrast two writing assessments (e.g., Oral and Written Language Scales; analyzing writing samples with a rubric). Consider how a practitioner would use information from each assessment to inform instruction. Compare the strengths and weaknesses of each assessment. Describe a situation for which each assessment would provide useful information.

3. A preschool classroom teacher asks for your help in creating an environment more conducive to writing development. Based on research, what advice would you offer? What advice would you offer to a kindergarten teacher? A first-grade teacher? A second-grade teacher?

EXERCISES

1. Collect three writing samples from a child or group of children. In addition, observe these children over the course of a week during different times in the day in the classroom setting. Determine each child's level of writing development. Provide evidence of the level of development based on your observations and informal examination of writing samples.

2. To analyze spelling development, administer a spelling inventory (e.g., DSA). Be sure to note the spelling features the students are using but confusing. Determine the level of spelling development indicated by the inventory. Examine children's spelling errors in writing samples to provide confirmatory evidence. Plan appropriate word-study instruction.

3. Elicit a writing sample from a child (Levels III and IV). In addition, obtain written samples from the classroom teacher. Assess the child's composition using an informal tool (e.g., The Writing Process and Product Worksheet).

4. Prepare a case study for a child or group of children, modeled after the case study presented in this chapter. Be sure to include assessment results, observational notes, and writing interventions. Justify your recommendations based on your knowledge of writing development.

References

Anthony, J. L., Lonigan, C. J., Driscoll, K., Phillips, B. M., & Burgess, S. R. (2003). Phonological sensitivity: A quasi-parallel progression of word structure units and cognitive operations. *Reading Research Quarterly, 38,* 470–487.

Aram, D., & Biron, S. (2004). Intervention programs among low-SES Israeli preschoolers: The benefits of joint storybook reading and joint writing to early literacy. *Early Childhood Research Quarterly, 19,* 588–610.

Bear, D. R., & Barone, D. (1998). *Developing literacy: An integrated approach to assessment and instruction.* Boston: Houghton Mifflin.

Bear, D. R., Invernizzi, M., Templeton, S., & Johnston, F. (2008). *Words their way: Word study for phonics, vocabulary, and spelling instruction* (4th ed.). Upper Saddle River, NJ: Pearson Education.

Beck, I. L., McKeown, M. G., & Kucan, L. (2002). *Bringing words to life: Robust vocabulary instruction.* New York: Guilford Press.

Beck, I. L., McKeown, M. G., & Kucan, L. (2008). *Creating robust vocabulary* (2nd ed.). New York: Guilford Press.

Berninger, V. W., Abbott, R. D., Jones, J., Wolf, B. J., Gould, L., Anderson-Youngstrom, M., et al. (2006). Early development of language by hand:

Composing, reading, listening, and speaking connections; three letter-writing modes; and fast mapping in spelling. *Developmental Neuropsychology, 29,* 61–92.

Biemiller, A., & Slonim, N. (2001). Estimating root word vocabulary growth in normative and advantaged populations: Evidence for a common sequence of vocabulary acquisition. *Journal of Educational Psychology, 93,* 498–520.

Bloodgood, J. W. (1996). *What's in a name? The role of name writing in children's literacy acquisition.* Unpublished doctoral dissertation, University of Virginia, Charlottesville.

Boroski, L. (2004). An introduction to interactive writing. In G. E. Tompkins & S. Collom (Eds.), *Sharing the pen: Interactive writing with young children* (pp. 1–4). Upper Saddle River, NJ: Pearson.

Bromley, K. (2003). Building a sound writing program. In L. M. Morrow, L. B. Gambrell, & M. Pressley (Eds.), *Best practices in literacy instruction* (2nd ed., pp. 143–165). New York: Guilford Press.

Bus, A. G., Both-De Vries, A., de Jong, M., Sulzby, E., de Jong, W., & de Jong, E. (2001). *Conceptualizations underlying emergent readers' story writing* (CIERA Report No. 2-015). Ann Arbor, MI: University of Michigan, School of Education, Center for the Improvement of Early Reading Achievement.

Cabell, S. Q., Justice, L. M., Zucker, T. A., & McGinty, A. S. (2009). Emergent name-writing abilities of preschool-age children with language impairment. *Language, Speech, and Hearing Services in Schools, 40,* 53–66.

Carrow-Woolfolk, E. (1996). *Oral and written language scales.* Circle Pines, MN: American Guidance Service.

Casbergue, R. M., & Plauché, M. B. (2005). Emergent writing: Classroom practices that support young writers' development. In R. Indrisano & J. R. Paratore (Eds.), *Learning to write, writing to learn: Theory and research in practice.* Newark, DE: International Reading Association.

Cassar, M. T., & Treiman, R. (1997). The beginnings of orthographic knowledge: Children's knowledge of double letters in words. *Journal of Educational Psychology, 89,* 631–644.

Cassar, M., & Treiman, R. (2004). Developmental variations in spelling: Comparing typical and poor spellers. In C. A. Stone, E. R. Silliman, B. J. Ehren, & K. Apel (Eds.), *Handbook of language and literacy: Development and disorders* (pp. 627–643). New York: Guilford Press.

Clay, M. M. (1993). *Reading recovery: A guidebook for teachers in training.* Portsmouth, NH: Heinemann.

Craig, G. J., Kermis, M. D., & Digdon, N. L. (2001). *Children today* (2nd Canadian ed.). Toronto, Canada: Prentice Hall.

Curenton, S. M., & Justice, L. M. (2004). African American and Caucasian preschoolers' use of decontextualized language: Literate language features in oral narratives. *Language, Speech, and Hearing Services in Schools, 35,* 240–253.

Dyson, A. H. (2001). Writing and children's symbolic repertoires: Development unhinged. In S. B. Neuman & D. K. Dickinson (Eds.), *Handbook of early literacy research* (pp. 126–141). New York: Guilford Press.

Ehri, L. C. (1997). Learning to read and learning to spell are one and the same, almost. In C. A. Perfetti, L. Rieben, & M. Fayol (Eds.), *Learning to spell: Research, theory, and practice across languages* (pp. 237–269). Mahwah, NJ: Erlbaum.

Ehri, L. (2005). Learning to read words: Theory, findings, and issues. *Scientific Studies of Reading, 9,* 167–188.

Ferreiro, E. (1986). The interplay between information and assimilation in beginning literacy. In W. Teale & E. Sulzby (Eds.), *Emergent literacy: Reading and writing* (pp. 15–49). Norwood, NJ: Ablex.

Fey, M., Catts, H., & Larrivee, L. (1995). Preparing preschoolers for the academic and social challenges of school. In M. Fey, J. Windsor, & S. Warren (Eds.), *Language intervention: Preschool through the elementary years* (pp. 3–37). Baltimore: Brookes.

Fey, M. E., Catts, H. W., Proctor-Williams, K., Tomblin, J. B., & Zhang, X. (2004). Oral and written story composition skills of children with language impairment. *Journal of Speech, Language, and Hearing Research, 47,* 1301–1318.

Fiderer, A. (1993). *Teaching writing: A workshop approach.* New York: Scholastic.

Ganske, K. (1999). The developmental spelling analysis: A measure of orthographic knowledge. *Educational Assessment, 6,* 41–70.

Ganske, K. (2000). *Word journeys: Assessment-guided phonics, spelling, and vocabulary instruction.* New York: Guilford Press.

Gee, J. P. (2000). New people in new worlds: Networks, the new capitalism, and schools. In B. Cope & M. Kalantzis (Eds.), *Multiliteracies: Literacy learning and the design of social futures* (pp. 43–68). London: Routledge.

Graves, D. H. (1983). *Writing: Teachers and children at work.* Portsmouth, NH: Heinemann.

Greenhalgh, K. S., & Strong, C. J. (2001). Literate language features in spoken narratives of children with typical language and children with language impairments. *Language, Speech, and Hearing Services in Schools, 32,* 114–125.

Hansen, J. (1998). Young writers: The people and purposes that influence their literacy. In J. Osborn & F. Lehr (Eds.), *Literacy for all: Issues in teaching and learning* (pp. 205–236). New York: Guilford Press.

Invernizzi, M., Abouzeid, M., & Gill, J. T. (1994). Using students' invented spelling as a guide for spelling instruction that emphasizes word study. *Elementary School Journal, 95,* 155–167.

Invernizzi, M., Juel, C., Swank, L., & Meier, J. (2004). *Phonological awareness literacy screening: Kindergarten.* Charlottesville, VA: University of Virginia Printing.

Invernizzi, M., Justice, L., Landrum, T. J., & Booker, K. (2004). Early literacy screening in kindergarten: Widespread implementation in Virginia. *Journal of Literacy Research, 36*, 479–500.

Invernizzi, M., Sullivan, A., Meier, J., & Swank, L. (2004). *Phonological awareness literacy screening: Pre-Kindergarten.* Charlottesville, VA: University of Virginia Printing.

Johnston, F. R. (1999). The timing and teaching of word families. *The Reading Teacher, 53*, 64–75.

Johnston, F. R., Invernizzi, M., & Juel, C. (1998). *Book buddies: Guidelines for volunteer tutors of emergent and early readers.* New York: Guilford Press.

Justice, L. M., Chow, S., Capellini, C., Flanigan, K., & Colton, S. (2003). Emergent literacy intervention for vulnerable preschoolers: Relative effects of two approaches. *American Journal of Speech–Language Pathology, 12*, 320–332.

Justice, L. M., & Ezell, H. K. (2004). Print referencing: An emergent literacy enhancement technique and its clinical applications. *Language, Speech, and Hearing Services in Schools, 35*, 185–193.

Justice, L. M., & Kaderavek, J. N. (2004). Embedded–explicit emergent literacy intervention: I. Background and description of approach. *Language, Speech, and Hearing Services in Schools, 35*, 201–211.

Justice, L. M., Pence, K., Bowles, R. B., & Wiggins, A. (2006). An investigation of four hypotheses concerning the order by which 4-year-old children learn the alphabet letters. *Early Childhood Research Quarterly, 21*, 374–389.

Kaderavek, J. N., & Justice, L. M. (2004). Embedded-explicit emergent literacy intervention: II. Goal selection and implementation in the early childhood classroom. *Language, Speech, and Hearing Services in Schools, 35*, 212–228.

Karchmer, R. A., Mallette, M. H., & Leu, D. J. (2003). Early literacy in a digital age: Moving from singular book literacy to the multiple literacies of networked information and communication technologies. In D. M. Barone & L. M. Morrow (Eds.), *Literacy and young children: Research-based practices* (pp. 175–194). New York: Guilford Press.

Klein, M. L. (1985). *The development of writing in children: Pre-k through grade 8.* Englewood Cliffs, NJ: Prentice Hall.

Lerner, J. W., Lowenthal, B., & Egan, R. W. (2003). *Preschool children with special needs: Children at risk and children with disabilities* (2nd ed.). New York: Allyn & Bacon.

Levin, I., Both-De Vries, A., Aram, D., & Bus, A. (2005). Writing starts with own name writing: From scribbling to conventional spelling in Israeli and Dutch children. *Applied Psycholinguistics, 26*, 463–477.

Lombardino, L. J., Bedford, T., Fortier, C., Carter, J., & Brandi, J. (1997). Invented spelling: Developmental patterns in kindergarten children and guidelines for early literacy intervention. *Language, Speech, and Hearing Services in Schools, 28*, 333–343.

Longcamp, M., Zerbato-Poudou, M. T., & Velay, J. L. (2005). The influence of writing practice on letter recognition in preschool children: A comparison between handwriting and typing. *Acta Psychologica, 119,* 67–79.

Lonigan, C. J. (2006). Conceptualizing phonological processing skills in prereaders. In D. K. Dickinson & S. B. Neuman (Eds.), *Handbook of early literacy research* (Vol. 2, pp. 77–89). New York: Guilford Press.

Lyon, G. R. (1999). Reading development, reading disorders, and reading instruction: Research-based findings. *ASHA Special Interest Division 1 Newsletter: Language Learning and Education, 6*(1), 8–16.

Mäki, H. S., Voeten, M. J. M., Vauras, M. M. S., & Poskiparta, E. H. (2001). Predicting writing skill development with word recognition and preschool readiness skills. *Reading and Writing: An Interdisciplinary Journal, 14,* 643–672.

Martin, B., Jr., & Carle, E. (1996). *Brown bear, brown bear, what do you see?* New York: Holt.

Martlew, M., & Sorsby, A. (1995). The precursors of writing: Graphic representation in preschool children. *Learning and Instruction, 5,* 1–19.

McCabe, A., Bliss, L., Barra, G., & Bennett, M. (2008). Comparison of personal versus fictional narratives of children with language impairment. *American Journal of Speech–Language Pathology, 17,* 194–206.

McFadden, T. U., & Gillam, R. B. (1996). An examination of the quality of narratives produced by children with language disorders. *Language, Speech, and Hearing Services in Schools, 27,* 48–56.

Morris, D. (2005). *The Howard Street tutoring manual: Teaching at-risk readers in the primary grades.* New York: Guilford Press.

Morris, D., Bloodgood, J., Lomax, R., & Perney, J. (2003). Developmental steps in learning to read: A longitudinal study in kindergarten and first grade. *Reading Research Quarterly, 38,* 302–328.

Morrow, L. M. (2005). *Literacy development in the early years* (5th ed.). Boston: Allyn & Bacon.

Nelson, N. W., Bahr, C. M., & Van Meter, A. M. (2004). *The writing lab approach.* Baltimore: Brookes.

Neuman, S. B., & Roskos, K. (1992). Literacy objects as cultural tools: Effects on children's literacy behaviors in play. *Reading Research Quarterly, 27,* 202–225.

Neuman, S. B., & Roskos, K. (1993). Access to print for children of poverty: Differential effects of adult mediation and literacy-enriched play settings on environmental and functional print tasks. *American Educational Research Journal, 30,* 95–122.

Nicholls, J., Bauers, A., Pettitt, D., Redgwell, V., Seamam, E., & Watson, G. (1989). *Beginning writing.* Philadelphia: Open University Press.

Norris, J., & Huffman, P. (1993). *Whole language intervention for school-age children.* San Diego, CA: Singular.

Pearson, P. D., Hiebert, E. H., & Kamil, M. L. (2007). Vocabulary assessment: What we know and what we need to learn. *Reading Research Quarterly, 42,* 282–296.

Pollo, T. C., Treiman, R., & Kessler, B. (2008). Three perspectives on spelling development. In E. L. Grigorenko & A. J. Naples (Eds.), *Single-word reading* (pp. 175–189). New York: Psychology Press.

Read, C. (1971). Pre-school children's knowledge of English phonology. *Harvard Educational Review, 41,* 1–34.

Read, C. (1975). *Children's categorization of speech sounds in English* (Report No. 17). Urbana, IL: National Council of Teachers in English.

Richgels, D. J. (2001). Invented spelling, phonemic awareness, and reading and writing instruction. In S. B. Neuman & D. K. Dickinson (Eds.), *Handbook of early literacy research* (pp. 142–155). New York: Guilford Press.

Ritchie, S., James-Szanton, J., & Howes, C. (2003). Emergent literacy practices in early childhood classrooms. In C. Howes (Ed.), *Teaching 4- to 8-year-olds* (pp. 71–92). Baltimore: Brookes.

Roskos, K. A., Christie, J. F., & Richgels, D. J. (2003). The essentials of early literacy instruction. *Young Children, 58,* 52–60.

Roskos, K. A., Tabors, P. O., & Lenhart, L. A. (2004). *Oral language and early literacy in preschool: Talking, reading, and writing.* Newark, DE: International Reading Association.

Schickedanz, J., & Casbergue, R. (2004). *Writing in preschool: Learning to orchestrate meaning and marks.* Newark, DE: International Reading Association.

Scott, C. M. (2005). Learning to write. In H. W. Catts & A. G. Kahmi (Eds.), *Language and reading disabilities* (2nd ed., pp. 233–273). Boston: Pearson.

Stauffer, R. (1970). *The language-experience approach to the teaching of reading.* New York: Harper & Row.

Stiggins, R. J. (1997). *Student-centered classroom assessment.* Upper Saddle River, NJ: Prentice Hall.

Sulzby, E. (1985). Children's emergent reading of favorite storybooks: A developmental study. *Reading Research Quarterly, 20,* 458–481.

Sulzby, E. (1986). Kindergarteners as writers and readers. In M. Farr (Ed.), *Advances in writing research: Vol. 1. Children's early writing.* Norwood, NJ: Ablex.

Sulzby, E. (1990). Assessment of emergent writing and children's language while writing. In L. M. Morrow & J. K. Smith (Eds.), *Assessment for instruction in early literacy* (pp. 83–109). Englewood Cliffs, NJ: Prentice Hall.

Tannen, D. (1982). Oral and literate strategies in spoken and written narratives. *Language, 58,* 1–21.

Treiman, R. (1993). *Beginning to spell: A study of first-grade children.* New York: Oxford University Press.

Treiman, R. (1994). Use of consonant letter names in beginning spelling. *Developmental Psychology, 30,* 567–580.

Treiman, R. (2000). The development of spelling skill. *Topics in Language Disorders, 20*(3), 1–18.

Treiman, R., Kessler, B., & Bourassa, D. (2001). Children's own names influence their spelling. *Applied Psycholinguistics, 22,* 555–570.

Treiman, R., Tincoff, R., & Richmond-Welty, E. D. (1996). Letter names help children to connect print and speech. *Developmental Psychology, 32,* 505–514.

Vukelich, C., & Christie, J. (2004). *Building a foundation for preschool literacy: Effective instruction for reading and writing development.* Newark, DE: International Reading Association.

Vygotsky, L. S. (1978). *Mind in society.* Cambridge, MA: Harvard University Press.

Welsch, J. G., Sullivan, A., & Justice, L. M. (2003). That's my letter!: What preschoolers' name-writing representations tell us about emergent literacy knowledge. *Journal of Literacy Research, 35,* 757–776.

Westby, C. E. (1985). Learning to talk—talking to learn: Oral-literate language differences. In C. Simon (Ed.), *Communication skills and classroom success: Therapy methodologies for language-learning disabled students* (pp. 181–213). San Diego, CA: College-Hill.

Wiig, E. H., Secord, W. A., & Semel, E. (2004). *Clinical Evaluation of Language Fundamentals: Preschool—Second edition.* San Antonio, TX: Harcourt Assessment.

CHAPTER FIVE

Children's Early Narratives

FROMA P. ROTH

This chapter addresses the development of narration during the preschool years (prior to first grade) and discusses assessment and intervention/instructional considerations for children who demonstrate difficulties acquiring or using this discourse form. Oral narration is a type of discourse that involves the comprehension, production, and recall of extended units of speech. Stories and oral exposition (or explanatory discourse) are two major genres of narration. Stories involve characters that engage in goal-directed actions to resolve problems or complications. Early developing oral expository text consists mainly of scripts and personal narratives that informally describe or recount one's experiences.

According to Halliday and Hasan (1976), narratives are a major form of text/discourse because they are linguistic passages of varying lengths that create a unified whole. A more sophisticated discourse form than conversation, narration requires macro-organization of discourse units involving the ability to sequence events, understand cause–event relationships and structures, and create a unified text. Specifically, narratives require the production of multiple linguistic propositions. They are expected to contain an introduction and an organized sequence of events that lead to a logical conclusion, and they require the narrator to carry on a monologue (versus a dialogue) during which the listener assumes a relatively passive role. Thus, it is the narrator's responsibility to present information in an organized, complete, and coherent manner without the expectation of substantial informational or extra-linguistic support from the listener (Halliday & Hasan, 1976; Roth & Spekman, 1986).

Why Is the Narrative an Important Linguistic Form?

The study of narratives is motivated by both conceptual and practical considerations. Conceptually, the narrative is considered a primary mode of human thought that is learned and used by children to organize and make sense of the world (Bruner, 1985). It also is a universal linguistic vehicle for constructing and transmitting meaning, and for acquiring knowledge. Further, narratives reflect the integration of an individual's linguistic knowledge, world knowledge, and sociocultural background, and provide a mechanism for language socialization—the means by which children become members of their linguistic and cultural communities (Hardy, 1978; Sutton-Smith, 1986).

From a practical perspective, several factors are important for our understanding of narrative development. This set of factors includes both language and background variables.

Oral Narrative as a Major Transition between Oral and Literate Language Styles

Like written text, oral narratives (1) are more formal (contain fewer pauses, false starts, and repetitions); (2) involve more concise and complex syntax; (3) contain more sophisticated and unfamiliar vocabulary; (4) comprise topics that are frequently unfamiliar and abstract; and (5) represent a decontextualized language form involving past or made-up events that are removed from the immediate context (Dickinson & Snow, 1987; Snow, 1983; Snow & Ninio, 1986; Westby, 1991). The decontextualized nature of narratives is thought to promote children's transition from talking in the "here and now" to a capacity to use language for talking in the "there and then," which is increasingly required in school as children encounter written text and other types of instructional discourse.

Associations between Background and Language Factors and Narrative Proficiency during the Emergent Literacy Period (Birth–5 Years)

Children who are from economically disadvantaged families, sparse home literacy environments, English language learners (ELLs), and those who are at risk for or have identified language disabilities often perform more poorly than matched peers on various types of narrative tasks (Manhardt & Rescorla, 2002; Neuman & Dickinson, 2001; Snow, Burns, & Griffin, 1998; Snow, Tabors, & Dickinson, 2001). It is important to note, however, that most studies documenting significant positive connections between narrative performance and background variables are correlational in nature. Thus, the specific nature of the reported associations between background variables and their relative impact on language and literacy development are not definitive. Background variables that have been examined include the child's socioeconomic status (SES), home literacy environment, cultural/linguistic background, and history of language impairment.

Socioeconomic Status

Economic disadvantage is a risk factor associated with the acquisition of many aspects of emergent literacy, including narrative discourse. Findings of some studies indicate that when asked to produce stories in the language of instruction, 3- to 5-year-old children reared in poverty produce stories with less sophisticated episodic (i.e., plot) structure than those of higher-income peers (Fazio, Naremore, & Connell, 1996; Heath, 1989, 1990; Karweit & Wasik, 1996; Neuman, 2006; Rogoff & Mistry, 1990). It is important to consider the findings of such studies in light of the influences of culture on the home literacy environment. Although children from low-SES backgrounds are at a greater risk for delayed development of literacy skills (including narrative discourse), there are studies that illustrate that book-sharing interventions with low-income parents have been effective in facilitating the children's development of more complex narratives. Peterson, Jesso, and McCabe (1999), for example, randomly assigned low-SES preschool children (mean age = 3 years, 7 months) to experimental or control groups. Mothers of children in the experimental group were instructed to ask open-ended and context-eliciting questions during book reading. Open-ended questions were queries and directions that prompted open-ended information about events (e.g., "What happened then?"). Context-eliciting questions were those that requested specific pieces of information (e.g., "Who chased the bunny?"). At the end of the 1-year intervention program and again on follow-up testing 1 year later, children in the experimental group produced longer narratives, achieved higher receptive vocabulary scores, and provided more setting information than control-group children whose mothers used their usual reading style. Although the findings of Peterson et al. (1999) revealed better developed narratives for the low-income children whose mothers received the book-sharing intervention, the study did not establish a strong direct correlation between low SES and narrative complexity. (Battle, Chapter 6, this volume, addresses cultural influences on emergent literacy and early literacy development.)

Home Literacy Environment

Children with limited access to and infrequent experiences with literacy activities and materials have been found to display lower levels of early literacy development than do children with more frequent exposure and experiences (Frijters, Barron, & Brunello, 2000; Snow et al., 1998; Sulzy & Teale, 1991). Shared book reading is one aspect of the home literacy environment that contributes to children's oral language development and provides a rich source for the acquisition of other emergent literacy skills. It most commonly involves a reading experience between a child and parent (or other caring adult) in which the pair share the content, language, and images of children's books (Ninio & Bruner, 1978). Frequent, regular storybook reading that begins at an early age is a factor that distinguishes children who go on to perform well on reading and writing tasks (e.g., Whitehurst et al., 1994). Moreover, it is a context that prompts verbalizations and adult–child verbal interactions. Ninio and Bruner (1978), for example, reported that the most frequent situation in which mothers labeled objects in the environment was during shared book reading, whereas Wells (1985) found that about 5% of the day-to-day speech of 2-year-old children occurred during story time with an adult.

Cultural/Linguistic Background

Like any aspect of language acquisition, narrative development occurs within a cultural context. Narratives are culture specific and reflect the values of the society that are absorbed by children through their family socialization experiences and the cultural milieu to which they are exposed (Price, Roberts, & Jackson, 2006; Wang & Leichtman, 2000). Children in schools today are more and more diverse in their backgrounds than in years past. Because of these between-culture variations, it is common to find wide ranges of narrative skills among children within the same age range (Demorest & Alexander, 1992; Sperry & Sperry, 1996). Moreover, cross-cultural differences exist regarding what constitutes a well-formed narrative, and these variations affect narrative performance. For instance, most narratives encountered by children in American public schools are based in the European North American tradition. Children from Hispanic, African American, and Asian backgrounds are reared in different narrative traditions and may struggle with narratives presented in the preschool curriculum (Burt & McCabe, 1996; Pritchard, 1990). For example, personal narratives in the European North American tradition generally concern single experiences, contain a number of specific actions that occur in the past tense, and are in chronological sequence (Champion, 1998). In contrast, the narratives in some Hispanic cultures deemphasize event sequencing and instead emphasize maintaining a conversational flow of information (Silva & McCabe, 1996).

History of Language Impairment

Compared to preschool children with typical language development, youngsters with language deficits have difficulty producing and recalling both structure and content aspects of narratives. Structurally, their narratives include fewer story components, fewer pieces of relevant information (e.g., Paul & Smith, 1993), and fewer elaborative comments (Manhardt & Rescorla, 2002), the latter of which contribute to the richness and texture of narratives and can affect the overall perception of story quality. The content of their narratives is marked by a shorter mean length of utterance, fewer sentences per narrative, and reduced grammatical accuracy (e.g.,

Norbury & Bishop, 2003; Paul & Smith, 1993). Further, Bishop and Edmondson (1987) showed that narrative recall at 4 years of age was the best single predictor of the successful resolution of pre-school language impairment. Longitudinal work also suggests that narrative structure deficits (i.e., story grammar) are often indepen-dent of SES and of performance on traditional measures of linguis-tic knowledge such as expressive vocabulary, word retrieval, and sentence formulation (Allen, Kertoy, Sherblom, & Pettit, 1994; Man-hardt & Rescorla, 2002; Paul, Hernandez, Taylor, & Johnson, 1996; Paul & Smith, 1993). Data such as these suggest that some children with language impairments have specific difficulty internalizing the linguistic structure (i.e., semantics and syntax) of the narrative, while others achieve age-appropriate performance on semantic and syntactic measures of language, but continue to perform more poorly than do normal-language peers on measures of narrative dis-course.

Importantly, these deficits frequently persist into the school years. Research demonstrates that many mid-elementary school-age students with language and learning deficits do not possess the narrative skills of typically developing 4- and 5-year-old children (Fey, Catts, Proctor-Williams, Tomblin, & Zhang, 2004; Manhardt & Rescorla, 2002; Paul et al., 1996; Roth & Spekman, 1986). Even those with age-appropriate language performance at the single-sentence level may have difficulties with the more advanced ability to structure extended discourse units required by narration. Thus, narrative knowledge may be an important index of risk for language and literacy learning problems.

Association of Narrative Knowledge with Literacy Development

The nature of this association is unclear as most studies have incor-porated group designs, have used correlation analyses, or have shown that narrative tasks contribute very small or no significant amounts of unique variance in the prediction of literacy skills. How-ever, some prospective data do exist. Tabors, Snow, and Dickinson (2001) followed children enrolled in Head Start programs from 3 years of age over a 10-year period, periodically administering a comprehensive battery of language and literacy measures, includ-ing measures of narrative production. Their findings showed that a measure of narrative production in kindergarten was one of four measures to correlate significantly with reading comprehension and receptive vocabulary in both fourth and seventh grades. Paris and Paris (2003) demonstrated that macrostructure features such as number of narrative elements were more closely related to beginning reading than micro-level features such as syntactic complexity for children between kindergarten and fourth grade. From another perspective, Griffin, Hemphill, Camp, and Palmer (2004) showed that children's oral expositions (i.e., descriptions) at 5 years of age predicted the amount of informational context provided in written narratives at the age of 8 years, whereas fictional story narratives did not predict 8-year-old performance on any of the administered reading or writing measures. (See Kaderavek, Cabell, & Justice, Chapter 4, this volume, for another perspective on early writing and spelling development.)

Development of Early Narrative Abilities

In literate cultures, children develop a "sense of story" naturally during their preschool years through experiences with various forms of narration (Westby, 1991). These incidental learning experiences include engaging in shared storybook reading, hearing and listening to stories and anecdotes told by others, observing stories through media, participating in storytelling and retelling, role playing daily activities, and participating in activities such as sharing time and show-and-tell.

The study of narrative development has centered on both text content and text structure features. Text content analyses, or microanalyses, typically analyze narratives at the word, phrase, or sentence level and identify surface features of texts, including measures of productivity (e.g., total number of words, utterance length) and measures of grammatical organization (i.e., grammatical complexity, grammaticality accuracy, and linguistic cohesion). Macroanalysis is a more global approach that examines underlying text meaning and text structure at the level of connected discourse. It typically utilizes text grammar approaches (e.g., story grammar, high-point analysis) that represent theories of the internal structure of stories. Such approaches focus on the identification of the basic components of a story, event sequences, and episodic structure of stories.

Both microanalytic and macroanalytic approaches have been used to study the development of expository and story narratives. Available research centers mainly on narrative production acquisition; little information exists that documents the development of narrative comprehension skills, either from longitudinal or cross-sectional perspectives (McCabe & Bliss, 2003; Tabors et al., 2001). Consequently, the information presented in this chapter concentrates on the emergence of children's narrative production abilities.

Microanalysis/Text Content Approaches

Our understanding of content development of narratives is relatively general, but it shows a progression of linguistic sophistication. Between 1 and 3 years of age, children use a great deal of prosodic elements to carry the story line (e.g., intonation, repetition of sounds and words), presumably because they have greater mastery over the phonological system than the semantic and syntactic systems (Sutton-Smith, 1986). Narratives are related in the first person, rather than in the conventional third person. Between the ages of 3 and 5 years, children's narratives increase in semantic complexity and diversity (Berman & Slobin, 1994) and length (Allen et al., 1994). For example, prosody is replaced by content events (i.e., prose) to carry the story line, and story markers (e.g., "Once upon a time," "The end") begin to signal the beginning and ending points of stories. Stories also become longer and contain a greater number of story elements (Berman, 1988; Hudson & Shapiro, 1991). Advancements in syntactic complexity (Gillam & Johnston, 1992; Paul & Smith, 1993) also occur during this period. Conjunctions are used more frequently to link events together, an increase in prepositions is notable, and events are sequenced in a logical chronology. Narratives increasingly take place in the past tense, reflecting children's growing ability to decontextualize or distance linguistic events from the constraints of everyday reality.

Macroanalysis/Structure Approaches

More extensive study has been conducted at the macroanalytic level. Children's earliest narratives emerge at about 2 to 3 years of age with the appearance of *scripts*, which are event sequences that recount very familiar routine experiences such as going to a birthday party or taking a trip to the zoo. Scripts are considered a type of narrative schemata because they reflect an organized representation of a child's experiences and knowledge about narratives (Kintsch, 1974). These narrative sequences begin to become regular parts of adult–child conversational interactions as early as 2 years of age (Eisenberg, 1984; Miller & Sperry, 1988; Sachs, 1983). At first, these scripts are constructed largely by adults, who provide scaffolding through prompting and the provision of content (Beals, 2001). The following examples illustrate the type and degree of scaffolding provided by adults:

MOTHER: Did you like the kitty?

CHILD: She lick my hand.

MOTHER: He licked your hand?

CHILD: Then he chase me.

MOTHER: He chased you into the kitchen?

CHILD: Yeah. And I fall down.

MOTHER: What happened at school?

CHILD: Make mud pies.

MOTHER: You made pies. I bet they taste good. Where are they?

CHILD: School.

MOTHER: You put them away for snack tomorrow?

CHILD: Yes, in the pantry.

MOTHER: (*laughing*) I hope nobody eats them.

Scripts are relatively easy for children to construct because the order of events is predictable, only one tense is required, and they pose limited cognitive challenges to the child (Hudson & Shapiro, 1991).

   Personal event narratives (PENs) emerge somewhat later than, and may overlap with, scripts. PENs entail recounts of past events that have been experienced by the child or someone else. This form is cognitively more complex because it requires some planning and sequencing of events without an a priori-provided structure. It also entails a degree of perspective taking to determine what a listener already knows and needs to know (McCabe & Peterson,

1991; McCabe & Rollins, 1994). These early narrative forms provide the basis on which children acquire the ability to construct fictional narratives, or imaginary stories.

Story narratives emerge by about 5 years of age. Children acquire the basic structure of stories, referred to as the "story schema," which involves knowledge that a story has a beginning, middle, and end with a theme or plot that ties events together. This knowledge gives rise to fictional narratives, and children begin to understand and produce stories about made-up experiences that are not part of the immediate context. By the time children enter school, their stories contain physical descriptions of the characters and have simple but well-developed plot structures with story events logically connected to one another and linked to a central theme (see Table 5.1; Applebee, 1978; Botvin & Sutton-Smith, 1977; McCabe & Rollins, 1994; Peterson, 1990; Stein & Glenn, 1979).

Cross-sectional and longitudinal studies from a variety of developmental disciplines have contributed to our understanding of story structure development (Applebee, 1978; Berman & Slobin, 1994; Botvin & Sutton-Smith, 1977; Stein, 1986; Sutton-Smith, 1986; Trabasso, Stein, Rodkin, Munger, & Baughn, 1992). Based on this work, and particularly that of Applebee (1978) and Stein and Glenn (1979), five stages that characterize children's early story development have been described and are outlined in Table 5.1.

The information in the table illustrates that at first, children's stories (2–3 years) are "heaps" or strings of unrelated events that are enumerated in no particular order (prenarratives). In an intermediate stage, between 3 and 4 years of age, children begin to chain events together that are sequenced temporally, but the event sequences are not anchored to or motivated by a central theme. Frequently, children at this stage describe a series of events in an additive fashion. At about 5 years of age, a qualitative shift occurs in children's narratives, and their stories now reflect knowledge of basic plot structure. These true/classic narratives contain a clearly demarcated beginning, middle, and end, and the events are goal-oriented, or linked to a central theme or character. Moreover, causation is evident; story events are linked to events that precede or follow in true temporal relationships. While story knowledge continues to develop into more complex narrative forms, it is at this point that children are said to have internalized knowledge of the story form, and use this knowledge to understand, remember, and construct stories.

TABLE 5.1. Stages of Story Development

Stage	Definition and example
1. Heap (2–3 years)	Simple listing of ideas in no particular order. Example: The cat is climbing on the tree. It's raining and the children are there and the cats. The sky is all blue and the clouds.
2. Description	Contains information about the personality and physical characteristics of the main character. Example: Once there was a big black cat who lived in a house. He was mean and scary. He had giant black eyes and big claws and scratched people in the face. And he chased dogs. The end.
3. Action sequence	Story events are connected through temporal relationships but not causally. Example: Once there was a big black cat. Every day, he came out and chased dogs. Then he played with his friends. Then he found some lunch. Then he purred and licked his fur. Then he went home and went to sleep. The end.
4. Primitive/abbreviated narrative: (3–4 years)	Events are linked temporally and causally, but there is no goal-based action. Example: Once there was a boy named Bob who lived by the train tracks. Bob was playing by the tracks, hopping over the rails, when along came a train, and Poosh, that was the end of Bob. The end.
5. True/classic narrative (5 years)	Events are chained logically to one another and to a central character or theme. Example: Once there was a big black cat who lived in the city. One day he decided he was very hungry and that he needed to get something for dinner. So he went into the alley and spotted a little bird, caught him, and had him for dinner. The end.

During the later preschool years, typically developing children's stories also reflect increased understanding of intentionality (Trabasso et al., 1992), and their plot lines begin to include the internal states (i.e., mental, physical, and emotional) of characters that motivate characters to act (e.g., anger, injuries, death, fear). By the age of 6 years, these causal and purposeful features are common elements of children's narrative constructions (Kemper & Edwards, 1986).

Presumably, children bring their basic knowledge of story structure to literacy learning tasks, and apply this knowledge in their efforts to decipher, understand, recall/retell, and compose written text. Although the logic of this thinking is sound, the precise relationship between a well-developed sense of story and literacy acquisition remains unclear (Roth, Speece, & Cooper, 2002; Roth, Speece, Cooper, & De La Paz, 1996). However, it has been repeatedly demonstrated that children (and adolescents) with reading and writing deficits have difficulty understanding stories, producing stories of their own, and retelling stories told or written by others (Newcomer & Barenbaum, 1991; Roth & Spekman, 1986; Roth, Spekman, & Fye, 1995; Vallecorsa & Garriss, 1990). Thus, narrative discourse is an emergent literacy skill that demonstrates the interrelatedness among the domains of speaking, listening, reading, and writing (Roth, 2000).

Prevention, Assessment, and Intervention

The challenges for practitioners and researchers are to reduce the probability that narrative deficits will occur (prevention), identify potential problems early (assessment), and provide effective narrative discourse intervention/instruction to promote the development of narrative skills as an important aspect of emergent literacy acquisition (intervention). Early childhood specialists assume a variety of service delivery roles in these instructional/clinical process areas that extend beyond the provision of direct services, including professional staff development; collaborative consultation with teachers and resource professionals; parent and community education; and dissemination of information about narrative development and its relationship to other emergent literacy acquisitions (American Speech–Language–Hearing Association, 2001).

The Prevention Process

The main goal of prevention is to promote opportunities for children to have meaningful and successful interactions with narrative forms. Prevention involves collaboration among early childhood specialists (e.g., preschool teachers and speech–language pathologists [SLPs]) and parents to ensure that young children have opportunities to participate in narrative activities, both at home and in preschool/day care environments. Prevention also involves providing access to such experiences for older children or those with developmental delays who have missed such opportunities. Further, prevention programs reflect the increased attention being paid to the early identification of children who are vulnerable to language and literacy learning difficulties. Once identified, children can be referred for further assessment. Early interventions can then be implemented to foster growth in areas of potential or identified deficit and reduce the likelihood or magnitude of continued difficulties. Adoption of a preventative model means taking a proactive stance to identify problems before kindergarten and first grade, when children are propelled into formal literacy instruction and may not be equipped to maintain the pace of instruction and increasing demands for story and expository knowledge (Justice, Invernizzi, & Meier, 2002).

Principles of Assessment and Intervention/Instruction

The evaluation and treatment of narrative discourse problems are guided by a number of general principles:

1. Assessment and intervention/instructional activities must be developmentally appropriate and supportive, based on a child's age, level of cognitive and linguistic functioning, and stage of narrative development. Further, different tasks require differing levels of processing; for example, story recall tasks are generally easier than spontaneous story construction tasks, so that performance variation across tasks is likely to occur. To apply this principle, all early childhood specialists must be familiar with the stages of narrative growth and with performance expectations at different ages/stages of acquisition.

2. Instructional procedures must be sensitive to children's cultural and linguistic background as these variables directly influence all aspects of the assessment and intervention processes. Yet, instructional tools and procedures are inherently culture bound; they reflect the linguistic and social beliefs, and values and interaction styles of a given society (Johnston & Rogers, 2001). In some cultures, emphasis is placed on what a child can learn independently, whereas others focus on what a learner can accomplish in collaboration with peers (Barrs, Ellis, Hester, & Thomas, 1989). Therefore, children's different learning styles necessitate different assessment

and intervention strategies. Children (and individuals, in general) comprehend and remember more information from narratives that conform to the kinds of narratives heard at home. As a result, their sense of story may not be aligned with the types of stories encountered at school (Gutierrez-Clennen, 1996; Pritchard, 1990). Further, different cultures have different expectations for narrative performance. In the Western European tradition, children are expected to be able to construct narratives independently by about 5 years of age, whereas, in some Hispanic cultures, narratives are viewed as collaborative efforts between an adult and child. In still other cultures, such as Asian Japanese, narratives are expected to be concise and absent of repeated references and elaboration. Thus, depressed narrative task performance may reflect unfamiliarity with expectations rather than a narrative deficiency (Gutierrez-Clennen, 1996; Gutierrez-Clennen & Peña, 2002). For these reasons, narrative assessment and intervention for children from diverse cultures requires knowledge of the narrative structures of their cultures as well as their cultural values. McCabe and Bliss (2003) suggest several questions to pose when assessing the narrative performance of children from different linguistic or cultural backgrounds:

a. What is the child's home language background?
b. Who spends a lot of time with the child at home? In day care? And what language(s) is (are) used?
c. How long has the family been in the United States?
d. Does the child have siblings or extended family for whom English is the dominant language?
e. Is there someone familiar with the child who can elicit a representative narrative sample?

Responses to these questions can provide early childhood specialists with an ecologically valid context within which to interpret narrative assessment findings with respect to the overall quality, coherence, and adequacy of a child's narrative performance. (See Battle, Chapter 6, this volume, for a detailed perspective on cultural considerations in emergent literacy assessment and intervention.)

3. Assessment and intervention practices should be based on scientific evidence. Evidenced-based practice necessitates incorporating and translating the highest quality and most recent research information on narrative development and disorders in conjunction

with informed clinical judgment and expertise of an early childhood specialist acquired through professional experience (e.g., American Speech–Language–Hearing Association, 2005). Strict adherence to published levels of evidence is problematic in the area of narrative discourse. There are few large-scale, replicated studies with randomized controlled trials. Therefore, to evaluate the efficacy and effectiveness of assessment results and treatment procedures, early childhood specialists, including speech–language pathologists (SLPs) and preschool teachers, must establish specific short- and long-term objectives and rely on session-to-session data collection procedures to monitor progress and inform program modifications.

4. Instruction should occur in authentic and natural (i.e., ecologically valid) contexts. Authentic environments increase the likelihood of obtaining representative appraisals of children's narrative abilities and maximizing young children's acquisition of functional narrative communication skills (Norris & Hoffman, 1990).

5. No one assessment tool or teaching approach is likely to be effective for all children or for all aspects of narrative development. Assessment and intervention must be individualized based on the nature of each child's needs and learning style. Therefore, both processes need to be accomplished through a range of activities implemented in multiple authentic contexts (e.g., Dollaghan, 2004; Neisworth & Bagnato, 2004).

6. Assessment and intervention often are most fruitful when conducted in collaborative relationships among professionals and family members. Collaborative efforts enhance the quality and generalizability of assessment results and intervention gains because each partner possesses specialized knowledge and skills (Paul, Blosser, & Jakubowitz, 2006; Roth & Troia, 2006). For example, SLPs have a deep understanding of the linguistic underpinnings of literacy in both typically developing children and children with learning problems. Classroom teachers and special educators, on the other hand, have expertise in varied strategies, materials, and standards for implementing classroom-based instruction. Rather than working on common goals in isolation, professionals and families can coordinate their expertise more efficiently to target mutually shared narrative learning objectives (Peña & Quinn, 2003; Silliman, Ford, Beasman, & Evans, 1999).

The Assessment Process

For early childhood specialists, such as SLPs and classroom teachers, the goals of assessment are to (1) determine whether a child has a deficit in narrative discourse; (2) identify the nature and dimensions of the deficit; and (3) gather enough information to make informed and appropriate recommendations about the management of the deficit (i.e., referral for additional testing, type and structure of intervention). It is important to sample both story and expository genres because intrachild narrative differences exist, and different narrative forms are related to different aspects of literacy development (e.g., Allen et al., 1994). Ideally, multiple narratives of any given type should be collected (the rule of thumb is three) to increase the likelihood that the sample obtained reflects a fair estimate of a child's ability.

Narrative assessment necessitates administration of informal and criterion-referenced measures because norm-referenced and standardized tests are not available to evaluate this dimension of linguistic knowledge in young children. Fortunately, an advantage of nonstandardized measures is that they can be tailored to the needs of individual children. Moreover, narrative samples provide an index of a child's higher-level language functioning and are relatively easy to elicit from young children in everyday contexts, thereby serving as a valuable, early risk indicator for language and learning disabilities in the preschool years. Finally, narrative sampling tends to be less biased than traditional measures of expressive language, and therefore may yield more reliable and valid information for ELL children (Fazio et al., 1996; Muñoz, Gillam, Peña, & Gulley-Faehnle, 2003).

In the absence of formal, standardized tests, a framework for narrative evaluation is guided by the developmental literature on narrative acquisition in children with typical language development. This body of literature suggests the use of several elicitation procedures for different narrative forms at different points in development.

Elicitation Procedures

Different types of narratives can be elicited depending on the age or developmental stage of the child, the child's verbal abilities, and the goals of assessment. For young (and lower-functioning) children, the three most common narrative genres are scripts, personal event narratives, and story narratives.

Scripts, or everyday event sequences, can be solicited from preschool children by posing a question about a familiar activity (e.g., "What do you do when … you go to the zoo?"; " … you go to a birthday party?"). *PENs* are most well suited for slightly older preschool children and can be gathered with prompts such as "Tell me what you did this summer"; "Tell me about your family." *Story narratives* most often involve two main tasks: story recall and fictional story construction. Story recall is a highly structured task in which a child is asked to repeat a story to an adult. Several presentation formats can be used including video recorded sequences, picture series, wordless books, and oral story telling. A variation of a recall task involves asking a child to tell about a favorite TV show or other familiar event. Fictional stories are generally elicited in two ways: (1) asking a child to make up a story of his or her own; or (2) providing a story stem or prompt such as "Once upon a time, there was a bear who lived in the forest. … " (McCabe & Rollins, 1994).

Narrative Analysis Strategies

If feasible, it is best to analyze all of the narrative samples elicited. McCabe and Peterson (1991) found that the narrative length was a gross indicator of its complexity, and therefore suggested scoring the longest story. It is important to remember, however, that a child's most advanced narrative might not be the longest one.

Oral stories and expositions can be examined at both the macrostructure and microstructure levels. Macrostructure analyses involve evaluation of the overall construction of narratives and examine variables such as story components, number of subplots/episodes, completeness of subplots/episodes, and number of relevant pieces of information (Berman & Slobin, 1994; Paul & Smith, 1993; Trabasso et al., 1992; Van Dongen & Westby, 1986). Various approaches to macrostructure analysis can be used. Regardless of the approach(es) selected, stage assignment for the child's level of narrative development should be based on the dominant pattern of story organization that the child exhibited. It also is possible to categorize a child's performance level as transitional/emergent; that is, between two different levels of story organization.

One approach involves categorization of a story narrative into one of the five developmental stages based on Applebee's (1978) study of 2- to 5-year-old children described earlier in this chapter (i.e., heap, description, action sequence, primitive/abbreviated narrative, true/classic narrative). To facilitate decision making, an adaptation of Westby's (1991) story structure decision-making tree can be helpful (see Figure 5.1). This binary decision-making tree is intended as a screening measure to quickly establish a general level of story development. The teacher or SLP reads through a story and then systematically asks the questions detailed in the tree.

Another approach to the assessment of story organization is completion of a high-point analysis, which focuses on a determination of whether the narrative has a climax and whether the climax is followed by a resolution (i.e., logical conclusion). A climax is a decisive moment or turning point in a narrative sequence. Labov (1972) developed the high-point analysis as a means of appraising PENs and anecdotes. It has been adapted for use with story narratives by McCabe and Rollins (1994), whose scoring guidelines for preschool children consist of a series of questions and answers, as summarized in Figure 5.2. Answers to these questions can assist in the determination of overall narrative structure through an examination of the basic components of a narrative. First, the child's discourse sample is assigned a narrative structure level. Then a narrative profile is developed that includes specific strengths and areas

Does the story consist of a simple listing of events in no particular order?

If Yes → Heap

If No, Does the story have a temporally related sequence of events?

If No → Descriptive Sequence

If Yes, Does the story have a causally related sequence of events?

If No → Action Sequence

If Yes, Does the story imply goal-directed behavior?

If No → Primitive/Abbreviated Narrative

If Yes, Does the story contain events that are logically related to one another and to a central theme?

If Yes → True/Classic Narrative

FIGURE 5.1. Story structure decision tree. Based on Westby (1991).

1. Are there two past events (actions)?

If No → *One-Event Narrative*

2. If Yes, Are there more than two past-tense events?

If No → *Two-Event Narrative*

3. If Yes, Is there a logical or causal sequence to these events?

If No → *Miscellaneous Narrative* (a narrative that cannot be categorized elsewhere)

4. If Yes, Are the events ordered in the same way as they must have occurred logically?

If No → *Leapfrog Narrative* (more than two events conveyed in random order)

5. If Yes, Is there a high point?

If No → *Chronological Narrative* (series of actions that are not causally related)

6. If Yes, Is there a resolution following the climax?

If No → *End-at-High-Point Narrative* (contains all narrative elements except for resolution)

If Yes → *Classic Narrative*

FIGURE 5.2. High-point scoring guidelines. Based on McCabe and Rollins (1994).

of need. This profile serves as a basis for developing intervention goals and strategies. For example, if the answer to the first three questions is "yes," and the answer to question 4 is "no," then the child's narrative likely represents a leapfrog structure (i.e., events that are in no particular sequence with the omission of important information or with the inclusion of contradictory information). An example of a leapfrogging narrative is "I got hair. I got braids in my hair. I like them. My mom helped me and she washed them. But the water was hot. When I cry, she stopped. The end."

Finally, the macrostructure of stories can be examined for inclusion of story structure elements, or episodic structure. A story can contain one or more episodes or subplots. An episode consists of one or more story grammar components and can be complete or incomplete. An episode is considered complete if it contains a minimum of three specific story components: initiating event/problem, attempt, and consequence. Episodes that omit one of these elements are considered incomplete. From a story grammar perspective, these elements or components represent the internal structure of classic narratives, called the "story schema," and are outlined in Table 5.2.

TABLE 5.2. Story Grammar Components

Category	Definition
Setting	Information about character description and story context (social, physical, temporal)
Initiating event/problem	Occurrence that influences character to act
Response	A character's reaction to the initiating event/problem
Plan	A character's strategy for attaining the goal
Attempt	A character's actions to attain the goal
Consequence	A character's success or failure to attain the goal
Resolution	A character's thoughts or feelings regarding the consequence

Note. Based on Stein and Glenn (1979).

A story grammar analysis also can include coding the presence and absence of story markers that introduce and end a story.

Microstructure analyses focus on the content aspects of narratives, examining variables such as story length and grammatical organization. Story length can be calculated as the total number of words and/or total number of propositions (usually main clauses). Grammatical organization involves analysis of grammatical complexity and grammatical accuracy. Measures of grammatical complexity include (1) mean length of utterance (MLU); (2) average T-unit length (main clause plus any subordinate clauses or nonclausal units); (3) use of cohesive ties such as pronominal reference (pronouns that refer to another element in the discourse for its interpretation, e.g., *he* for *the man*; *she* for *the woman*), conjunction (logical relationships between clauses, e.g., *so, but, and, next*), and ellipsis (omission of redundant information, e.g., Q: "Have you been swimming?" A: "Yes, I have" [omitting "been swimming."]); (4) number of different words and number of different word roots; and (5) clause density (average number of clauses per T-unit). Measures of grammatical accuracy include calculations of percent of grammatical T-units and percent of correctly used cohesive ties.

The combination of macrostructure and microstructure analyses permits the identification of a profile of strengths and needs for a particular child, which then can be used for intervention programming and planning. This information also can guide the selection of target areas for collaborative efforts with significant others in the child's daily environment (e.g., preschool teacher, SLP, day care personnel, family members). Children with narrative deficits present with different areas of need, and thus require different intervention foci. For example, one child may produce adequate utterance-length output but have difficulty ordering events in a logical sequence. Another child may show proficiency with simple PENs, but struggle to comprehend and generate story narratives. This variability is supported by research. For example, late talkers with persistent language deficit show continued difficulties in story coherence and cohesion with normal growth trajectories for narrative content and form (Paul et al., 1996; Paul & Smith, 1993). In other words, their stories may contain substantive and plausible information that is encoded in relatively grammatical utterances. Yet, the interutterance connections are omitted, ambiguous, or incorrect. In contrast, expression of themes in PENs by children with specific language impairment (SLI) is delayed in comparison to same-age peers (Liles, Duffy, Merritt, & Purcell, 1995).

The Intervention/Instruction Process

Narrative discourse instruction is important for all young children, and particularly those at risk for or with language learning impairments. The primary aim of the instruction is to maximize children's receptive and expressive narrative discourse skills. Narrative development needs to begin early in the preschool period to prepare children for literacy instruction and access to the educational curriculum. For example, the written texts used in first grade for beginning reading instruction are in the narrative discourse genre and contain simple, chronologically ordered events that are linked to one another by causal and temporal connectors. Promoting narrative development, however, is not confined to young children. Older children, particularly those with communication impairments, may be functioning developmentally in the emergent literacy stage and require intervention aimed at establishing and solidifying early developing narrative comprehension and production skills.

The three-stage instructional model of Snow, Burns, and Griffin (1998) is ideal for narrative intervention with young children. The three stages include (1) explicit instruction, during which models of correct performance are provided, elicited, and reinforced;

(2) guided practice, where children try out their newly learned behaviors with scaffolding from an adult (e.g., teacher, SLP, parent); and (3) independent practice, during which children work on their own.

Intervention Principles and Guidelines

Narrative discourse instruction and intervention are informed by several "best-practice" principles and guidelines. For the purposes of this chapter, the term "best practices" refers to our current knowledge base on early narrative discourse and development that has been garnered through a combination of experimental research studies and expertise of seasoned early childhood educators.

1. *Implement and embed strategies in natural, authentic environments and interactive activities, including preschool curricula.* Young children learn best through active exploration, meaningful experiences, and interactive participation with materials that sustain their interest. They benefit from regular opportunities to talk about what is read; active use of their narrative knowledge helps them transfer what they know to new situations. This is especially important for young children, who need to be engaged in experiences that make narration meaningful and which build on prior learning (i.e., what children already know and can do). Children can be asked to share their own experiences with the character's dilemma/problem or talk about what they would do in the protagonist's situation. Role playing story lines also helps to concretize information gained from narrative text. Further, small peer groupings can be given the task of predicting what would happen next if the story were to continue or what would happen if the story were set in another climate/location.

2. *Expose children to developmentally appropriate, high-quality literature with respect to both content and complexity.* For example, children under the age of 5 years benefit most from simple linear stories that follow the activities of one main character over time (e.g., *The Snowy Day*; Keats, 1962), whereas older children can follow the simultaneous actions of two main characters (e.g., *Two Good Friends*; Delton, 1974). In *The Snowy Day*, a little boy goes out to play in the snow and comes home with a snowball in his jacket pocket. The following morning there is only a wet spot in his

pocket. The plot line of *Two Good Friends* involves two characters, Bear and Duck, who each do a chore for the other as a surprise.

3. *Consider the emotional content of books.* Children as young as 5 years differentiate between positive and negative emotions such as happiness and sadness, respectively, but cannot yet recognize the emotions of others, especially when the feelings are different from their own. They also have difficulty integrating more than one emotion at a time. Many books for young children, however, do not explicitly state characters' emotions, assuming that youngsters will recognize the emotion portrayed based on the situation or attributes of the character. This assumption cannot be made for young children, especially those with language impairments (Westby, Maggart, & Van Dongen, 1984). Rather, books should be selected that make emotions explicit throughout the story line (e.g., the Care Bear series and the Berenstain Bears series).

4. *Use discourse hierarchies.* This organizational approach involves progressing from simple to more complex genres (e.g., scripts → personal narratives → fictional narratives). It also includes a gradual increase in the length of narratives introduced, addition of more actions and participants into narrative sequences, increasing the displacement of narratives in time and location, and gradually introducing mental states and motivations of characters (Norris & Hoffman, 1990).

5. *Use recounts of true, familiar events.* As children become more comfortable with the event sequence, scaffold the youngsters to gradually take over parts of the narrative, and then encourage elaboration (e.g., include new incidents, add other characters). In preschool classrooms, the teacher, SLP, or other early childhood specialist can begin with well-known folktales or familiar stories from books into which variations in story line can be introduced gradually.

6. *Introduce a variety of narrative genres, including fictional and informational books.* Different genres stimulate conversations about different ideas and concepts beyond everyday experiences. Genres provide interesting and diverse content to talk and think about, increasing children's funds of background world knowledge. Moschovaki and Meadows (2005) studied shared book reading between teachers and kindergarten classes and showed that information books (e.g., *The Four Elements: Fire*; Rius & Parramon, 1992—describing features of fire and different uses of fire) elicited

more comments about personal experiences, whereas fiction books elicited more prediction responses. Further, familiar fiction books prompted more predictive and analytical comments than unfamiliar fiction books, which encouraged more labeling responses.

7. *Choose books that maintain interesting language patterns, a sense of cadence, and rhyme and alliterative sequences.* Sound patterns rather than words may attract and sustain children's attention to the printed page. Suggestions include *Each Peach Pear Plum* (Ahlberg, 1979); *Pass the Fritters, Critters* (Chapman, 1993); *Mouse Mess* (Riley, 1997); and *Noisy Nora* (Wells, 1973).

8. *Read aloud to children on a daily basis using shared book reading and/or dialogic reading.* These reading strategies promote the development of story knowledge. It is through repeated exposure to stories that children begin to internalize a framework for understanding and generating narrative sequences (Westby, 1991). Shared book reading fosters social and affective aspects of literacy, expands children's understanding of story structure, and helps them form connections between speech and print. It also enhances their perception of the value of text and increases their enthusiasm for the narrative literate form. Dialogic reading is a specific form of shared book reading. Children actively participate throughout the book-reading experience as an adult poses different types of questions. Evidence indicates that children's understanding of story content and vocabulary increases through this interactive adult–child format (Morrow, 1988; Sénéchal, LeFevre, Thomas, & Daley, 1998; Snow, 1983; Thomas, 1985). Appropriate questions for younger preschool children (2–3 years) focus on individual pages and ask children to describe objects, events, and actions (e.g., "What is this?"; "What is the hen doing?"; "What color is Barney?"). For older preschool children (4–5 years), questions can focus on the narrative as a whole or the relationship between the story line and the child's own experiences (e.g., "Have you ever seen a dog swimming?"). Burns, Griffin, and Snow (1999) refer to these latter query types as "distancing questions" because these interrogatives move the story line to children's own experiences, and in so doing, promote decontextualized language. Whitehurst et al. (1988) showed that 2- to 3-year-old children whose mothers deliberately posed increased numbers of open-ended and wh-questions during shared book reading attained higher receptive and expressive vocabulary scores at the end of a 4-week intervention than the children whose

mothers read in their typical fashion. Some of the differences were maintained at follow-up testing 9 months later. Many other studies (e.g., Fivush, 1991; Reese, Haden, & Fivush, 1993) have shown similar results. Parents who asked more questions and prompted for contextualizing information (i.e., where and when events took place) had children who produced more complex narratives.

9. *Embed vocabulary instruction in narrative activities.* The narrative context provides natural opportunities to introduce new vocabulary words and strengthen familiar lexical items (e.g., Akhtar, Jipson, & Callanan, 2001; Hart & Risley, 1995, 1999; Tabors, Beals, & Weizman, 2001; Whitehurst et al., 1994). For example, a book about airplanes can be used to introduce less familiar synonyms (e.g., *jet, 747*) as well as serve as a basis for discussion about other things that fly but are not categorized as airplanes. This strategy can be particularly beneficial for young children who have difficulty learning new words and retaining the meaning of newly learned words. (See Vander Woude, van Kleeck, & Vander Veen, Chapter 2, this volume, on book sharing and the development of meaning.)

10. *Select books with well-developed plot structures.* Such books have logical event sequences that culminate in a clear resolution (e.g., *Frog, Where Are You?*; Mayer, 1969). This type of literature can be used to introduce and reinforce the traditional concept of "story"; that is, a story has beginning, middle, and end portions with logically connected event sequences.

11. *Use predictable pattern books.* The repetitive themes in these stories foster both comprehension and apprehension skills. Comprehension involves understanding what you have just heard; apprehension entails predicting what's coming next (e.g., *Polar Bear, Polar Bear;* Martin & Carle, 1991; *If You Give a Mouse a Cookie*; Numeroff, 1985).

12. *Direct children's attention to the printed word rather than just pictures.* This strategy supports the connection between spoken words and print forms. Introduce and reinforce book conventions including title, author, and left-to-right, top-to-bottom, and front-to-back orientations.

13. *Engage in storytelling in addition to story reading.* Storytelling brings children into the act of story making, thereby permitting the creation of stories *with* children, not just *for* or *to* children (Trousdale, 1990). Through reading, children learn about story structure; through storytelling, children learn to actively manipu-

late and control these structures. This cooperative enterprise helps children learn what a story is "from the inside out."

14. *Engage in repeated readings/tellings of the same book/stories rather than single readings of different books.* This rereading strategy increases participation, language output, and quality of contribution (Eller, Pappas, & Brown, 1998; Morrow, 1988; National Reading Panel, 2000; Pappas, 1991; Sénéchal et al., 1998; Teale & Sulzby, 1987).

15. *Choose the appropriate reading style.* Different styles are more conducive to different language levels. For example, children with strong receptive vocabularies benefit from a higher demanding "performance-oriented" style, in which the reader provides plentiful commentary before and after an uninterrupted story reading. Children with sparser receptive vocabularies profit from a "describer style," a less demanding mode that involves labeling and describing pictures during book sharing. The alignment of reading style with linguistic/cognitive level conforms to a fundamental tenet of effective instruction: scaffolding. Based on Vygotsky's (1986) zone of proximal development, interventions should be designed to advance a child's knowledge one step beyond his or her current level of functioning.

16. *Use a variety of scaffolding techniques to provide children with predictable verbal and nonverbal narrative language and instructional feedback.* Two specific examples are PEER and CROWD.

PEER is based on Ninio and Bruner's (1978) storybook reading routine and involves the following sequence of activities:

P = Parent/adult initiates exchange about book
E = Evaluates child's response
E = Expands child's response
R = Repeats initial question to check comprehension

Example

Parent initiates = "What is Mrs. Bear doing?" (standing on her toes)
Evaluate and Expand = "Yes, she *is* standing on her toes, and picking apples."
Repeat initial question = "What is Mrs. Bear doing? Do you remember?"

CROWD (Burns et al., 1999) consists of five types of questions or prompts that occur during book reading, each serving a different function:

C = Completion questions: focus on linguistic structure
R = Recall questions: focus on story content
O = Open-ended questions: focus on increasing amount of talk about book
W = Wh-questions: focus on teaching new vocabulary
D = Distancing questions: focus on linking book events to child's own experiences

Example

Completion = When Choco talked with Penguin, he cried. "You have (wings) just like me!" Child completes by saying, "wings."
Recall = "Do you remember how this book ended?"
Open Ended = "What is happening on this page?"
Wh = "What is a *search*"?
Distancing = "Does everyone in your family look the same?"
Wh- and open-ended questions are most appropriate with children who are from 2 to 3 years of age or functioning at this level developmentally, whereas the remaining three types are best suited for older preschool children (between 4 and 5 years of age).

17. *Provide specific suggestions to parents and other family members.* Sharing information with parents and caregivers can reinforce adult–child interactions and offer school-based professionals opportunities to scaffold these interactions. Examples include:

- Encouraging children to recount experiences at school, playgroup, or day care
- Rereading favorite stories
- Providing daily reading experiences
- Reading a variety of different book genres, including predictable pattern books, folktales, and nursery rhymes
- Engaging children in conversation and showing interest in what they say

- Elaborating on children's comments with descriptive and explanatory language
- Using a dialogic book-reading strategy
- Encouraging children to draw or recount a familiar story
- Demonstrating and reinforcing book conventions (e.g., left-to-right and top-to-bottom orientation)
- Talking about a child's favorite book or recent excursion activity during mealtime conversations
- Taking regular trips to library and community center story hours

Case Study

The following case study provides an illustration of how the information presented in this chapter on narrative development, assessment, and intervention can be applied in real-world educational settings. It emphasizes the importance and value of meaningful collaboration among early childhood professionals (e.g., general education teachers, special education teachers, and SLPs) in the design and implementation of instructional goals and strategies that are integrated into educational curricula.

Steven is a 4-year-old child who attends a Head Start program. The preschool curriculum contains specific learning objectives that are designed to promote various aspects of emergent literacy including narrative knowledge. For example, classroom activities encourage understanding the basic structure of stories, vocabulary development, appreciation of the functions and conventions of print, and "writing" stories and personal event narratives using invented spelling. Steven has not been formally identified with a language impairment, but the Head Start teacher is concerned about Steven's progress for a number of reasons. First, he demonstrates difficulty learning and retaining new vocabulary. For example, Steven does not remember word meanings contained in storybooks even after repeated readings of the same book during story time across several days. Second, while he recalls the events of a simple story or personal event narrative, he does not maintain the sequential order of the event sequences. Third, Steven does not exhibit the ability to convey a personal narrative when, for example, he is asked to describe a familiar event that he has experienced. Finally, Steven demonstrates difficulties in other areas of emergent literacy, including phonological awareness and letter-name knowledge.

Based on Steven's profile, the classroom teacher consulted with the SLP, and they decided to develop and implement a collaborative model to enhance the narrative discourse skills of Steven as well as his classmates. They selected a demonstration lesson, in which one professional teaches a lesson or lessons to target specific learning objectives, while the other professional initially observes and gradually assumes responsibility for lesson implementation. Like other evidence-based professional partnership models, demonstration lessons emphasize the critical role that early childhood professionals play in the education of young children (Roth & Troia, 2006).

Demonstration Lesson

The SLP and the teacher talked about the importance of narrative knowledge to emergent literacy development. The SLP offered to model a classroom lesson that targeted enhancing knowledge of the story form and development of expressive and receptive vocabulary. Dialogic reading, an interactive style of shared book reading, was selected as the instructional approach because it seemed an ideal instructional strategy for the classroom context. The SLP and the teacher agreed that, as an interactive model of storybook reading, dialogic reading provides natural opportunities to embed vocabulary teaching into an authentic reading experience. It also builds and reinforces children's knowledge of story structure, and may help Steven and his classmates to gradually internalize a framework for understanding and generating narrative sequences.

With the teacher's guidance, the SLP selected a book from the existing curriculum corresponding to a thematic unit and read the book with expression. Using this book, the SLP explicitly identified the main elements of the story, emphasizing the initiating event, the action, and the resolution. Another book was then selected with the same theme, and the dialogic reading technique of CROWD was implemented, in which the SLP asked five different kinds of instructional questions and prompts throughout the book reading. While reading the book, the clinician solicited information from the students and provided feedback about their responses to the questions posed in CROWD.

The SLP began with wh- and open-ended questions, as these are easier for young children and tend to engage them more readily. After finishing the story, the children were prompted to recap the main events of the book and were asked to identify the beginning (i.e., initiating event), middle (i.e., action sequence), and ending (i.e., resolution) parts of the story. To facilitate the children's recall, the SLP introduced the "Dinastory," a visual scaffold of a large dinosaur with three clearly demarcated parts, each representing a portion of the story. The SLP explained that the dinosaur's head is on top because it signifies the beginning of the story; the body is the biggest part because the middle is the largest part of a story; and the tail tapers off to indicate that a story needs an ending. The SLP deliberately selected Steven to respond to some of the questions and to contribute to the story recap. The SLP then reread the book, as repeated readings have been shown to increase children's degree of participation, amount of verbal output, and linguistic sophistication of their contributions (Teale & Sulzby, 1987).

New vocabulary words were taught as they were encountered within the context of the story line. The SLP identified the new words (e.g., "What is *roaring*?") and provided simple definitions for each word. Short descriptions and synonyms were presented to scaffold and strengthen vocabulary knowledge (e.g., "He built a *cocoon*— a warm comfy blanket"). The SLP focused on teaching both common words (e.g., *roaring*) and rare words (e.g., *cocoon*) because exposure to both kinds of words is associated with increased vocabulary size even in young children (Tabors et al., 2001). The class then engaged in constructing a semantic map for the target word *lion* that involved three sequential activities: brainstorming a list of words from the story; categorizing the words into groups (i.e., actions, foods, colors, body parts) using pictures; and then drawing lines to connect each category with the center node (i.e., *lion*). Steven and a more accomplished peer worked together to complete their own version of the semantic map with feedback from the SLP and the teacher. This helped provide a visual representation of the thematic vocabulary and their relationships and highlighted the semantic categorical organization of these words. After the SLP had modeled the dialogic storybook reading technique on several occasions, the teacher implemented the techniques on days when the SLP was not scheduled in the classroom, first with the same book and then with new books.

The SLP and the teacher consulted on a regular basis to monitor Steven's progress. Steven gradually began to participate more fully and spontaneously in the shared book-reading activities and began to use some of the new vocabulary in sociodramatic play situations during center time.

The intent of this case study was to highlight the importance of narrative discourse to the acquisition of language and emergent literacy and how narrative discourse difficulties may manifest themselves in the preschool years. It also focused on specific ways that early childhood professionals can work in tandem to help young children develop the language skills necessary to gird their narrative discourse abilities in natural contextualized learning environments.

Summary

Oral narrative discourse is an aspect of language that has its developmental onset during the preschool years and constitutes a chief component of emergent literacy. This chapter described story and expository discourse acquisition in typical language learners and those at risk for or with identified language impairments. A central theme of this chapter was the relationship between oral narrative development and other emergent literacy factors that affect language and literacy acquisitions and outcomes. Several key points were underscored:

1. All professionals working with young children must be knowledgeable about the developmental connections between narration, other language skills, literacy, and associated risk factors.
2. Preschool experiences must include developmentally sensitive and systematic instructional opportunities for children to learn and practice narrative discourse forms.
3. The early identification of children who require additional supports and/or intervention is critical to ensure appropriate referral for assessment and timely provision of needed intervention/instructional services.

To this end, the concluding section addressed "best-practice" approaches to narrative prevention, assessment, and intervention, as well as the variety of roles that early childhood professionals play in the effective and successful implementation of these clinical processes.

DISCUSSION QUESTIONS

1. Given that conversation and narrative are both forms of discourse, why is narration considered a more difficult discourse form for young children to learn?

2. How would a child's semantic and syntactic difficulties reflect themselves in a narrative discourse task such as storytelling?

3. Why is early oral narrative development thought to be important for the acquisition of literacy skills?

4. What factors require consideration by an SLP in the assessment of narrative discourse of a child whose dominant language is not English?

EXERCISES

1. Identify the types of narrative samples and the microstructure and macrostructure features that an early childhood professional (e.g., SLP) may want to obtain and analyze in the evaluation of a 4-year-old child's narrative discourse skills.

2. Design two developmentally appropriate learning objectives for a 3½-year-old child with a language impairment that would focus on the overall goal of improved oral narrative discourse skills. Describe the factors that went into making your decision.

3. Hypothetical situation: You are an SPL or other early childhood professional working in an elementary school that has an all-day preschool program. Ms. Smith, the principal, is dissatisfied with the "story-time" component of the curriculum for both the preschool and kindergarten levels. She has asked you to review it and make suggestions for improving it. What would you look for in this review?

References

Ahlberg, J. (1979). *Each peach pear plum*. New York: Viking.
Akhtar, N., Jipson, J., & Callanan, M. A. (2001). Learning words through overhearing. *Child Development, 72*, 416–430.

Allen, M., Kertoy, M., Sherblom, J., & Pettit, J. (1994). Children's narrative production: A comparison of personal event and fictional stories. *Applied Psycholinguistics, 15*, 149–176.

American Speech–Language–Hearing Association. (2001). *Roles and responsibilities of speech–language pathologists with respect to reading and writing in children and youth*. Rockville, MD: Author.

American Speech–Language–Hearing Association. (2005). *Evidence-based practice in communication disorders* [Position statement]. Rockville, MD: Author.

Applebee, A. N. (1978). *The child's concept of story*. Chicago: University of Chicago Press.

Barrs, M., Ellis, S., Hester, H., & Thomas, A. (1989). *The primary language record: Handbook for teachers*. London: London Education Authority.

Beals, D. E. (2001). Eating and reading: Links between family conversations with preschoolers and later language and literacy. In D. K. Dickinson & P. O. Tabors (Eds.), *Beginning literacy with language* (pp. 75–92). Baltimore: Brookes.

Berman, R. A. (1988). On the ability to relate events in narrative. *Discourse Processes, 11*, 469–497.

Berman, R. A., & Slobin, D. I. (1994). *Relating events in narrative: A cross-linguistic development study*. Mahwah, NJ: Erlbaum.

Bishop, D. V. M., & Edmondson, A. (1987). Language-impaired 4-year-olds: Distinguishing transient from persistent impairment. *Journal of Speech and Hearing Disorders, 52*, 156–173.

Botvin, G., & Sutton-Smith, B. (1977). The development of structural complexity in children's fantasy narratives. *Developmental Psychology, 13*, 377–388.

Bruner, J. (1985). Narrative and paradigmatic modes of thought. In E. Eisner (Ed.), *Learning and teaching the ways of knowing* (pp. 97–115). Chicago: University of Chicago Press.

Burns, M. S., Griffin, P., & Snow, C. E. (1999). *Starting out right: A guide to promoting children's reading success*. Washington, DC: National Academy Press.

Burt, B. S., & McCabe, A. (1996). Chameleon writers? Narrative styles in written story books. In A. McCabe (Ed.), *Chameleon readers: Teaching children to appreciate all kinds of good stories*. New York: McGraw-Hill.

Champion, T. B. (1998). Tell me somethin' good: A description of narrative structure among African American children. *Linguistics and Education, 9*, 251–286.

Chapman, C. (1993). *Pass the fritters, critters*. New York: Four Winds Press.

Delton, J. (1974). *Two good friends*. New York: Crown.

Demorest, A. P., & Alexander, I. E. (1992). Affective scripts as organizers of personal experiences. *Journal of Personality, 60*, 645–663.

Dickinson, D. K., & Snow, C. E. (1987). Interrelationships among prereading and oral language skills in kindergarteners from two social classes. *Early Childhood Research Quarterly, 2,* 1–26.

Dollaghan, C. (2004). Evidence-based practice in communication disorders: What do we know and when do we know it? *Journal of Communication Disorders, 37,* 391–400.

Eisenberg, A. R. (1984). Learning to describe past experiences in conversation. *Discourse Processes, 8,* 177–204.

Eller, R., Pappas, C., & Brown, E. (1998). The lexical development of kindergarteners: Learning from written text. *Journal of Reading Behavior, 20,* 5–24.

Fazio, B., Naremore, R., & Connell, P. (1996). Tracking children from poverty at risk for specific language impairments: A 3-year longitudinal study. *Journal of Speech and Hearing Research, 39,* 611–624.

Fey, M. E., Catts, H. W., Proctor-Williams, K., Tomblin, B. J., & Zhang, X. (2004). Oral and written story composition skills of children with language impairment. *Journal of Speech, Language, and Hearing Research, 47,* 1301–1318.

Fivush, R. (1991). The social construction of personal narratives. *Merrill–Palmer Quarterly, 37,* 59–81.

Fritjers, J. C., Barron, R. W., & Brunello, M. (2000). Direct and mediated influences of home literacy on preschoolers' oral vocabulary and early written language skill. *Journal of Educational Psychology, 92,* 466–477.

Gillam, R. B., & Johnston, J. R. (1992). Spoken and written language relationships in language/learning-impaired and normally achieving school-age children. *Journal of Speech and Hearing Research, 35,* 1303–1315.

Griffin, T. M., Hemphill, L., Camp, L., & Palmer, D. (2004). Oral discourse in the preschool years and later literacy skills. *First Language, 24,* 123–147.

Gutièrrez-Clennen, V. F. (1996). Language diversity: Implications for assessment. In K. Cole & D. Thal (Eds.), *Assessment of communication and language* (pp. 29–56). Baltimore: Brookes.

Gutièrrez-Clellen, V. F., & Penã, E. (2002). Dynamic assessment of diverse children: A tutorial. *Language, Speech, and Hearing Services in Schools, 32,* 212–224.

Halliday, M., & Hasan, R. (1976). *Cohesion in English.* London: Longman.

Hardy, B. (1978). Narrative as a primary act of mind. In M. Meek, A. Warlow, & G. Barton (Eds.), *The cool web.* New York: Atheneum.

Hart, B., & Risley, T. (1995). *Meaningful differences.* Baltimore: Brookes.

Hart, B., & Risley, T. (1999). *The social world of children learning to talk.* Baltimore: Brookes.

Heath, S. B. (1989). Oral and literate traditions among Black Americans living in poverty. *American Psychologist, 44,* 367–373.

Heath, S. B. (1990). The children of Trackton's children: Spoken and written language in social change. In J. W. Stigler, R. A. Shweder, & G.

Herdt (Eds.), *Cultural psychology* (pp. 496–519). Cambridge, MA: Cambridge University Press.

Hudson, J. A., & Shapiro, L. R. (1991). From knowing to telling: The development of children's scripts, stories, and personal narratives. In A. McCabe & C. Peterson (Eds.), *Developing narrative structure* (pp. 89–136). Hillsdale, NJ: Erlbaum.

Johnston, P. H., & Rogers, R. (2001). Early literacy assessment development: The case for "informed assessment." In S. B. Neuman & D. K. Dickinson (Eds.), *Handbook of early literacy research* (pp. 377–389). New York: Guilford Press.

Justice, L. M., Invernizzi, M., & Meier, J. D. (2002). Designing and implementing an early literacy screening protocol: Suggestions for the speech–language pathologist. *Language, Speech, and Hearing Services in Schools, 33,* 84–101.

Karweit, N., & Wasik, B. (1996). The effects of storytelling programs on literacy and language development of disadvantaged preschoolers. *Journal of Education for Students Placed At-Risk, 4,* 319–348.

Keats, E. J. (1962). *A snowy day.* New York: Viking.

Kemper, S., & Edwards, L. (1986). Children's expression of causality and their construction of narratives. *Topics in Language Disorders, 7,* 11–20.

Kintsch, W. (1974). *The representation of meaning in memory.* Hillsdale, NJ: Erlbaum.

Labov, W. (1972). *Language in the inner city.* Philadelphia: University of Pennsylvania.

Liles, B. Z., Duffy, R. J., Merritt, D. D., & Purcell, S. (1995). Measurement of narrative discourse ability in children with language disorders. *Journal of Speech and Hearing Research, 38,* 415–425.

Manhardt, J., & Rescorla, L. (2002). Oral narrative skills of late talkers at ages 8 and 9. *Applied Psycholinguistics, 23,* 1–21.

Martin, B., & Carle, E. (1991). *Polar bear, polar bear, what do you hear?* New York: Dial Press.

Mayer, M. (1969). *Frog, where are you?* New York: Dial Books for Young Readers.

McCabe, A., & Bliss, L. S. (2003). *Patterns of narrative discourse: A multicultural lifespan approach.* New York: Allyn & Bacon.

McCabe, A., & Peterson, C. (1991). Getting the story: A longitudinal study of parental styles in eliciting oral personal narratives and developing narrative skill. In A. McCabe & C. Peterson (Eds.), *Developing narrative structure* (pp. 217–253). Hillsdale, NJ: Erlbaum.

McCabe, A., & Rollins, P. R. (1994). Assessment of preschool narrative skills: Prerequisite for literacy. *American Journal of Speech–Language Pathology, 3,* 45–56.

Miller, P. J., & Sperry, L. L. (1988). Early talks about the past: The origins of conversational stories of personal experience. *Journal of Child Language, 15,* 293–315.

Morrow, L. M. (1988). Young children's responses to one-to-one story readings in school settings. *Reading Research Quarterly, 23*, 89–107.

Moschovaki, E., & Meadows, S. (2005). Young children's spontaneous participation during classroom book reading: Differences according to various types of books. *Early Childhood Research and Practice, 7*, 1–17.

Muñoz, M. L., Gillam, R. B., Peña, E. D., & Gulley-Faehnle, A. (2003). Measures of language development in fictional narratives of Latino children. *Language, Speech, and Hearing Services in Schools, 34*, 332–342.

National Reading Panel. (2000). *Report of the National Reading Panel.* Bethesda, MD: National Institute of Child Health and Human Development.

Neisworth, J. T., & Bagnato, S. J. (2004). The mismeasure of young children. *Infants and Young Children, 17*, 198–212.

Neuman, S. B. (2006). The knowledge gap: Implications for early education. In D. K. Dickinson & S. B. Neuman (Eds.), *Handbook of early literacy research: Vol. 2* (pp. 9–40). New York: Guilford Press.

Neuman, S. B., & Dickinson, D. K. (2001). *Handbook of early literacy research.* New York: Guilford Press.

Newcomer, P. L., & Barenbaum, E. M. (1991). The written composing ability of children with learning disabilities: A review of the literature from 1980–1990. *Journal of Learning Disabilities, 24*, 578–593.

Ninio, A., & Bruner, J. (1978). The achievement and antecedent of labeling. *Journal of Child Language, 5*, 1–14.

Norbury, C. F., & Bishop, D. V. M. (2003). Narrative skills of children with communication impairments. *International Journal of Communication Disorders, 38*, 287–313.

Norris, J. A., & Hoffman, P. R. (1990). Language intervention within naturalistic environments. *Language, Speech, and Hearing in Schools, 21*, 72–84.

Numeroff, L. (1985). *If you give a mouse a cookie.* New York: Harper Row.

Pappas, C. (1991). Young children's learning the "book language" of information books. *Discourse Processes, 14*, 203–225.

Paris, A. H., & Paris, S. G. (2003). Assessing narrative comprehension in young children. *Reading Research Quarterly, 38*, 36–76.

Paul, D., Blosser, J., & Jakubowitz, M. D. (2006). Principles and challenges to forming successful literacy partnerships. *Topics in Language Disorders, 26*, 5–23.

Paul, R., Hernandez, R., Taylor, L., & Johnson, K. (1996). Narrative development in late talkers: Early school age. *Journal of Speech and Hearing Research, 39*, 1295–1303.

Paul, R., & Smith, R. (1993). Narrative skills in four year olds with normal, impaired, and late-developing language. *Journal of Speech and Hearing Research, 36*, 592–598.

Peña, E. D., & Quinn, R. (2003). Developing effective collaboration teams in speech–language pathology: A case study. *Communication Disorders Quarterly, 24,* 53–63.

Peterson, C. (1990). The who, when, and where of early narratives. *Journal of Child Language, 17,* 433–455.

Peterson, C., Jesso, B., & McCabe, A. (1999). Encouraging narratives in preschoolers: An intervention study. *Journal of Child Language, 26,* 49–67.

Price, J. R., Roberts, J. E., & Jackson, S. C. (2006). Structural development of the fictional narratives of African American preschoolers. *Language, Speech, and Hearing Services in Schools, 37,* 178–190.

Pritchard, R. (1990). The effects of cultural schemata on reading processing strategies. *Reading Research Quarterly, 25,* 273–295.

Reese, E., Haden, C., & Fivush, R. (1993). Mother–child conversations about the past: Relationships of style and memory over time. *Cognitive Development, 8,* 381–405.

Riley, L. (1997). *Mouse mess.* New York: Blue Sky Press.

Rius, M., & Parramon, J. M. (1992). *The four elements: Fire.* Athens: Kedros.

Rogoff, B., & Mistry, J. (1990). The social and functional context of children's remembering. In R. Fivush & J. Hudson (Eds.), *Knowing and remembering in young children* (pp. 197–222). New York: Cambridge University Press.

Roth, F. P. (2000). Narrative writing: Development and teaching with children with writing disorders. *Topics in Language Disorders, 20,* 15–28.

Roth, F. P., Speece, D. L., & Cooper, D. H. (2002). A longitudinal analysis of the connection between oral language and early reading. *Journal of Educational Research, 95,* 259–272.

Roth, F. P., Speece, D. L., Cooper, D. H., & De La Paz, S. (1996). Unresolved mysteries: How do metalinguistic and narrative skills connect with early reading? *Journal of Special Education, 30,* 257–277.

Roth, F. P., & Spekman, N. J. (1986). Narrative discourse: Spontaneously generated stories of learning-disabled and normally achieving students. *Journal of Speech and Hearing Disorders, 51,* 8–23.

Roth, F. P., Spekman, N. J., & Fye, E. C. (1995). Reference cohesion in the oral narratives of students with learning disabilities and normally achieving children. *Learning Disability Quarterly, 18,* 25–40.

Roth, F. P., & Troia, G. A. (2006). Collaborative efforts to promote emergent literacy and efficient word recognition skills. *Topics in Language Disorders, 26,* 24–41.

Sachs, J. (1983). Talking about the there and then: The emergence of displaced reference in parent–child discourse. In K. E. Nelson (Ed.), *Children's language* (Vol. 4, pp. 1–28). Hillsdale, NJ: Erlbaum.

Sénéchal, M., LeFevre, J., Thomas, E. M., & Daley, K. E. (1998). Differential effects of home literacy experiences on the development of oral and written language. *Reading Research Quarterly, 33,* 96–116.

Silliman, E. R., Ford, C. S., Beasman, J., & Evans, D. (1999). An inclusion model for children with language learning disabilities: Building classroom partnerships. *Topics in Language Disorders, 19*, 1–18.

Silva, M. J., & McCabe, A. (1996). Vignettes of the continuous family ties: Some Latino American traditions. In A. McCabe (Ed.), *Chameleon readers: Teaching children to appreciate all kinds of good stories* (pp. 116–136). New York: McGraw-Hill.

Snow, C. E. (1983). Literacy and language: Relationships during the preschool years. *Harvard Educational Review, 53*, 165–189.

Snow, C., Burns, M. S., & Griffin, P. (1998). *Preventing reading difficulties in young children*. Washington, DC: National Academy Press.

Snow, C. E., & Ninio, A. (1986). The contracts of literacy: What children learn from learning to read books. In W. H. Teale & E. Sulzby (Eds.), *Emergent literacy: Writing and reading* (pp. 116–138). Norwood, NJ: Ablex.

Snow, C. E., Tabors, P. O., & Dickinson, D. K. (2001). Language development in the preschool years. In D. K. Dickinson & P. O. Tabors (Eds.), *Beginning literacy with language* (pp. 1–25). Baltimore: Brookes.

Sperry, L. L., & Sperry, D. E. (1996). Early development of narrative skills. *Cognitive Development, 11*, 443–465.

Stein, N. L. (1986). *The development of storytelling skills*. Paper presented at the Eleventh Annual Boston University Child Language Conference, Boston, MA.

Stein, N., & Glenn, C. (1979). An analysis of story comprehension in elementary school children. In R. Freedle (Ed.), *Directions in discourse processing* (pp. 53–120). Norwood, NJ: Ablex.

Sulzby, E., & Teale, W. (1991). Emergent literacy. In R. Barr, M. Kamil, P. B. Mosenthal, & P. D. Pearson (Eds.), *Handbook of reading research* (pp. 727–757). New York: Longman.

Sutton-Smith, B. (1986). The development of fictional narrative performance. *Topics in Language Disorders, 7*, 1–10.

Tabors, P. O., Beals, D. E., & Weizman, Z. O. (2001). "You know what oxygen is?": Learning new words at home. In D. K. Dickinson & P. O. Tabors (Eds.), *Beginning literacy and language* (pp. 93–110). Baltimore: Brookes.

Tabors, P. O., Snow, C. E., & Dickinson, D. K. (2001). Homes and schools together: Supporting language and literacy development. In D. K. Dickinson & P. O. Tabors (Eds.), *Beginning literacy with language* (pp. 313–334). Baltimore: Brookes.

Teale, W. H., & Sulzby, E. (1987). Literacy acquisition in early childhood: The roles of access and mediation in storybook reading. In D. A. Wagner (Ed.), *Future of literacy in a changing world* (pp. 111–130). Elmsford, NY: Pergamon.

Thomas, K. F. (1985). Early reading as social interaction. *Language Arts, 62*, 469–475.

Trabasso, T., Stein, N. L., Rodkin, P. C., Munger, M. P., & Baughn, C. R. (1992). Knowledge of goals and plans in the online narration of events. *Cognitive Development, 7*, 133–170.

Trousdale, A. M. (1990). Interactive storytelling: Scaffolding children's early narratives. *Language Arts, 67,* 165–173.

Vallecorsa, A. L., & Garriss, E. (1990). Story composition skills of middle-grade students with learning disabilities. *Exceptional Children, 57,* 48–54.

Van Dongen, R., & Westby, C. E. (1986). Building the narrative mode of thought through children's literature. *Topics in Language Disorders, 7,* 70–83.

Vygotsky, L. S. (1986). *Thought and language.* Cambridge, MA: MIT Press.

Wang, Q., & Leichtman, M. D. (2000). Same beginnings, different stories: A comparison of American and Chinese children's narratives. *Child Development, 71,* 1329–1346.

Wells, G. (1985). *Language development in the preschool years.* Cambridge, England: Cambridge University.

Wells, R. (1973). *Noisy Nora.* New York: Dial Press.

Westby, C. (1991). Learning to talk—talking to learn: Oral–literate language differences. In C. S. Simon (Ed.), *Communication skills and classroom success* (pp. 181–218). San Diego, CA: College Hill.

Westby, C., Maggart, Z., & Van Dongen, R. (1984, July). *Oral narratives of students varying in reading ability.* Paper presented at the International Child Language Congress, Austin, TX.

Whitehurst, G. J., Epstein, J. N., Angell, A. L., Payne, A. C., Crone, D. A., & Fischel, J. E. (1994). Outcomes of an emergent literacy intervention in Head Start. *Journal of Educational Psychology, 86,* 542–555.

Whitehurst, G. J., Falco, F. L., Lonigan, C. J., Fischel, J. E., DeBaryshe, C. L., Valdez-Menchaca, M. C., et al. (1988). Language development through picture books. *Developmental Psychology, 24,* 552–559.

CHAPTER SIX

Multiculturalism, Language, and Emergent Literacy

Dolores E. Battle

Literacy is a right for all Americans, including the typically developing, people living in urban/rural communities, individuals who are gifted and those with developmental delays, persons with severe disabilities, and the socioeconomically and culturally/linguistically diverse. Environmental factors, such as parenting, family income level, and the education of the mother play an important role in the development of literacy for all children. These factors often overshadow and challenge traditional literacy learning objectives, including literacy socialization, vocabulary development, and phonological awareness. For culturally and linguistically diverse children, other factors confound the process of learning to read and write (Rickford, 1999) beyond what is explainable by socioeconomic and racial/ethnic issues. Geneticists and neurobiologists are also raising questions about the role of genetics in the development of literacy, particularly as answers are sought to explain the process of emergent literacy among culturally and linguistically diverse children. This chapter explores the relationship between emergent literacy and cultural and linguistic diversity. It attempts to answer several questions, such as What roles do culture and language play in the development of literacy? What are the major sources of variation in children's exposure to social, intellectual, and material resources that are directly related to emergent literacy and language development? How important are genetics in the development of literacy? What are the appropriate assessment and intervention programs for culturally and linguistically diverse children?

There are a number of children in America who have difficulty learning to read. This chapter shows that children from low-income homes perform less well in the development of literacy than those from middle- and upper-income households. In the United States, there is a disproportionate representation of persons from certain racial and ethnic minority groups in low-income households. Therefore, it is easy to conclude that there is a higher degree of difficulty in learning to read among those from racial and ethnic minority groups. However, most research does not disaggregate the factors that contribute to literacy development, particularly among racial and ethnic minority groups. This chapter also seeks to separate language, literacy, race, and culture in the attempt to reach an understanding of the relative impact of each factor on emergent literacy.

In any discussion of emergent literacy, language, and culture it is important to ensure that the characteristics of the child are considered. Emergent literacy in culturally and linguistically diverse children must also consider that the children have speech, language, and hearing abilities within the normal range. Speech, language, or hearing impairment will most likely increase the complexity of emergent literacy related to cultural and linguistic diversity. Thus, it is important to ensure that the children with cultural and linguistic diversity be articulate and competent in the language of their home and community. The discussion of emergent literacy in culturally and linguistically diverse children in this chapter continues with this general assumption.

Defining Culture

What is culture? "Culture is a framework that guides and bounds life practices" (Lynch & Hanson, 2004, p. 4). It is a combination of knowledge, experiences, values, beliefs, and attitudes that affects the behaviors of individuals in social contexts. Culture is an organizing construct, not a prescription for categorizing people, individuals, or groups. Just as all families, children, and individuals are unique, no classification of ethnic, racial, or language descriptors can fully define or describe individuals. An understanding of cultural and linguistic differences should enhance our understanding of individuals rather than form or reinforce stereotypes of groups identified by race and ethnicity.

One's culture is continually evolving as it is influenced by new information, new experiences, and new interactions. Children are socialized or taught within a social context such that particular acts have particular meaning and certain behaviors are appropriate and others are not. These behaviors are governed by many factors including, but not limited to, socioeconomic status, gender, age, length of residence in a community, acculturation, assimilation, languages spoken, and education of the family members, especially that of the mother. Culture influences how parents rear their children; what parents understand about their role in the education and development of their children; and how their children present themselves, understand the world, and interpret experiences. Culture affects people's shared understandings about what children need to know, how they learn, and how best to teach them. It is the prism through which all experiences are filtered. It affects the experiences through which children's earliest knowledge about literacy and numbers are acquired.

Connecting Culture and Emergent Literacy

Emergent literacy is a social practice that is closely related to social constructs including variables such as the family's socioeconomic status, social and political relations, beliefs, and relationships to the environment (Delgado-Gaitan, 1990, 1994). Important variables in emergent literacy are the cultural values related to education and literacy. The cultural values of a family will influence family literacy practices, such as the types of reading material found in the home, the emphasis placed on the importance of reading, and the types of reading activities. Family literacy practices, in turn, are related to income level and the education of the parents, especially the mother. It is important to look at parenting behaviors to understand the ways that they impact the literacy development of culturally and linguistically diverse children.

It is also important then to define the meaning of "family" as it is used in this chapter. The "family" includes any form of what naturally occurs in the child's home, whether it be one generation, multiple generational, or intergenerational, and includes whomever provides "parenting" in the home without concern for the biology, except in the discussion of the influence of genetics on emergent literacy.

Parenting and the Development of Literacy

Parents' attitudes and beliefs about early learning have an effect on their children's literacy development. Literacy and numeracy interactions in the home directly reflect parents' views about how children learn to read, write, use numbers, and acquire other competencies. Parents have "theories" about their role in the development of literacy and learning before children enter school. Their beliefs manifest themselves in their behavior at home and the expectations of teachers. The nature and extent of parent–child interactions that support learning and literacy and social conventions affect the ways knowledge and skills pertinent to early learning are communicated among and used by family members. If parents believe that literacy development is a school activity, they may not engage in emergent literacy activities with their preschool children. If they believe that it is their role to prepare the children for school, they may provide emergent literacy activities for the children at an early age.

Parenting encompasses a host of activities used in rearing children. The Home Observation Measurement Environment (HOME) Inventory (Linver, Brooks-Gunn, & Cabrera, 2004) includes several items that focus on the foundation of literacy in the home environment. The HOME inventory includes seven categories of parenting behavior: (1) nurturing or expressing love, affection, and care; (2) disciplining or responding to inappropriate behavior; (3) teaching or conveying information or skills to the child; (4) teaching language; (5) providing literacy materials; (6) monitoring development; and (7) managing home-life activities. Of these categories, teaching language, providing literacy materials, monitoring development, and managing home-life activities have been shown to have the greatest impact on literacy.

The *teaching language* section of the HOME inventory focuses on the availability of books for children in the home; whether the family buys and reads the newspaper and whether the child has two or more books of his or her own. The *providing literacy materials* section focuses on whether there are materials other than books in the home that are indicative of literacy, including educational toys and other resources for learning numbers, the alphabet, and learning to draw, as well as other materials that are cognitively and linguistically stimulating. The *monitoring development* section focuses on whether the parents engage in activities that enhance the child's development, such as providing language-enriching activities (e.g., trips to the zoo and involvement in play groups or library reading groups). The *managing home-life activities* section of the inventory refers to the rhythm of the household, including bedtime routines with story reading, family mealtime, and the importance of television as family entertainment. The underlying premise is that children who are exposed to more books, reading, and educational materials at home, and whose parents engage them in educational activities, are likely to spend more time being read to by their parents than children who do not have these advantages.

A recent longitudinal study using the HOME inventory showed that after controlling for maternal education, maternal reading skills, and the child's gender, the HOME global measure of the home environment was the most consistent predictor of children's language and literacy skills (Roberts, Jurgens, & Burchinal, 2005). The HOME inventory predicted receptive vocabulary at 3 years of age and at entry to kindergarten, and receptive and expressive language at 4 years of age and at entry to kindergarten. It also predicted early literacy skills at 4 years of age and at entry to kindergarten. The HOME global measure of overall responsiveness and support in the home environment contributed over and above the specific literacy practices in predicting children's early language and literacy skills. These results underscore the importance of considering the education of the mother and the general home environment in any study of emergent literacy.

Language and Culture

Just as children learn language within the culture of the home and family, the development of literacy is formed in a full array of cognitive, social, cultural, institutional, and historical contexts within the home (Gee, 2001). People from different cultures adopt different perspectives of "literacy" with different purposes and functions.

Thus, culture and ethnicity can be expected to influence literacy development.

Although there is much research on the importance of various factors in the development of literacy, it is not known whether the behaviors are causal or the result of other interacting variables. What can be safely said is that at least four factors influence literacy development, none of which can be isolated from the others regardless of cultural and linguistic differences. These factors are: (1) family social, educational, and economic conditions; (2) genetic similarities between parent and child; (3) child characteristics; and (4) other immeasurable characteristics.

Socioeconomics and Emergent Literacy

The culture of the home and family are of critical importance in the way a child develops literacy. Culture is the foundation for the skills, attitudes, and behaviors that the child brings to the task of learning to read and write. The family influences the development of language and literacy through a complex interaction of social, economic, and political forces within their community (García & Beltran, 2001). Children bring an individualized inventory of cultural and linguistic experiences from home to school for reading and writing instruction. Their experiences are continually embellished as they develop through the school years. Family support for literacy, especially opportunities for book reading and letter knowledge, is a predictor of later success in reading comprehension (Craig, Connor, & Washington, 2003).

Socioeconomic Effects on Emergent Literacy

Most studies of the development of literacy have focused on literacy development in White families that provided numerous opportunities for children to be exposed to reading materials (Westby, 1994). The works of Heath (1983) and Anderson-Yockel and Haynes (1994) underscore the differences in the importance of reading and writing in culturally different families. Heath's (1983) study of early literacy in the Piedmont Carolinas was among the earliest studies of the effects of cultural differences and income level on literacy development. Heath (1983) used a sample of Black families from Trackton and White families from Readville in the Piedmont Carolinas, including 13 high-income White professional families, 23 middle-income White working-class families, and six low-income African American families. The low-income families had fewer books to read, read less often to their children, placed less emphasis on literacy-related activities, and used a different style of interacting with their children during book-reading activities than the other families. According to Heath (1983), sociocultural practices are intractably intertwined with "ways" of talking, thinking, believing, knowing, acting, interacting, valuing, and feeling. These practices apply to both oral and printed words because the understanding and use of words and print are developed in and governed by their use in a sociocultural context.

Hart and Risley (1995) reported differences in literacy and book-reading practices in low- and middle-income families. They found that children in middle-income homes had 1,000 to 1,700 hours of one-on-one book reading at home prior to entering school, whereas children from low-income families had fewer than 25 hours of book reading, and often there were few books in the home other than the telephone book and a few magazines. There was also a significant difference by family income level in the vocabulary and amount of language directed at the children by their parents. In low-income families, parents directed an average of 616 words to their children ages birth to 3 years compared to an average of 1,251 words that parents of middle-income families directed to their children, a number that was nearly doubled in upper-income professional families, where parents directed an average of 2,153 words to their children. The trend continued in the preschool years, where parents in low-income families directed only an average of 1,840 words toward their children per hour and parents in middle-income families directed an average of more than 2,383 words per hour toward their children.

Coley (2002) reported similar results in a longitudinal study of family literacy practices for children entering kindergarten. In the study, 46% of all of the parents reported that they read to their children every day; however, there was a significant difference in the frequency of reading by the parents based on income level. Whereas 63% of parents from high income levels reported that they read to their children every day, only 36% of parents with low income levels reported reading to their children every day. Denton, Hasbrouck,

Weaver, and Riccio (2000) followed children through the second grade and found that children from upper-income levels who were read to at least three times a week by a family member were almost twice as likely to score in the top 25% of their class in reading as children from lower-income families who were read to fewer than three times a week. These patterns are consistent with other studies. For example, Lonigan et al. (1999) found that preschool children from middle-income households had significantly higher levels of skills across all print awareness tasks than children from low-income households.

Questionable Socioeconomic Effects on Emergent Literacy

The available research does not clearly support the notion that differences in literacy readiness are dependent on family income; in fact, not all low-income children show low achievement in emergent literacy. The Abecedarian Project in Piedmont, North Carolina (Feagans & Haskins, 1986; Vernon-Feagans, Emanuel, & Blood, 1997) replicated the work of Heath (1983) and found that low-income rural African American children had excellent oral language, including vocabulary and narrative skills, compared to middle-class White children. African American kindergarten males were more proficient at telling stories, had more words, and had better storytelling skills than White males or Black females. However, their storytelling scores were not related to school literacy and achievement and the skills did not transfer to the classroom. Others (e.g., Pelligrini, Perlmutter, Galda, & Brody, 1990) reported that when low-income mothers of children enrolled in a Head Start program used strategies similar to those of middle-class mothers during joint book reading, there was little difference in the achievement of the low-income children. (Roth, Chapter 5, this volume, also addresses cultural influences on narrative development.)

Walter (1994) observed a group of Native American preschool children in a Head Start program on a reservation for over a year. He observed that there were three levels of literacy engagement among the children. Twenty-two percent of the children had high literacy engagement, as evidenced by their attempts to read and their ability to tell and retell stories. Thirty-nine percent of the children showed little literacy engagement, as evidenced by their lack of interest in or ability to tell and retell stories. The remaining 39% comprised a mild-literacy engagement group that fell between the low- and high-literacy engagement groups. Although it was assumed that the children were homogeneous because they were all from the same tribe and lived on the same reservation, their home literacy experiences prepared them differently for the literacy expectations of school.

Explaining the Gap in Emergent Literacy Preparation

Although there are differences in the influence that the preschool classroom can have on the development of literacy among children from low-income homes, it is more often that the quality of the preschool program is also impacted by social and economic factors in the community. Children in low-income communities have fewer independent experiences with books than children from middle-income communities (Marvin & Miranda, 1993). The libraries have fewer resources to supplement the availability of literacy materials in the homes, and families may not have the ability to access the libraries. Schools in poorer neighborhoods may have more discipline problems, lower academic expectations, fewer instances of positive reinforcement, fewer resources in the classroom, and fewer opportunities to explore the world beyond the immediate community through field trips to zoos and museums, and fewer opportunities for other enriching activities.

Long-term poverty has a lasting effect on families, even after the parents have entered the middle class. Ladson-Billings (1999) reported for first-generation college-educated parents, the roots of their academic and economic success may not be as firmly established in their families as in families where education has a longer tradition. Because these parents may not have been socialized to support literacy activities in their own lives, they may limit the exposure to literacy activities and experiences for their children.

Despite the abundance of evidence that shows a relationship between family income and academic achievement in reading, there is limited evidence to show that the relationship is *causal*. A longitudinal study compared the achievement of children in families whose average income fell below the poverty level when the children were between birth and age 5 years with that of children in families whose average income stayed above the poverty level for the 5-year period (Brooks-Gunn, 2003; Smith, Brooks-Gunn, &

Klebanov, 1997). Control variables included the mother's education level, the child's birth weight, and family structure. The income level of the family accounted for only 0.30 standard deviation of the gap in achievement between the two groups of children. Fryer and Levitt (2004) reported that investigations of several socioeconomic status measures indicate that socioeconomic status can account for no more than half a standard deviation in Black–White achievement scores regardless of the assessments used or the population tested.

Parents from low-income families want their children to succeed in school and will respond to direction and guidance on how to improve literacy and preparation for reading by their young children when given the opportunity and resources. Morrow and Young (1997) focused on improving literacy achievement (reading and writing) by involving inner-city parents in a year-long family literacy program. The parents in the program valued literacy and expected achievement in their children. By involving the parents in the literacy program, the achievement level of their children increased. The teachers in the program had not previously realized how important parent involvement in the program was in working toward literacy development of children.

Race/Ethnicity and Literacy Practices

There is considerable data to support the notion that children from racial minority groups perform less well in reading when compared to majority groups. Much of the research has focused on the differences between African American children from low-income families and White children from middle-class families in emergent literacy in the preschool years (Burns, Griffin, & Snow, 1999; Byrd & Weitzman, 1994; Jencks & Phillips, 1998; Patterson, 1997). There has been no research on the relationship between ethnicity and race as disaggregated from socioeconomic factors such as income level and the factors previously discussed. There is a relationship between income level and reading achievement. There is also a relationship between income level and racial/ethnic diversity. These relationships do not mean, however, that there is a direct relationship between race/ethnicity and literacy levels. All reports of low achievement of racial/ethnic groups must be considered with these facts in mind.

Race/Ethnicity, Poverty, and Reading

According to the U.S. Census Bureau (2006), families with low incomes or living below the poverty level are more likely to be from racial/ethnic minority groups. While only 8.0% of White families live below the poverty level, 22.1% of African American families, 19.7% of Hispanic families of any race, and 9.0% of Asian American families live below the poverty level. Although race and ethnicity appear to be related to income level, most research does not separate the data; that is, when the report speaks of African Americans, information on interactions of family income levels with other cultural variables usually is not provided.

The report from the National Center for Education Statistics (NCES; 1999) on the National Assessment of Educational Progress (Lee, Grigg, & Donahue, 2007) provides average scores and achievement levels for children in grades 4 and 8 on reading assessment. According to the report, children from racial/ethnic minority families have lower scores on the assessment than children from nonminority families. The report also gives the achievement in reading for children who are eligible for free and reduced lunch according to the standards established by the National School Lunch Program (2004), which is based on family income level. As shown in Table 6.1, White children showed greater achievement in reading at grade 4 than Black, Hispanic, or Native American/Alaskan Native children. The report indicates that when the data are analyzed by race, all children made significant gains in reading over their achievement

TABLE 6.1. Average Scale Scores and Achievement Levels in NAEP Reading for Fourth-Grade Public School Students, by Race/Ethnicity: 2007

	National average score	% at or below basic	% at or above basic	% at or above proficient	% advanced
White	230	23	77	42	10
Black	203	54	46	14	2
Hispanic	204	51	49	17	3
Asian/Pacific Islander	231	24	76	45	14
Native American/ Alaskan Native	206	49	51	20	4

Note. Data from Lee, Grigg, and Donahue (2007, Table A-9).

TABLE 6.2. Average Scale Score and Achievement Level Results in NAEP Reading for Fourth-Grade Public School Students by Eligibility for Free/ Reduced School Lunch: 2007

	National average score	% at or below basic	% at or above basic	% at or above proficient	% advanced
Eligible for free/ reduced school lunch	205	50	50	17	2
Not eligible for free/reduced school lunch	232	21	79	44	12

Note. Data from Lee, Grigg, and Donahue (2007, Table A-11).

in 2005. However, children who were eligible for free or reduced lunch made no measurable gain since 2005, regardless of their ethnic group. As shown in Table 6.2, children eligible for free or reduced lunch achieved at a level below the national average with nearly 50% scoring at or below the basic level established for children in grade 4. The data in Tables 6.1 and 6.2 show that although the reading scores of racial/ethnic minority children improved from 2005, the reading scores of Hispanic and African American children consistently fall behind that of European American children. Children from Asian families consistently achieve at higher levels than their European American peers.

Home Literacy Experiences in Ethnic-Minority Families

Results from the School Readiness Survey of the National Household Education Survey Program (National Center for Education Statistics, 1999) reported on family involvement in home literacy activities between 1993 and 1999. Family members were asked to report whether they read to their children three or more times in a week, told them a story, taught them letters or numbers, or visited a library with them within the last month. There was little difference in the family reports. The percentages ranged from 39% for White families to 30% and 31% of the Hispanic and Black families, respectively. Different results were obtained, however, when children's actual school-readiness skills were assessed. School-readiness skills involving the ability to recognize all letters, count to 20 or higher, write one's name, and read or pretend to read storybooks were tracked for children between the ages of 3 to 5 years. At least 43% of the White children, 35% of the Black children, and 22% of the Hispanic children had at least three of the four skills.

Similar findings were reported by Hammer, Miccio, and Wagstaff (2003) in a study of the availability of reading materials in low-income Hispanic families, who often are learning English and may have a low level of education even in their home language. Low-income Hispanic families had fewer types of reading materials and fewer books in the home. They also read less frequently to their children than did the parents in the White families. In 46% of the low-income Hispanic families, parents read to their children every day, whereas parents in 64% of the White families read to their children every day. The Federal Interagency Forum on Child and Family Statistics (2005) also reported that in contrast to the middle-income families, the low-income Hispanic families did not press their children for achievement by taking children to the library or teaching colors, shapes, letter sounds, and numbers. They spent less time helping their children with homework and believed that children should not be given an opportunity to write, "scribble," or talk about books. Many believed their efforts to encourage young children to read or write before they entered school were inappropriate and could interfere with school learning. Families kept books outside the reach of children until they were 3 to 5 years of age, believing that children could not understand storybook content until age 5 years (Madding, 2002; Reese & Gallimore, 2000). According to Karrass, VanDeventer, and Braungart-Ricker (2003), while 67% of middle-class families report sharing books with infants under the age of 12 months, only 22% of Hispanic parents report sharing books with children under 12 months of age. As a result, there are reports that 60–70% of low-income children cannot recognize letter names at kindergarten entry (Goldenberg, 1989).

Turning to the effects of recent immigration, Auerbach's (1995) review of family literacy refutes statements that poor, minority, and immigrant families do not value or support literacy development. Many low-income new immigrant families see literacy and schooling as the key to changing their lives and preventing their children from having the difficulties they had. According to Auerbach (1995), Southeast Asian families view school rather than home as having a greater influence on student attitudes and abilities in literacy. Hispanic families also are very trusting of schools to educate and work in the best interest of their children. Similarly, African American, Asian American, and Native American parents desire a quality education for their children.

Literacy and Language Differences

If reading is a function of language, then it can be assumed that variation in language can play a role in the ability of children to read (Silliman, Bahr, Wilkinson, & Turner, 2002). The process of reading shares phonological, lexical, and morphological knowledge with oral language. Language dialects of English such as Black English (BE) or African American English (AAE) differ in phonological, morphological, lexical, and syntactic variables from Standard American English (SAE). However, the degree to which variations in language and dialect contribute to beginning reading and spelling has not been systematically explored.

African American Children and Literacy

The gap between the performances of African American children and White children (see Tables 6.1 and 6.2) is evident at entry to school and widens through grade 12 (Phillips, Crouse, & Ralph, 1998). Numerous reports show that African American students also perform significantly lower than White students in vocabulary, writing, science, math, and geography (e.g., Donahue, Voelkl, Campbell, & Mazzeo, 2001). There have been numerous attempts to explain this disparity, some of which related the disparity to differences in the language system used by African American children. Given that reading success is related to vocabulary development, phonological awareness, and letter–sound knowledge, it is hypothesized that because African American children use the sound system of AAE, they have difficulty matching their sound system to that of SAE, which is used in most emergent literacy programs. In the 1970s, it was believed that African American children should be taught to read using texts that were written using AAE, sparking the Ebonics discussion in the 1990s of the use of AAE in schools as a foundation for teaching reading (O'Malley, 1997). (See Hester and Hodson, Chapter 3, this volume, for a discussion of the relationship between phonological awareness and emergent literacy development.)

Some researchers (e.g., Manning & Baruth, 2000) attribute the low achievement of African American students in literacy and other academic areas to the influence of speaking AAE on language activities for literacy. They hypothesize that the use of AAE slows the development of the grammatical rules of SAE, which are necessary for reading and writing in the SAE that is necessary for school success. Craig, Thompson, Washington, and Potter (2003) stress the importance of understanding the phonology of AAE speakers because of its relationship to reading, particularly to phonological awareness and other phonological skills essential to early reading. Craig and Washington (2002) showed that students who were considered "low-density" AAE users out-performed "high-density" AAE users on standardized reading and vocabulary tests, thus lending support to the idea that the density of AAE use is related to literacy development. The density of AAE is also related to income level, social environment, and education of the family (Craig et al., 2003; Washington & Craig, 2000).

Recent research deemphasizes the connection between acquiring SAE and developing skills in print recognition in favor of the family literacy beliefs and values as primary factors in the reading competence of children in families (Adger, Wolfram, & Christian, 2007). Earlier research (Craig et al., 2003) showed that low-income African American children who were exposed to an enriched literacy program in the early school grades could reach and exceed the reading levels of more economically advantaged groups by the end of third grade. Thus, an enriched literacy preschool environment can mediate the effects of prior environments and family practices on literacy development. Craig and Washington (2006) showed, however, that the deficits may persist through fifth grade and beyond despite enriched early preschool experiences.

Attempts to identify predictors of later reading skills examined variables such as letter knowledge, phonological awareness, and family literacy practices (especially opportunities for storybook reading at home for African American children) (Bus, van IJzendoorn, & Pellegrini, 1995). Craig et al. (2003) and Hammer and Miccio (2001) cautioned, however, that there is little known about the development of phonological awareness in African American children, particularly because research typically has not disaggregated the African American children who used AAE from those who used SAE. Recent research has shown that dialect density measures based solely on the use of the phonological features of AAE explained few differences in phonological processing scores (Craig & Washington, 2006; Kohler et al., 2007). The research indicated that children with higher dialect densities produced more nonword spelling errors influenced by AAE, an effect most evident in grade 3. Heath (1983, 1989) suggested home literacy practices might differ for families in frequency and style as a function of income rather than race.

There has been a variety of attempts to explain the degree to which language variations impact on reading. For example, Labov (1970) discussed the cultural conflict hypothesis, which held that the difficulty that children who used nonmainstream dialects had in learning to read was because of the beliefs and values of their vernacular culture rather than in the linguistic aspects of their dialect. Recent hypotheses deemphasize the connections between dialect or language variation in learning to read, and attribute more of the discrepancy between speakers of dialect and SAE to cultural factors such as insufficient phonological awareness, insufficient knowledge of letter names, and insufficient knowledge of letter–sound correspondence (Adger et al., 2007; Delpit, 1998).

Phonological Awareness: Grapheme–Phoneme Association

Several theories attempt to explain the role of dialect variations in the development of the ability to read (Butler & Silliman, 2002; Terry, 2006). The general belief is that because children who use language variations or dialects other than SAE receive language input from SAE and their dialect, they must incorporate both systems into their phonological system. Dialect creates more variants, thus making the task of learning letter–sound relationships more difficult. In learning to read, children that use dialects other than SAE must learn all of the possible variations that SAE speakers use and then incorporate any phonological variations that interfere with their production or ability to read a word (Silliman et al., 2002). This speculation places a special burden on the children in accounting for the difficulty they have in developing literacy skills. The hypothesis is counter to the studies that essentially show that the spoken language development of African American children in the preschool years is virtually the same as that of children exposed to SAE (e.g., Steffensen, 1974). According to Stockman's (1996) extensive review of African American phonology, African American children who use

AAE dialect produce the same phonetic inventory as speakers of SAE dialects with few exceptions. The differences are primarily in the distribution of phonemes and frequency of phoneme use. There are fewer differences in the initial position of words, which are usually the focus of sound–letter relationships in early literacy, than in the medial and final positions.

If there is to be an answer to the question of the relationship between dialect variation and reading, perhaps it lies in the study of children learning a language other than English as a first language. If a child who has no literacy difficulty in the first language struggles with literacy in English, the difficulty may be related to phonological differences between the first and the second language. For example, grapheme–phoneme relationships in Spanish are regular; however, the relationships in English may be irregular, such as *sug/sugar*. In addition, graphemes in Spanish may have different representations such as *ball* versus *tortilla*, or *n* versus *ñ*. They thus have a more difficult task to form relationships between phonological systems and the critical distinctions necessary for letter–sound relationships.

Unfortunately, the theory has not been investigated in studies that controlled for the effects of income level, dialect usage, or other factors that were controlled. Silliman et al. (2002) reported that studies of phonological processing and other factors related to reading often do not consider dialect in their design. Only nine studies in 23 years included African American students along with some statement on their socioeconomic status. Others identified the families as African American or "inner city" with no other demographic characteristics; none of the studies addressed dialect issues either directly or indirectly.

Without systematic research on the relationship between dialect use and reading ability, it must be left that the reading difficulties of children who do not use SAE may be related to factors such as home literacy experiences, motivation to read, opportunities to analyze SAE as a written form, book-reading experiences, and other exposure to print (Silliman et al., 2002; Washington & Craig, 2000). Children who have no exposure to the excitement of reading books are apt to be unenthusiastic about learning to read and write, regardless of the dialect or language used. Those who experience reading failure are less likely to enjoy reading and will read less. Thus, they do not undertake the most important means of improving the ability to read; that is, reading more (Snow, Barnes, Chandler, Goodman, & Hemphill, 1991).

Bilingualism and Literacy

This country is becoming a nation where English is not the first language of an increasing number of residents. According to the 2000 U.S. Census, nearly 18% (21.5 million) of the population over the age of 5 years speaks a language other than English at home and 8% (21 million) speak English less than very well. Nearly 9 million children between the ages of 5 and 17 years speak English as a second language. Less than half of all students who are English language learners (ELLs) are foreign born. The majority of the ELL students were born in the United States and many are children of U.S.-born parents (Capps et al., 2005). One in every five children in the United States has an immigrant parent and 72% of children in immigrant families do not speak English at home. Twenty-six percent of the children of immigrants live in households where no one age 14 years or older speaks English very well (Capps et al., 2005).

Most ELLs have Spanish as their first language (79%), however, more than 400 other languages, including Haitian Creole, Arabic, Russian, French, German, Hindi, Vietnamese, Hmong, Chinese (Cantonese), Japanese, Korean, Tagalong (Philippines), and Navajo, are spoken by the remaining 21% of children in school. There are increasing numbers of children who use languages of the Middle East and Africa. Reportedly, 42% of teachers in the United States have at least one ELL student in their classroom (Moss & Puma, 1995); two-thirds of ELLs are from low-income families (Capps et al., 2005).

The No Child Left Behind Act of 2001 (Public Law 107-110; 2002) defines an English language learner (ELL) as a person ages 3 to 21 years who has a first, home, primary, or native language other than English; who either was not born in the United States; is a Native American or Native Alaskan; or comes from an environment where a language other than English has had a significant impact on the individual's level of English proficiency and whose difficulties in speaking, reading, writing, or understanding the English language may be sufficient to deny the individual the ability to successfully achieve in classrooms where English is the language of instruction. The primary challenge of ELL children is to acquire concepts and skills for literacy in a language they have not mastered orally. While some have mastered oral language in their first language, they must transfer those skills to a language that differs in vocabulary, sound system, and grammar.

Complex Relationships

In a study of language and literacy development of Puerto Rican Head Start children, 19% of the mothers reported using English only or more English than Spanish at home; 41% used both English only or more English than Spanish; and 34% used only Spanish at home (Hammer & Miccio, 2001; Hammer et al., 2003). The studies did not account for the relative English language use by the children who spoke a language in addition to English. According to the mothers, 41% of the children used English only or used more English than Spanish; 39% used equal amounts of Spanish and English; and 20% used Spanish only. The mothers reported that 53% of the children were simultaneous bilinguals (learning two languages simultaneously) and 47% sequential bilinguals (learning two languages sequentially) with considerable variation in the children's ability to comprehend and express themselves in English and/or Spanish. The findings indicted that there was a critical level of home literacy activity during the early school years that could result in improved literacy in young children learning English as a second language. The preliminary results illustrated the complexity of understanding the relationship between literacy and cultural and linguistic diversity. What is known is that literacy and language development are related. What is not known is the relationship between the development of languages other than English and literacy, and the effects of factors in the home environment where English is not the first language (e.g., maternal education and home support for literacy) that have been shown to influence literacy development in American families.

This complexity extends to Native American families as well. Nieto (1999) reported that home cultures and native languages get in the way of student learning, not because of the nature of the home cultures or native languages themselves, but because they do not conform to the way the schools define learning. Cleary and Peacock (1998) cited numerous differences between Native American and non-Native American worlds. For example, people from oral traditions, such as Native Americans, contextualize their articulation of thought, depend on shared knowledge, and do not necessarily articulate what others already know. Cultural conflict arises when children from the Native American homes function in settings with American cultural expectations.

The findings described here indicate that parents who speak a language other than English at home have little access to books and reading materials in English and cannot assist their children who are learning English for school tasks such as reading and writing. With the growing number of ELL children in the schools, there is increased interest in understanding literacy development among children for whom English is not their first language.

Literacy development is a complex multifaceted process that becomes more complex when the child's primary language differs from the language used in the school. The challenge of developing literacy in English is even greater for those learning English as a second or third language. ELL children may acquire literacy skills in English in a manner similar to mono-English children, dependent on their level of alphabetic knowledge, phonological awareness, and phonological processing skills in their first language. The challenges are different for those who are bilingual; that is, they have at least conversational ability in two or more languages. Their alphabetic knowledge may precede and actually facilitate the acquisition of phonological awareness in English (Chiappe, Siegel, & Gottardo, 2002).

According to Gutièrrez-Clellan (1999), children from different linguistic backgrounds who are learning English as a second language may face challenges that are independent of their familiarity with the written code of their first language. Some written codes, such as English, Spanish, and other western languages, are alphabetic such that a written letter matches a particular sound, which serves as a guide to word pronunciation. In contrast, codes such as Chinese, Japanese, or Korean are logographic, requiring the reader to associate the meaning of a specific logogram with its phonological form. Writing in these codes involves ideas and words or meanings. Reading fluency depends more on the frequency and, thus, familiarity of the logogram, than on its phonological component. Young children who are familiar with reading logograms may have a greater challenge in transferring to a system that is more alphabetic than do children who are transferring from one alphabetic system to another. However, older children who have developed phonological awareness in their first language can transfer the skills to the second language with little difficulty. It appears to be an easier task, however, when the grapheme–phoneme relationship between the languages is predictable and transparent, as between English and Spanish or Italian than when the relationship is less apparent, as between English and Arabic, Chinese, or Japanese.

In addition to differences in the written code, the phonology of languages differs. According to the National Reading Panel (2000), children learning English must be able to distinguish between the phonemes of English. ELLs also must be able to match sounds to letters and letter combinations. When the sound systems of the first language (L1) and the second language (L2) differ, children may have difficulty distinguishing between the sounds of the two systems, making the process of decoding the sound system more challenging. For example, speakers of Japanese may have difficulty distinguishing between /l/ and /r/; /v/ and /b/ may be indistinguishable to Spanish speakers. Another consideration in decoding words in a language is the degree of transparency of the code. Spanish and Italian, for example, are highly transparent; that is, there is a close letter–sound correspondence so that a child can readily decode unfamiliar words. In opaque languages, such as English, the letter–sound correspondence is not always direct, making it more challenging for children in decoding written words. However, cross-language transfer has been found for children ages 9 to 12 years with well-developed phonological awareness abilities in their L1 even when the languages differ in orthographies, such as English and Arabic (Abu-Rabia & Siegel, 2002). The grapheme–phoneme conversions are more difficult because of the number of irregularities in pronunciations. For example, in English, words such as *meet* and *meat* are pronounced the same. Words such as *Christmas* and *choose* appear to have the same initial sound and the same final sounds, but do not. Children using decoding skills will have difficulty when they apply regular decoding rules to words with irregularities.

Other Influential Variables

Not only must the children distinguish the sound systems, they also must have a basic vocabulary and understand the multiple meanings of words and homophones (such as *to, too,* and *two*), and differences in syntax and discourse styles. They must accomplish this all within a context of rapidly produced speech and in a context that may be unfamiliar. In addition, persons who are learning English as a second language have cultural experiences that affect their adjustment to American classrooms and teacher–student relationships. They must bring these challenges to developing literacy in a context where they may also be learning spoken English while adjusting to a new environment, a new lifestyle, and different expectations of school.

Educational researchers generally agree that the child's primary language should play a role in literacy development of ELLs. When a child's home language differs from the language that is used in school to teach literacy, the likelihood of reading difficulty increases for the child, particularly if reading instruction begins before the child has acquired oral proficiency in English (August & Hakuta, 1997; Fillmore & Snow, 2000; Fitzgerald, García, Jiménez, & Barrera, 2000; Gersten & Baker, 2000; Goldenberg, 2001; Strickland, 2001; Tharp, 1997). The problem is compounded when the children are from lower-income families in poorer neighborhoods. The compounding of the negative factors makes the task of having language experiences that enrich literacy an even greater challenge.

Research related to the reading achievement of children who are bilingual or ELLs is inconclusive because of the many compounding circumstances such as the level of language competence in English, instruction in literacy in the first language, and other social and cultural factors that influence the ability to read. Studies of older children with literacy skills in their first language of Arabic (Abu-Rabia & Siegel, 2002), Turkish (Durgunoglu & Oney, 1999), Italian (D'Angiulli, Siegel, & Serra, 2001), Cantonese (Gottardo, Yan, Siegel, & Wade-Wolley, 2001), Hebrew (Geva & Siegel, 2000), Spanish (Denton et al., 2000), and Portuguese (Dafontoura & Siegel, 1995) suggest that bilingualism does not negatively affect beginning reading development in either language if a child has acquired phonological awareness and an understanding of reading in L1 and oral language proficiency in L2. To the contrary, bilingualism may enhance the child's ability to develop literacy in L2 because of transferable skills. However, if a child has difficulty with or has not acquired phonological processing and awareness skills in L1, it will be more difficult to close the gap in literacy skills between the child and monolingual English learners or those ELLs with a strong basis in L1.

Slavin and Cheung (2003) conducted an evidence-based meta-analysis of effective reading programs for ELLs. They reported that although the number of high-quality studies is small, the evidence does support bilingual reading approaches that teach reading in the native language and English at the same time. They reported that whether taught in English or the native language, ELLs have been found to benefit from direct systematic instruction in phonics in small-group tutorial programs.

Levels of Proficiency

The theory of Cummins regarding the level of proficiency in the primary language that is necessary for a child to be successful in language-based academic tasks is well published (Cummins, 1984, 1991, 1992; Cummins & McNeely, 1987). According to Cummins (2000), knowledge of two types of language proficiency or registers is important to understanding the language needs of ELLs. Basic interpersonal communication skills (BICS) include social skills used to communicate with peers and other native speakers in conversations or social situations. Cognitive academic language proficiency (CALP) or academic register refers to skills that are necessary for the child to handle the language and cognitive demands of the academic environment. According to the theory, it takes a normally developing second-language learner approximately 2 years after immersion in L2 to develop proficiency in the social or conversational register. ELLs are able to use cues in a context-embedded learning environment that is enriched with pictures and other present visual and oral cues to comprehend and express themselves in social situations. However, it is believed that it will take approximately 5 to 7 years to develop the CALP sufficient to be successful in academic tasks with a high cognitive demand in context-reduced environments where cues are less available to aid comprehension.

According to the theory, it is essential that students developing literacy in their L2 continue to develop L1 while developing the skills necessary for success in L2, and this may take several years. It is also important to embed literacy instruction in contexts with low cognitive demands until the child has sufficient language skills in L2 to handle literacy tasks in context-reduced cognitively demanding environments. Cummins (2000) advanced the theory of the differences between social and academic language demands as a guard against moving children from language supports in bilingual education before they have developed proficiency in academic language skills necessary to support comprehension and expression in English. The supports may be necessary through middle school and beyond as the linguistic demands of the curriculum increase. The recent findings of August, Shanahan, and Shanahan (2006) indicate that ELLs at the elementary and secondary levels who receive instruction in their L1 perform better on English reading measures than children instructed only in English. August et al. (2006) reported, "there is no basis in research findings to suggest that bilingual programs are in any way disadvantageous to English academic outcomes" (p. 639).

Summary

The National Literacy Panel on Language-Minority Children and Youth (August et al., 2006) reviewed the quantitative and qualitative research on literacy development of language-minority children. The panel concluded that oral proficiency in English is linked to English reading comprehension skills. The evidence suggested that English vocabulary knowledge, listening comprehension, syntactic skills, and the ability to handle the metalinguistic aspects of language, such as providing definitions of words, are linked to English reading and writing proficiency. The panel also concluded that successful literacy instruction must incorporate extensive oral language skills; programs that focus only on reading are insufficient to result in academic achievement in school.

Although additional research is needed on literacy development in language-minority children, the literature generally supports the following conclusions:

1. Gaps in reading comprehension between English- and Spanish-speaking children are associated with gaps in vocabulary knowledge (Tabors & Snow, 2001). Teaching word analysis

and explicit vocabulary can lead to significant gains in reading. To increase success in reading, children should encounter new words in meaningful texts in L1. Introduction of new words in multiple contexts builds a fuller understanding of word meanings, multiple meanings, and better reading comprehension (Hess & Halloway, 1984; Snow, Burns, & Griffin, 1998).

2. Many children who learn English as a second language are taught to read in L2 (English) when they are in the initial stages of learning oral English. Initiating reading instruction in L1 reduces the risk of reading problems for students facing the additional challenge of learning to read in a second language (Snow et al., 1998).

3. Teaching a child who is learning English as a second language to read in L1 while learning L2 increases the possibility of producing a student who is biliterate; that is, has the ability to read in both languages.

4. Children whose first language is Spanish are at risk for poor literacy outcomes in the United States. They are twice as likely as non-Hispanic Whites to read below grade level (Snow et al., 1998).

5. ELLs can benefit from reading instruction focused on four components—phonemic awareness, reading fluency, vocabulary, and reading comprehension—if instruction is adjusted to meet the student's specific needs. However, programs that do not also include support for English language development, including speaking, reading, listening, and writing, are insufficient to support the student's academic success (Callahan, 2006). If children receive effective instruction with appropriate scaffolding in language, they are able to master early reading skills in English.

6. ELL students who are instructed in their L1, in addition to English at both the elementary and secondary levels, perform better on English reading measures than students instructed only in English. Instruction must include development of oral language skills in addition to reading or written language skills.

McCardle (2001), in collaboration with Hammer and Miccio (2001) and Hammer et al. (2003) have been engaged in a multi-year project sponsored by the National Institute of Child Health and Human Development and the U.S. Department of Education's Office of Educational Research and Improvement to address three unanswered questions related to bilingual children and the development of literacy:

1. How do children whose first language is Spanish learn to read and write in English?
2. Why do some Spanish-speaking children have difficulties acquiring English-language reading and writing skills?
3. For children whose first language is Spanish, which instructional approaches and strategies are most beneficial at which stages for reading and writing development and under what conditions?

The hope is that the study will shed light not only on how Spanish-speaking children develop literacy in English, but more broadly, on how children with linguistic and cultural backgrounds that differ from that of mainstream American schools develop literacy in English for success in school.

Genetics and Literacy

Is it *all* about culture? Do biology and genetics play a role in shaping literacy? In this chapter it has been shown that literacy development has a strong relationship to sociocultural and socioeconomic factors including family income level, family education level (especially the mother), and other language and linguistic factors. Which of these factors can be attributed to genetics?

The Human Genome Project (2009) has attempted to decipher the more than 3 billion units of DNA that make up human beings. Recent research attempting to find the gene that regulates language has found that genes play a causal role in the development of neural brain activity that underlies speech and language. Recent study of a family with a history of speech–language disorders has lead to the identification of *FOXP2* as the gene that has some relationship to the evolutionary origins of speech and language (Bishop, 2002; Fisher, 2007). Recent advances in understanding the genetics of reading and spelling (Gërd, 2001; Wagner, 2005) indicate that reading and spelling are complex behaviors strongly influenced by genetic factors. There is some evidence that a single gene, such as

FOXP2, may be responsible for language/learning both for language and reading. However, the role of influences in the environment, such as shared reading and book sharing, also should be considered significant in the development of reading and spelling (van Kleeck, 2006). (See Vander Woude, van Kleeck, & vander Veen, Chapter 2, this volume, on book sharing and the development of meaning.) Given the rapid expansion of research into the genetic influences in both language and reading, the answers to the questions about this relationship will open more doors and raise more questions in the future.

The relationship between literacy development and the competency in literacy of members of the family, especially the mother, has been shown in this chapter. What has not been shown is whether the education of the family members is related to a genetic disposition or to environmental effects that persist over generations.

A recent study of behavioral genetics attempts to separate genetic effects from environmental effects in literacy and language. Gilger (1995) reported that chromosome 3 is linked to reading and cognition; chromosome 7 is linked to grammar and the effect on single-word reading, phonological awareness, sight vocabulary, rapid naming, intelligence quotient, and language-related skills, such as reading. Chromosome 15 is related to reading. Although the genetic structures have been identified, research also shows that the genes related to language and reading interact with other genes and the environment to form and operate the systems required for human behavior (Gilger, 1995). Based on indirect evidence from recent research, it is believed that the human genome might hold some answers to the relationship between language and reading. Recent research confirms the discovery of specific genetic changes that appear sufficient to derail speech and language development. According to Fisher (2007), researchers are already using information from genetic studies to aid early diagnosis and to shed light on the neural pathways that are perturbed in these inherited forms of speech and language disorder.

Attempts have been made to relate difficulty in literacy to genetic differences between racial groups. According to Wagner (2005), 50% or more in most language areas including reading is attributable to genetic variation. However, *none* of the traits related to literacy development within racial and ethnic groups have a heritability of

100% or 1.0. The environment also makes a contribution. Risk is a problematic statement that refers to chance and varies as a function of both environmental and genetic factors. If a child is genetically predisposed to having difficulty with literacy, and if negative environmental factors are added to genetic factors, the risk of having a reading disorder may increase. Family risk studies (e.g., Dickens, 2005) have shown that there is a 5–10% risk of a reading disorder in the general population. The risk increases to 20–60% if a first-degree relative has a history of reading difficulty. If a parent has a reading disorder, the risk increases that the child will have a reading disorder. Males are five times more likely to have a reading disorder when there is at least one parent with a reading disorder. Females are four times more likely to have reading difficulty when there is one parent with a reading disorder. Despite the apparent relationship between genetics and reading disorders, environmental factors such as parenting, exposure to print and reading resources, and family literacy practices explain *most*, if not all of the differences between racial/ethnic groups in literacy development (Dickens, 2005). Research into the role that genetics plays in the development of language and reading will influence our thinking for many years to come.

Assessment of Language and Literacy in Culturally and Linguistically Diverse Children

The Individuals with Disabilities Education Improvement Act of 2004 (IDEA) requires that the assessment of children who are ELLs be provided in their native language to the extent feasible or with language accommodations. The No Child Left Behind Act of 2001 (U.S. Department of Education, 2002) mandates that assessment methods and materials used with culturally and linguistically different children be nonbiased and nondiscriminatory. This is to ensure that the underlying language ability of the child is appropriate for the development of literacy. Because the assessment of language and emergent literacy must be nonbiased, the assessment process must not rely on standardized or normative measures because of their inherent bias against culturally and linguistically different children (Wyatt, 2002).

Preevaluation and Nonstandardized Assessments

The assessment of emergent literacy in young ELLs must include a preevaluation process, as well as nonstandardized assessment. The preevaluation process is intended to develop a thorough understanding of the language and literacy history of the child, usually obtained from information provided by the parent or person with knowledge of the child's background. The language history should include information such as the language used by the family in addressing the child, the language of the home, and the opportunities that the child has had to be exposed to other languages. Given the importance of the home environment for emergent literacy development, the language history must include questions about the parents' involvement in literacy activities with the child such as the availability of books in the home; book-reading practices; storytelling experiences and expectations; beliefs and practices related to teaching the alphabet, numbers, and words; and visits to the library.

The speech–language pathologist (SLP) and other professionals involved in literacy assessment must have knowledge of *dynamic assessment techniques* and how to reduce bias when assessing the reading and writing abilities of students, including those with cultural and linguistic differences, emotional or behavioral issues, cognitive limitations, severe physical impairments, or multiple disabilities. Every effort should be made to eliminate any effects of dialectal, linguistic, or cultural factors on the assessment of the child's language and literacy status. Assessment must include an analysis of the family's role in literacy development, the language of the home, access to literacy materials at home, and home literacy practices that influence literacy development.

ELL Assessment

The assessment of emergent literacy in ELLs must not only address the cultural issues, but must also include an assessment of phonemic awareness and other phonological skills. Standardized assessments in languages other than English are not readily available. Caution must be used in any attempt to use assessments standardized on the development of phonological awareness in English when assessing phonological awareness in a language other than English.

Peinado (2001) investigated the effects of eight variables on the reading achievement of 68 first-grade ELLs from Spanish-speaking homes. The variables included intelligence level, oral language skills, initial early literacy skills, initial reading skills, the method used by the teacher to teach reading, family income, education of the parents, and the occupation of the parents. The results indicated that the educational variables accounted for 64% of the variance in predicting reading achievement in English. Family variables accounted for 30% of the variance and student variables accounted for 35% of the variance. Peinado (2001) concluded that, for first-grade ELLs, educational variables were most important in predicting later reading achievement in English; family and child variables were equally important in the assessment of reading achievement.

Phonological awareness appears to be the best indicator of later reading skills among ELLs (Licata, 2002; Smith, 2005), as is the case for monolingual children. The Dynamic Indicators of Basic Early Literacy Skills (DIBELS) (Kaminski & Cummings, 2007; Kaminski & Good, 1996, 1998) has been used to measure knowledge of letter names and sounds and the ability to identify phonemes in Spanish-speaking children who are learning to read. Smith (2005) evaluated alliteration identification and the relative contributions of phonemic awareness and syllabic awareness in predicting early literacy skills. The results indicated that phonological awareness in children who spoke Spanish was a predictor of later success in reading. Phonological awareness appeared to be a stronger predictor of success than syllabic awareness for young ELLs. Phonological awareness, as a basic skill, should be assessed in both English and Spanish.

Oral language proficiency in English appears to be a poor predictor of subsequent ability to decode words, but does play an important role in discourse comprehension (Geva & Wade-Woolley, 2004). Licata (2002) monitored and contrasted the reading development of first-grade bilingual Spanish-speaking children and monolingual English-speaking children with the Nonsense Word Fluency and Curriculum-Based Measurement Reading components of the DIBELS. After phonological awareness remediation, the groups were not significantly different in the rate at which the children learned to read nonsense words or the curriculum-based words and both appeared to read equally well. Thus, the recent research indicates that there is no need to wait until a child has good oral language proficiency before teaching reading. Reading instruction with ELLs can begin by focusing on phonological skills while building oral language proficiency.

ELL Intervention

Intervention strategies for supporting emerging literacy development with children who are not considered ELLs are discussed elsewhere in this volume (see Chapters 1 through 5). Intervention strategies for children from culturally and linguistically different families have the added dimension of the complexities of learning to read according to the expectations of mainstream cultures while being reared in a family that may have cultural values and language use that differ from the mainstream. Intervention for culturally and linguistically diverse children and adolescents must also be culturally appropriate, nonbiased, and culturally sensitive to the needs of the children and their families (American Speech—Language–Hearing Association, 2001; Gutièrrez-Clellan, 1999). Otherwise, the intervention may be perceived as patronizing, demeaning, or unintentionally alienating, resulting in implicit or explicit rejection (van Kleeck, 2006).

Some General Principles

Several researchers have developed principles from successful prevention and intervention programs with culturally and linguistically diverse children. (Duffy-Hester, 1999; Pikulski, 1994; Snow et al., 1998; van Kleeck, 2006; Wasik, 1998). Based on a review of several successful programs, the researchers drew the following conclusions:

1. Intensive, systematic early intervention is preferable to extended remediation.
2. A systematic program of home support is essential. Family culture, beliefs, and practices must be considered in any intervention effort. Intervention should involve the parents where they are, and with consideration of their literacy level. Parents must be given opportunities to interact with their children in the development of literacy through joint interactions with print, picture books, or

other emergent literacy activities to strengthen family literacy in the social context.

3. Children considered at risk require more time than do others. They require multiple and redundant exposures to text material to establish a firm basis for comprehension and vocabulary development.

4. ELLs should be given twice the time devoted to beginning literacy because many of them must learn to read English at the same time they are still learning oral English.

5. Students must be given culturally appropriate materials they can handle successfully and that are relevant to their homes and communities. Reading materials should relate to the experiences that the child and family have had while expanding their exposure to new, but appropriate areas that will be encountered in school. Building on what the children and families know helps them relate the reading material to their lives.

6. ELLs should be taught using a systematic phonics and phonological awareness approach with emphasis on the sound–symbol relationships in English, especially where they contrast with the relationships of their first language.

7. Children should be given print materials to share with their parents, such as worksheets, picture stories, and other messages to involve the parents in the literacy development of the children.

8. Children should be encouraged to involve their parents in story reading and storytelling at the level appropriate for the parents. Using books without words encourages children to engage the parents in book sharing regardless of the literacy level or language of the parents.

9. Attention must be given to providing enriched language learning experiences that allow the children to relate the content and context in text to their reality.

10. Individual progress must be monitored in a regular, ongoing basis to ensure that skills are emerging in an efficient manner to foster development.

11. Professionals (e.g., educators and SLPs) must continually develop their understanding of the cultural and language systems of the family so they can foster literacy development in all children who bring to the learning situation their individual and unique selves.

Selecting the Language of Instruction

According to the Five Standards for Excellence in pedagogy developed by the Center for Research on Education, Diversity, and Excellence (CREDE; 2002; Dalton, 1998), the primary language use is essential and must be included in the literacy instruction for all ELLs. Native language or primary language use supports literacy development. Educators must recognize the value of initial instruction in the native or home language and acknowledge that education in the official language and the home language are not mutually exclusive. Cummins (1981) stressed the principle that literacy instruction for ELLs must begin with L1 instead of L2.

There is much research to support the notion that extensive use of L1 throughout the elementary grades will increase the student's English reading performance and lead to greater academic success (Ramirez, Pasta, Yuen, Billings, & Ramey, 1991). Children must continue using L1 while they learn English to develop their natural language and to continue cognitive growth. The use of L1 to teach higher-order thinking and introduce new complex concepts will foster the child's continued concept development while learning English. Teachers should point out differences between L1 and L2 while the child is learning L2. In this way the child's academic and cognitive development will continue while the child is developing L2 (Gersten & Baker, 2000). There is need for research with sufficient controls to support current views of literacy development in ELLs.

The challenges in providing oral language and reading instruction to ELLs increase when the SLP and the classroom teacher do not speak the language of the child or the family. Kohnert (2008) provides suggestions for facilitating the language development in L2 in the academic environment. It is important for the SLP and the classroom teacher to collaborate to assist the ELL child to develop comprehension of the language of instruction and social interaction in the classroom. She suggests that making attempts to increase the acoustic saliency of teacher talk during instructional time using such devices as sound field systems, preferential seating, and other strategies to improve the acoustic environment for the child. Assigning a peer–partner could assist the child with classroom instructions and routines, such as "turn to page 56 in your history book." The SLP should collaborate with the classroom teacher to identify vocabulary used in instruction and classroom routines as well as vocabulary and expressions used in social conversations with peers. The goal is to facilitate the oral language skills of ELLs to function in the social environment of the classroom as well as develop the language skills necessary for academic success.

Conclusion

There is a considerable body of literature regarding literacy development of children from diverse cultural and linguistic backgrounds. Much of the literature indicates that students from diverse backgrounds do not achieve in reading as well as their majority peers; however, studies have not disaggregated the variables that may contribute to this discrepancy. The education of the mother, home environment, and home literacy practices are important factors in understanding the bases for the discrepancy. Collaboration among the family, the SLP and the classroom teacher is essential for the development of language and literacy in children from diverse cultural and linguistic backgrounds.

Assessment of the children's literacy development, just as assessment of oral language, must consider home, cultural, and linguistic variables. Intervention programs must address the underlying issues that contribute to literacy development so that programs can be designed to meet the individual needs of the children. Without these considerations, the reports will continue to identify discrepancies and entire groups will be denied their right to literacy education and their rightful place in society.

DISCUSSION QUESTIONS

1. Define culture. Explain how a child's cultural background can affect his or her emergent literacy development.
2. How could a family's socioeconomic status (SES) influence the emergent literacy development of the children in the family?
3. What explanations have been offered for the gap in literacy performance that has been shown to exist between African American children and White children when they enter school?
4. What is an English language learner (ELL)? What are important

considerations for early childhood professionals to make when assessing the emergent literacy development of ELL children?

EXERCISES

1. Generate a list of questions for early childhood professionals to use with families to obtain information on their home literacy practices. Explain the relevance of each question to emergent literacy assessment with children from culturally diverse backgrounds.

2. Describe three activities that early childhood professionals can incorporate within a classroom setting to facilitate the development of phonological awareness skills in English for a child who is an ELL.

3. Develop a guide for early childhood professionals on dynamic assessment of emergent literacy in children from culturally and linguistically diverse backgrounds.

4. Prepare a list of cultural factors to consider in emergent literacy assessment and intervention. Explain how each factor is considered in assessment and intervention.

References

Abu-Rabia, S., & Siegel, L. S. (2002). Reading, syntactic, orthographic, and working memory skills of bilingual Arabic-English speaking Canadian children. *Journal of Psycholinguistic Research, 31,* 661–678.

Adger, C. T., Wolfram, W., & Christian, D. (2007). *Dialects in schools and communities* (2nd ed.). New York: Taylor & Francis.

American Speech–Language–Hearing Association. (2001). Roles and responsibilities of speech–language pathologists with respect to reading and writing in children and adolescents. *ASHA Supplement, 21,* 17–28.

Anderson-Yockel, J., & Haynes, W. O. (1994). Joint book-reading strategies in working-class African American and White mother–toddler dyads. *Journal of Speech and Hearing Research, 37,* 583–593.

Auerbach, E. (1995). Deconstructing the discourse of strengths in family literacy. *Journal of Reading Behavior, 27,* 643–659.

August, D. A., & Hakuta, K. (Eds.). (1997). *Improving schooling for language-minority children: A research agenda.* Washington, DC: National Academy Press.

August, D., Shanahan, T., & Shanahan, L. (Eds.). (2006). *Developing literacy in second-language learners: Report of the national literacy panel on language-minority children and youth.* Mahwah, NJ: Erlbaum.

Bishop, D. V. M. (2002). The role of genes in the etiology of specific language impairment. *Journal of Communication Disorders, 35*, 311–328.

Brooks-Gunn, J. (2003). The black–white test score gap in young children: Contributions of test and family characteristics. *Applied Developmental Science, 7*, 239–252.

Burns, S., Griffin, P., & Snow, C. (Eds.). (1999). *Starting out right: A guide to promoting children's reading success.* Washington, DC: National Academy Press.

Bus, A. G., van IJzendoorn, M. H., & Pelligrini, A. D. (1995). Joint book reading makes for success in learning to read: A meta-analysis on intergenerational transmission of literacy. *Review of Educational Research, 65*(1), 1–21.

Butler, K., & Silliman, E. (2002). *Speaking, reading, and writing in children with language learning disorders.* Hillsdale, NJ: Erlbaum.

Byrd, R. S., & Weitzman, M. L. (1994). Predictors of early grade retention among children in the U.S. *Pediatrics, 93*, 481–487.

Callahan, R. M. (2006). The intersection of accountability and language: Can reading intervention replace English language development? *Bilingual Research Journal, 30*(1), 1–21.

Capps, R., Fix, M., Murray, J., Ost, J., Passel, J. S., & Hernandez, S. H. (2005, September). *The new demography of America's schools: Immigration and the No Child Left Behind Act* [Research report]. Washington, DC: Urban Institute.

Center for Research on Education, Diversity, and Excellence. (2002). *The five standards for effective pedagogy.* Retrieved February 8, 2006, from *www.crede.ucsc.edu/tools/research/standards/standards.html.*

Chiappe, P., Siegel, L. S., & Gottardo, A. (2002). Reading-related skills of kindergarteners from diverse linguistic backgrounds. *Applied Psycholinguistics, 23*, 95–116.

Cleary, L., & Peacock, T. (1998). *Collected wisdom: American Indian education.* Needham Heights, MA: Allyn & Bacon.

Coley, R. (2002). *An uneven start: Indicators of inequality in school readiness.* Princeton, NJ: Educational Testing Service.

Craig, H., Connor, C., & Washington, J. (2003). Early positive predictors of later reading comprehension for African American students: A preliminary examination. *Language, Speech, and Hearing Services in Schools, 34*, 31–43.

Craig, H., Thompson, C. A., Washington, J., & Potter, S. (2003). Phonological features of child African American English. *Journal of Speech, Language, and Hearing Research, 46*(3), 623–635.

Craig, H. K., & Washington, J. A. (2002). Oral language expectations for African American preschoolers and kindergartners. *American Journal of Speech–Language Pathology, 11*, 59–70.

Craig, H. K., & Washington, J. A. (2006). *Malik goes to school: Examining the language skills of African American students from preschool–5th grade.* Mahwah, NJ: Erlbaum.

Cummins, J. (1981). The role of primary language development in promoting educational success for language-minority students. In California State Department of Education (Ed.), *Schooling and language-minority students: A theoretical framework* (pp. 3–49). Los Angeles: Evaluation, Dissemination, and Assessment Center, California State University.

Cummins, J. (1984). *Bilingual education and special education: Issues in assessment and pedagogy.* San Diego, CA: College Hill.

Cummins, J. (1991). Language development and academic learning. In L. Malave & G. Duquette (Eds.), *Language, culture, and cognition.* Cleveland, OH: Multilingual Matters.

Cummins, J. (1992). Language proficiency, bilingualism, and academic achievement. In P. A. Richard-Amoto & M. A. Snow (Eds.), *The multicultural classroom readings for content-area teachers* (pp. 167–192). Reading, PA: Addison Wesley.

Cummins, J. (2000). *Language, power, and pedagogy: Bilingual children in the crossfire.* Buffalo, NY: Multilingual Matters.

Cummins, J., & McNeely, S. (1987). Language development, academic learning, and empowering minority students. In K. Tikunoff (Ed.), *Bilingual education and bilingual special education: A guide for administrators.* San Diego, CA: College Hill.

Dafontoura, H. A., & Siegel, L. S. (1995). Reading, syntactic, and working memory skills of bilingual Portuguese-English Canadian children. *Reading and Writing, 7,* 139–153.

Dalton, S. (1998). *Pedagogy matters: Standards for effective teaching practice* (Research Pre. No. 4). Retrieved January 31, 2006, from *www.caal. org/crede/pubs/research.RR4.pdf.* Washington, DC and Santa Cruz, CA: Center for Research on Education, Diversity, and Excellence.

D'Angiulli, A., Siegel, L. S., & Serra, E. (2001). The development of reading in English and Italian in bilingual children. *Applied Psycholinguistics, 22,* 479–507.

Delgado-Gaitan, C. (1990). *Literacy for empowerment: The role of parents in children's education.* London: Farmer Press.

Delgado-Gaitan, C. (1994). Sociocultural change through literacy: Toward empowerment of families. In B. Ferdman, R. Weber, & A. Ramirez (Eds.), *Literacy across languages and cultures* (pp. 143–170). Albany: State University of New York Press.

Delpit, L. (1998). What should teachers do: Ebonics and culturally responsive teaching. In T. Perry & L. Delpit (Eds.), *The real ebonics debate: Power, language, and the education of African American children* (pp. 17–26). Boston: Beacon Press.

Denton, C., Hasbrouck, J., Weaver, L., & Riccio, C. (2000). What do we know about phonological awareness in Spanish? *Reading Psychology, 21,* 335–352.

Dickens, W. T. (2005). Genetic differences and school readiness. *The Future of Children, 15*(1), 55–69.

Donahue, P., Voelkl, K., Campbell, J., & Mazzeo, J. (2001). *The nation's report card: Fourth-grade reading 2000.* Washington, DC: National Center for Education Statistics.

Duffy-Hester, A. (1999). Teaching struggling readers in elementary school classrooms: A review of classroom reading programs and principles for instruction. *The Reading Teacher, 52,* 480–495.

Durgunoglu, A. Y., & Oney, B. (1999). A cross-linguistic comparison of phonological awareness and word recognition. *Reading and Writing, 11,* 281–299.

Feagans, L., & Haskins, P. (1986). Neighborhood dialogues of black and white 5 year olds. *Journal of Applied Developmental Psychology, 7,* 181–200.

Federal Interagency Forum on Child and Family Statistics. (2005). *America's children: Key national indicators of well-being.* Washington, DC: U.S. Government Printing Office.

Fillmore, L., & Snow, C. (2000). *What teachers need to know about language.* Retrieved October 23, 2005, from *www.cal.org/ericoll/teachers.pdf.*

Fisher, S. E. (2007). Molecular windows into speech and language disorders. *Folia Phoniatrica et Logopedica, 59*(3), 130–140.

Fitzgerald, J., García, G., Jiménez, R. T., & Barrera, R. (2000). How will bilingual/ESL programs in literacy change in the next millennium? *Reading Research Quarterly, 35*(4), 520–523.

Fryer, R., & Levitt, S. (2004). Understanding the black–white test score gap in the first 2 years of school. *A Review of Economics and Statistics, 86,* 447–464.

García, G., & Beltran, D. (2001). Revisioning the blueprint: Building of the academic success of English learners. In C. Dowell (Ed.), *And still we speak . . . stories of communities sustaining and reclaiming language and culture* (pp. 197–226). Oakland, CA: California Tomorrow.

Gee, J. P. (2001). A sociocultural perspective on early language development. In S. B. Neuman & D. K. Dickinson (Eds.), *Handbook of early literacy research* (pp. 30–42). New York: Guilford Press.

Gërd, S. (2001). Recent advances in understanding the genetics of reading and spelling disorders. *Journal of Psychology and Psychiatry and Allied Disorders, 42,* 985–997.

Gersten, R., & Baker, S. (2000). What we know about effective instructional practices for English language learners. *Exceptional Children, 66*(4), 454–470.

Geva, E., & Siegel, L. S. (2000). Orthographic and cognitive factors in the concurrent development of basic reading skills in two languages. *Reading and Writing, 12,* 1–30.

Geva, E., & Wade-Woolley, W. (2004). Issues in the assessment of reading disability in second-language children. In I. Smythe, J. Everett, & R. Salter (Eds.), *The international book of dyslexia: A cross-language comparison and practice guide* (2nd ed., pp. 195–206). New York: Wiley.

Gilger, J. W. (1995). Behavioral genetics: Concepts for research in language and language disabilities. *Journal of Speech and Hearing Research, 38*, 1126–1142.

Goldenberg, C. (1989). Parents' effects on academic grouping for reading: Three case studies. *American Educational Research Journal, 26,* 329–352.

Goldenberg, C. (2001). Promoting early literacy development among Spanish-speaking children: Lessons from two studies. In E. H. Hiebert & B. Taylor (Eds.), *Getting ready right from the start: Effective literacy interventions* (pp. 171–199). Boston: Allyn & Bacon.

Gottardo, A., Yan, B., Siegel, L. S., & Wade-Woolley, L. (2001). Factors related to English reading performance in children with Chinese as a first language: More evidence of cross-language transfer of phonological processing. *Journal of Educational Psychology, 93*, 530–542.

Gutièrrez-Clellan, V. (1999). Mediating literacy skills in Spanish-speaking children with special needs. *Language, Speech, and Hearing Services in Schools, 30*, 285–292.

Hammer, C. S., & Miccio, A. W. (2001). Biliteracy: A pairing of research and funding. *The Asha Leader, 6*(21), 6.

Hammer, C. S., Miccio, A. W., & Wagstaff, D. A. (2003). Home literacy experiences and their relationship to bilingual preschools developing English literacy abilities: An initial investigation. *Language, Speech, and Hearing Services in Schools, 34*, 20–30.

Hart, B., & Risley, T. (1995). *Meaningful differences in the everyday experiences of young American children.* Baltimore: Brookes.

Heath, S. B. (1983). *Ways with words.* Cambridge, UK: Cambridge University Press.

Heath, S. B. (1989). Oral and literate traditions among black Americans living in poverty. *American Psychologist, 44*, 367–373.

Hess, R. D., & Halloway, S. D. (1984). Family and school as educational institutions. In R. D. Parks, R. H. Emde, H. P. McAdoo, & G. P. Sackett (Eds.), *Reviewing child development research (Vol. 7): The family* (pp. 179–222). Chicago: University of Chicago Press.

Human Genome Project. (2009). *ISCID encyclopedia of science and philosophy.* Retrieved April 7, 2009, from *www.iscid.org/encyclopedia/ Human_Genome_Project*

Individuals with Disabilities Education Improvement Act of 2004, 20 USCS § 1400 *et seq.* (2004).

Jencks, C., & Phillips, M. (1998). The black–white test score gap: An introduction. In C. Jencks & M. Phillips (Eds.), *The black–white test score gap* (pp. 1–51). Washington, DC: Brookings Institution.

Kaminski, R. A., & Cummings, K. D. (2007). Assessment for learning: Using general outcomes measures. *Threshold* [Online], 26–28. Available at *ciconline.org/threshold.*

Kaminski, R. A., & Good, R. H. (1996). Toward a technology for assessing basic early literacy skills. *School Psychology Review, 25*, 215–227.

Kaminski, R. A., & Good, R. H. (1998). Assessing early literacy skills in a problem-solving model: Dynamic indicators of basic early literacy skills. In M. R. Shinn (Ed.), *Advanced applications of curriculum-based measurement* (pp. 113–142). New York: Guilford Press.

Karrass, J., VanDeventer, M. C., & Braungart-Ricker, J. M. (2003). Predicting shared parent–child book reading in infancy. *Journal of Family Psychology, 17*(1), 134–146.

Kohler, C. T., Bahr, R. H., Silliman, E. R., Bryant, J. B., Apel, K., & Wilkinson, L. C. (2007). African American English dialect and performance on nonword spelling and phonemic awareness tasks. *American Journal of Speech–Language Pathology, 16*, 157–168.

Kohnert, K. (2008). *Language disorders in bilingual children and adults.* San Diego, CA: Plural.

Labov, W. (1970). *The study of nonstandard English.* Washington, DC: Center for Applied Linguistics.

Ladson-Billings, G. (1999, July 4). Reason is sought for lag by blacks in school effort. *New York Times*, p. 15.

Lee, J., Grigg, W., & Donahue, P. (2007). *The nation's report card: Reading 2007.* Washington, DC: National Center for Education Statistics, U.S. Department of Education.

Licata, C. M. (2002). *Measuring phonemic awareness in Spanish-speaking young children using dynamic indicators of basic early literacy skills.* Unpublished doctoral dissertation, California State University, Fresno.

Linver, M., Brooks-Gunn, J., & Cabrera, N. (2004). The home observation for measurement of the environment (HOME) inventory: The derivation of conceptually designed subscales. *Parenting: Science and Practice, 4*(2–3), 99–114.

Lonigan, C., Bloomfield, B., Anthony, J., Bacon, K., Phillips, B., & Samuel, C. (1999). Relations among emergent literacy skills, behavior problems, and social competence in preschool children from low- and middle-income backgrounds. *Topics in Early Childhood Special Education, 19*, 40–53.

Lynch, E. W., & Hanson, M. J. (2004). *Developing cross-cultural competence: A guide for working with children and their families.* Baltimore: Brookes.

Madding, C. C. (2002). Socialization practices of Latinos. In A. E. Brice (Ed.), *The Hispanic child: Speech, language, culture, and education* (pp. 68–84). Boston: Allyn & Bacon.

Manning, M. L., & Baruth, L. G. (2000). *Teaching learners at risk.* Norwood, MA: Christopher-Gordon.

Marvin, C., & Miranda, P. (1993). Home literacy experiences of preschoolers enrolled in Head Start and special education programs. *Journal of Early Intervention, 17*(4), 351–367.

McCardle, P. (2001). Biliteracy: A pairing of research and funding—collaboration and funding. *The ASHA Leader, 6*(21), 7.

Morrow, L., & Young, J. A. (1997). A family literacy program connecting school and home: Effects on attitude, motivation, and literacy achievement. *Journal of Educational Psychology, 89*, 736–742.

Moss, M., & Puma, M. (1995). Prospects: The congressionally mandated study of educational growth and opportunity. *First Year Report on Language Minority and Limited English Proficient Students.* Washington, DC: George Washington University.

National Center for Education Statistics. (1999). *Home literacy activities and signs of children's emerging literacy, 1993 and 1999.* Washington, DC: U.S. Department of Education, Office of Educational Research and Improvement.

National Reading Panel. (2000). *Teaching Children to Read* [Online], April 2000. Available at *www.nationalreadingpanel.org.*

National School Lunch Program. (2004, December 8). (P.L. 108-265) Federal Register [42 USC 1751]. Vol. 69, No. 235.

Nieto, S. (1999). Multiculturalism, social justice, and critical thinking. In I. Shor & C. Pari (Eds.), *Education is politics: Critical teaching across differences K–12* (pp. 1–32). Portsmouth, NH: Boynton/Cook.

No Child Left Behind Act of 2001 (Public Law 107-110). (2002). Washington, DC: United States Department of Education. Available at *www. ed.gov/nclb/landing.jhtml?src=pb.*

O'Malley, P. (1997). Ebonics–black English or boondoggle. *Psychiatric Times, 14*(3), 2–3.

Patterson, F. D. (1997). *The African American education data book, volume II: Preschool through high school edition.* Fairfax, VA: Frederick D. Patterson Research Institute of the United Negro College Fund.

Peinado, R. (2001). *The effects of student, familial, and educational variables on the English reading achievement of Spanish-speaking first-grade limited English-proficient children.* Doctoral dissertation, University of Oregon, Eugene.

Pelligrini, A. D., Perlmutter, J. C., Galda, L., & Brody, G. H. (1990). Joint reading between black Head Start children and their mothers. *Child Development, 61,* 443–453.

Phillips, M., Crouse, J., & Ralph, T. (1998). Does the black–white test score gap widen after children enter school? In C. Jencks & M. Phillips (Eds.), *The black–white test score gap* (pp. 229–272). Washington, DC: Brookings Institute Press.

Pikulski, J. (1994). Preventing reading failure: A review of five effecting programs. *Reading Teacher, 48,* 30–39.

Ramirez, J. D., Pasta, D. J., Yuen, S., Billings, D. K., & Ramey, D. R. (1991). *Final report: Longitudinal study of structural immersion strategy, early exit, and late-exit transitional bilingual education programs for language-minority children* [Report to the U.S. Department of Education]. (Vols. 1 & 2). San Mateo, CA: Aguirre International.

Reese, L., & Gallimore, R. (2000). Immigrant Latinos' cultural model of literacy development: An evolving perspective on home–school discontinuities. *American Journal of Education, 108,* 103–133.

Rickford, J. (1999). Language diversity and academic achievement in the education of African American students: An overview of the issues. In A. Adger, D. Christian, & O. Taylor (Eds.), *Making the connection:*

Language and academic achievement among African American students (pp. 1–30). Washington, DC: Center for Applied Linguistics.

Roberts, J., Jurgens, J., & Burchinal, M. (2005). The role of home literacy practices in preschool children's language and emergent literacy skills. *Journal of Speech, Language, and Hearing Research, 48,* 345–359.

Silliman, E. R., Bahr, R. H., Wilkinson, L. C., & Turner, C. (2002). Language variation and struggling readers: Finding patterns in diversity. In K. G. Butler & E. R. Silliman (Eds.), *Speaking, reading, and writing in children with language learning disabilities: New paradigms for research and practice* (pp. 109–148). Mahwah, NJ: Erlbaum.

Slavin, R., & Cheung, A. (2003). *Effective reading programs for English language learners: A best-evidence synthesis.* Baltimore: Johns Hopkins University.

Smith, J., Brooks-Gunn, J., & Klebanov, P. (1997). The consequences of living in poverty on young children's cognitive development. In G. Duncan & J. Brooks-Gunn (Eds.), *Consequences of growing up poor* (pp. 132–189). New York: Russell Sage Foundation.

Smith, J. L. (2005). *Spanish-speaking kindergarteners' detection of initial syllables or phonemes: Selecting an indicator of phonological awareness.* Unpublished doctoral dissertation, University of Oregon, Eugene.

Snow, C., Barnes, W. S., Chandler, J., Goodman, J. F. , & Hemphill, L. (1991). *Unfulfilled expectations: Home and school influences on literacy.* Cambridge, MA: Harvard University Press.

Snow C., Burns M., & Griffin, P. (Eds.). (1998). *Preventing reading difficulties in young children.* Committee on the Prevention of Reading Difficulties in Young Children, National Research Council, Washington, DC: National Academy Press.

Steffensen, M. (1974). *The acquisition of black English.* Unpublished doctoral dissertation, Ohio State University, Columbus.

Stockman, I. J. (1996). Phonological development and disorders in African American children. In A. G. Kamhi, K. E. Pollock, & J. L. Harris (Eds.), *Communication development and disorders in African American children: Research, assessment, and intervention* (pp. 117–153). Baltimore: Brookes.

Strickland, D. S. (2001). Early intervention for African American children at risk. In S. B. Neumann & D. K. Dickinson (Eds.), *Handbook of early literacy research* (pp. 322–332). New York: Guilford Press.

Tabors, P. O., & Snow, C. E. (2001). Young bilingual children and literacy development. In S. B. Neumann & D. K. Dickinson (Eds.), *Handbook of early literacy research* (pp. 159–191). New York: Guilford Press.

Terry, N. P. (2006). Relations between dialect variation, grammar, and early spelling skills. *Journal of Reading and Writing, 19*(9), 907–931.

Tharp, R. G. (1997). From risk to excellence: Research, theory, and principles for practice [Research Report 1]. The world outside and inside schools: Language and immigrant children. *Educational Researcher, 27*(6), 4–18.

United States Census Bureau. (2006). *Statistical abstract of the United States. Families below poverty level and below 125 percent of poverty by race and Hispanic origin: 1980 to 2005, Table 693*. Washington, DC: U.S. Government Printing Office.

van Kleeck, A. (2006). *Sharing books and stories to promote language and literacy*. San Diego, CA: Plural.

Vernon-Feagans, L., Emanuel, D. C., & Blood, I. (1997). The effect of otitis media and quality of day care on children's language development. *Journal of Applied Developmental Psychology, 18*(3), 395–410.

Wagner, R. (2005). Understanding genetics and environmental influence on the development of reading: Researching the higher field. *Scientific Study of Reading, 9*(3), 317–326.

Walter, E. (1994). A longitudinal study of literacy acquisition in a North American community: Observation of the 4-year-old classes at Lummi Headstart (Report No. EDRS RC019460). Bellingham, WA: Lummi Tribal Council. (ERIC Document Reproduction Service No. ED 366479)

Washington, J., & Craig, H. (2000). Reading performance and dialectal variation. In J. L. Harris, A. Kamhi, & K. Pollock (Eds.), *Literacy in African American communities* (pp. 147–168). Mahwah, NJ: Erlbaum.

Wasik, X. (1998). Using volunteers as reading tutors: Guidelines for successful practices. *The Reading Teacher, 51*(7), 562–570.

Westby, C. (1994). The effects of culture on genre, structure, and style of oral and written texts. In G. Wallach & K. Butler (Eds.), *Language and learning disabilities in school-age children and adolescents* (pp. 180–218). New York: Macmillan.

Wyatt, T. (2002). Assessing the communicative abilities of clients from diverse cultural and linguistic backgrounds. In D. E. Battle (Ed.), *Communication disorders in multicultural populations* (3rd ed., pp. 415–460). Woburn, MA: Butterworth-Heineman.

Index

f following a page number indicates a figure; *t* following a page number indicates a table